The Magical Realm

The Magical Realm

Kathleen Coyle

WOLFHOUND PRESS

First published in 1997 by
Wolfhound Press Ltd
68 Mountjoy Square
Dublin 1, Ireland

British Library Cataloguing in Publication Data
A catalogue record for this book is available from the British Library.

ISBN 0-86327-548-6

Cover Design: Slick Fish Design
Typesetting: Wolfhound Press
Printed in the Republic of Ireland by Colour Books, Dublin.

Contents

Kathleen Coyle

Chapter One

It is absurd to think that life begins for us at birth. The pattern is set far back, we merely step into the process. We pick it up as we take on the sins of our fathers, where they reach and touch us. What is directly important to us as individuals, about to set out upon periods of our own, is the state of the family when we join it. Families are either going up or down as families. Their stationary spells are either short or dull and dynastic — associated purely with human industry as an art or as a system, Ming or Capitalism.

The family I happened to join was in a *Cherry Orchard* condition. It was losing. It was walking upon water. It was one of those racial and social units that had the mark upon its brow. Its indications were tidal — and the tide was going out. Any chance of escape had to be both single and against the current. The process, of course, need not be deprived of splendour. We have but to regard salmon and eels to realise that they behave interestingly when they are going back. Retrogression can be very conscious in its retroaction. This is manifest in all *fin de siècle* surges and extinctions. It may be that Death is essentially a filter. It saves what it can. The ones who are nearest to the final gates carry the fullest meaning, for whatever that meaning may be worth. They are the asses for the new Jerusalems.

I had better lay down my load just here so that there may be no misconceptions. I was evidently never intended to cause, in the language of ships, much displacement anywhere. I belong definitely to the smaller creatures of the earth. I barely escaped being born a midget. I weighed something over four pounds at birth and the surgeon who brought me into this world is said to have held me out upon the palm of his hand on my second morning, and to have

demanded scoffingly: 'Have the ducklings had breakfast?'
He was a giant of a man, self-glorified by his own over-
weight offspring. His youngest daughter had but recently
presented herself and been christened Valetta, in memory of
unforgettable years spent by her parents in Malta. At a later
age I could never see Valetta without remembering that her
father had insulted me. I should never have been told, of
course, but parents have this very human habit of committing our infancy into our hands with the everlasting
endurance of the spoken word. They take no account of our
feelings at a stage when, in their estimation, anything at all
on our part is a sort of joke.

Another thing that I would much rather never have
heard about was that my mother insisted upon my newborn
body being bathed in milk and rose water. The only effect
that this pristine bath had upon me was that I have loathed
milk all my life and adored roses. No moral can therefore be
drawn. My mother was insuring my complexion. If it had
not been the last week in a northern October, with winds
blowing and leaves flying, she would probably have ordered me to be rolled in dewdrops.

These were my signals: a tiny being acquiring mockery
and flattery with my first breaths of carbon. To be quickened
with life is such a marvel that it is no wonder we ask ourselves so often for a law. We are tempted to rationalise
ourselves. It is so natural to wish to believe that there is a
purpose in our presence upon the earth. All that we ever
discover is that if there is a design it is decidedly impersonal.

I was born, in the strictest heritable sense of the term,
from a generation of grandaunts. Out of a family of twelve
my mother was the unique gift to her generation. As a link
she had the nature of a cipher, a medium of accidence. I was
very definitely what I was because she was what she was.
Behind her was my maternal grandmother and what my
maternal grandmother did to my mother had to be traced
clearly to one of the grandaunts. This took and kept me on
their line.

I loved my grandmother. She and my father were my first passionate images. They were stamped into the early waxy nature of my being. That they were deadly enemies made no difference to me.

The very first thing I remember was the white walls of a hospital. I was in bed, and my grandmother was going away from me along the white walls towards a door which opened, engulfed her and closed upon her. I was twenty-three months old and I was swept in those terrifying and desolating seconds from the oblivion of infancy into the most awful awareness. It was devastating. It sharpened everything about me, the presence of others, the bareness of the white walls to the right of me, the strangeness of being given a cup with a spout to it and the taste of coffee. Then the door closed. I was held there. The screen went down again.

I was in the hospital because of an accident that had occurred several months previously. I have not the faintest recollection of physical pain and, judging by what had been done to me, there must have been a good deal of it. What reached me was not physical; it was the deeper injury to my psyche, the separation from the last being who was part of my integral world.

The second thing that I remember was also associated with white walls and strangeness. I believe now that the setting of the second incident recalled the first by pure association. It also was stamped with separation. I had been moved from the hospital on the recommendation of Dr MacEwan, the famous hip specialist. I was under his care and he had discovered that the nurse in charge of me had not been kind to me. It was he who arranged for me to live in the private home of an old favourite nurse of his who had married the janitor of the Glasgow High School. It was the janitor who took me into the white-walled schoolroom which smelt strongly of carbolic acid. He went down on his knees and showed me how to draw a cat on a slate; two balls with tiny triangles for ears and nothing but the tail to prove that it was a cat. I can see the walls, smell the carbolic, and hear the pencil scraping to this day.

The third event that I remember also had to do with separation. I awoke at partings. This time I was in bed with these people, the janitor and his wife, and there was a letter. Something, I knew not what, was brought into my consciousness and then, again, blankness.

I remember standing between Dr MacEwan's knees. My grandmother was there but she was no longer important. I was far more conscious of gifts being taken from stacks of wrapping paper and being placed upon a table by Dr MacEwan.

I remember standing on a plush seat in the cabin of the steamboat to have a sash tied, a broad blue silken sash with yellow velvet stripes. That time there was the smell of the sea and men were laughing.

I remember nothing at all about my arrival home two years later except that there was a new sister in whom I absolutely refused to believe. I do not have any impression of her, merely this urgent feeling of resentment. She had not been there when I left so what right had she to be there when I returned? The fact of this resentment proves that there were definite recognitions in respect to others. Although nothing stands out with regard to my father and mother I must, at least, not have denied them. The only creature to whom I went out fully with all my senses was Major, the Newfoundland dog. I think the secret is that he must have welcomed me overwhelmingly. Father had bought him for me as a puppy. We had been very young together and here, clearly, we were again!

I was home. I was almost four years old.

Chapter Two

During the next three years only a few things stand out. There is still nothing consecutive.

I was on crutches and Major was my constant companion. Wherever he led, I followed. When he bounded up flights of stairs in obedience to his mistress' voice, at the rate of eight steps at a time, I bounded after at the rate of four. The voice proved often to be a decoy. Mother had a parrot which imitated her inflection perfectly and which hated Major. Her great delight was to make a fool of him. She would lure him with the alarm of 'cats', or 'rats', when neither cats nor rats were present and, as soon as he reached the threshold of my mother's room, she would burst into the most raucous laughter and, adding insult to injury, then ask 'pretty Mrs C. to give Pol a lump of sugar'. She always got her sugar while Major and I would stand there gasping, watching the vile-natured bird roll her eyes at us. She was such a glorious object, all bright green and scarlet. Her chain always jingled and made you think of African bangles. She always seemed to me, when I think of her now, to glisten with diamonds and rubies. Major and I would bound down the stairs again, expunging our hatred in danger — for we were always being told that sudden death awaited us at the bottom. The more we were warned the more we did it. Nothing could frighten me when Major was about. He was my great black friend in his astrakhan coat. His raven blue-black hair was curled as tightly as the fleece of unborn lambs. On our daily promenades with a nurse and a perambulator we sometimes had to pass a hotel with a wine cellar that was often opened to the street by a trap door in the pavement. When it was closed we bumped over it with a horrible hollow sound. This hotel had wire blinds on its lower windows. On these its name was printed, punctuated by the division of the panes so that the word 'hotel' came out with *hot* on one side and *el* on the other. When the cellar was open Major always took up his position between me and it and would even push me on occasions out of danger. I always believed that he was rescuing me from burning hell. I had returned home with strong convictions about heaven and hell.

The maternal side of my family was strictly Roman Catholic. My father's religion was a strict secret. I returned from Scotland to cast a bombshell into these strictures. I had become, in my absence, a devotée of the Salvation Army. A drum had but to beat or somebody touch a piano and I would burst out into urgent calls to 'Come quick to Jesus'. I used to sing hymns that were like miniature tom-toms, and I had the strongest notions about sins. Sins were things that should be shouted upon sidewalks. The janitor's wife had apparently taken me with her when she attended street meetings. My behaviour distressed my mother and grandmother. Father enjoyed it. So, encouraged by him, I remained immunised against my mother and grandmother and their influence. I remained faithful to the wife of the janitor and the Salvation Army.

There must have been a strong sense of religious controversy in the atmosphere which played upon my spirit. There was an altar in our nursery, built into the wall facing our three railed cots. It was draped with lace. Mother collected lace and china and rolls of silk. She was as acquisitive as a magpie. Our attics were full of Saratoga trunks filled to the brim with treasures. Whenever she allowed any of us to accompany her to the attic it always acted upon us like a visit to Ali Baba. The altar had three statues: Our Lord in the centre with Saint Joseph on one side and the Virgin Mary on the other. Flowers were always wilting in the ruby glow of a red bowl filled with colza oil and lit by a floating wick. When Mary O'Connell, our old nurse, tucked us into bed at night she always put out the lamp and left us to the mercy of the red altar light. I awoke one night in utter darkness.

Nothing glowed from the altar and all was black as pitch. That was the first time I felt fear. It was spiritual fear. It had nothing to do with the body. I was afraid because of the sins I had committed. I *saw* my soul. It was the size and shape of a sheep's kidney and it was as white as ivory, or suet. Gradually spots appeared upon the whiteness. My sins began to spread into the whiteness. The little white kidney became blacker and blacker and I became more and more terrified. I was convinced that the Devil had blown out the light and was after me in the darkness. That was the time that I had been reading forbidden literature. One of our servants indulged in what was known as penny dreadfuls. She had forbidden us to read these but I had yielded to the temptation. I had opened one at random and been caught by a realistic picture of a girl standing up in a boat in a raging sea. A man was attacking her with a raised dagger. I was compelled to read what it was about. Not to do so was equivalent to not going to the rescue. I read with terror and exaltation that the girl had either to be stabbed by the man or jump into the sea and when I read this much I had to read further. But I never got to the end of the story. I was interrupted and for days my mind was tormented with the girl's fate. Now, in the pitch-black night, in the presence of my blackened soul and the Devil, I knew that it was none of my business and that I should never have got mixed up in it. Vengeance was falling upon me who was, after all, not guilty of anything that approached murder. The whole thing was on top of me when suddenly a tall needle of light appeared at the edge of the door which Mary O'Connell had left ajar. This gave me the direction. I scrambled out of the cot and reached the door and went out upon the landing. Light was rising in the circle of the banisters. And from the pool below, on the drawing-room floor, my mother's precious voice soared towards me. She was singing. Her song had the sweetness of angels. I began to descend the stairs when a door banged and scared me as though the Devil had pounced. I think I must have yelled like mad. I don't know how I got to the bottom. There was no Major to save me. I know I called out for my mother. But it was Father who came, who picked me up into strong arms of salvation. That was my introduction to my father. I discovered that he had been there all the time — and that he loved me. By the time Mother appeared she had become secondary. Her comfort was so many degrees less than his. He was a new being to me, a sort of Mother and Major combined for he was black like Major — where he was not white. I relied upon him as I relied upon Major. His arms *felt* like Major.

I had returned from Glasgow also as a cactus emissary, for another place which I had frequented with the janitress was the Botanical Gardens. I had become intimate with the head gardener, a Mr Cherry. His name, you must admit, was perfect for a gardener. A man with such a name was predestined. He was, I believe now, in love with me. In spite of my crutches and a hateful steel patten I evidently attracted him for he involved my family in a correspondence which lasted for years. Almost every letter he sent was accompanied by a cactus. He had sent home with me enough pots to stack a conservatory. Our window sills, tables and shelves and whatnots bristled with these tiny plants with human gestures. My mother took great delight in them for she was an amateur botanist. She had that vile habit of giving you Latin roots and stems when she presented you with a flower for your buttonhole. I have no memory at all of Mr Cherry. He was bound to me solely over a period of years by the arrival of cactus pots. It is only when I enter a greenhouse that his influence comes back to me. The pungent odour of plants under glass always excites me like something primitive and racial; something far back in the blood such as Druid menhirs or the smell of gold and silver. Something forgotten and buried but *there* all the time. It is then that I know that I once stood in that atmosphere with Mr Cherry.

Chapter Three

I believe now that my family fought for my soul. I had become a changeling in my absence, a spiritual imponderable. There never was any doubt about Elizabeth or James. Even when James stopped in the middle of the recitation of the rosary to ask if wombs were orchards ('Blessed be the fruit of thy womb') nobody paid attention. But all questions on my part were referred to confessors, and had a peculiar habit of coming back to me. Father was always defending me. I never forgot his advice — to keep my religion to myself. I believed every word he uttered. But there was a period when my grandmother had me on the edge of miracles: she spoke to me with such earnestness about novenas that she actually converted me. I was not partly converted but completely. She had visited Lourdes and she convinced me that if one prayed with absolute faith to Our Lady one's prayers would be heard. I had once heard her tell Father that all reforms should begin with himself. Her voice was so distinct and her will so strong that I believed it when she said it. So now, caught in the absolute faith of miracles, I began with myself. I hated having to wear a steel patten. The gardener had once remarked that he could trace me all over the garden like a donkey. If miracles were possible then it was only logical to apply them to the abolition of pattens. I began to pray to Our Lady.

I do not believe that any child has ever prayed more fervently or with more complete faith. For nine days I kept the faith. For nine days I was one of God's saints. I ate my porridge for breakfast. I went without sugar. I smiled at James. I told no lies and I did everything on the minute. I was a model creature. I cannot recall that anybody noticed it. No sign rewarded me. I prayed the first thing in the morning and the last thing at night; lying in the dim glow of the altar lamp I deliberately pulled out hairs from my head by the roots as offerings of sanctity to the Blessed Virgin. I prayed that my shortened leg would become the same length as the other one. I believed to the very depths of my being that this would be done. On the ninth morning I expected to awake and leap out of bed like a hart.

On the ninth morning when I awoke I lay still and rigid, saying the prayer *first*. When I experimented I discovered that no miracle had occurred. All was as it had been before. My faith in Our Lady died in that moment. I never prayed to her again. Whatever aspect of her had been imbedded in me by the Scotch janitor and janitress, returned. She was decidedly not one to whom appeals were profitable.

Still, miracles were in the air. They stayed in the air. Whether she noticed anything about me or not I do not know but the next thing was that my grandmother had discovered a worker of miracles. She explained to me that whatever gift from God a young priest asked for at his ordination he invariably received it. This young priest, who had begun as a medical student, asked for the gift of healing. His burning desire was to heal the sick. She said to me quite simply: 'We will go to him and ask him to take away your crutches.' I was agreeable to go — but I was unable to believe. The difficulty was how to find this young priest. Daily newspapers were consulted. He had begun to work miracles in County Cavan and had healed so many sick persons that crowds had begun to follow him about upon the roads. His parish priest had been very perturbed about it and had written to the bishop and the bishop had written to Rome and it was published in the paper that he was definitely forbidden by the Pope to continue to work miracles. But the demand of those in need of miracles was so great that people followed him, sought him out and found him wherever he hid. My grandmother was one of these. She set forth with me to find him. We took trains. We rode in all sorts of vehicles. Finally the day came when we were close to his presence. We sat in the small crowded parlour of a country hotel and he was upstairs. His prayers reached us when the door opened, going up and down like the waves of the sea. People in the parlour kept going to the window and drawing back the curtains and peering across the little market place. We were called in turn. I do not remember when our turn came but I distinctly remember standing on the threshold of the room upstairs with a terrible excitement clutching at my heart. I do not remember a thing about this young priest except the bright purple, gold-edged stole that he kissed and placed around his neck. He ordered my shoes to be taken off and for me to be laid upon the bed. It was a very high featherbed that went down and down when I was laid on it. The prayers that I had heard downstairs began to rise and fall right against my ears. I did not follow them. *I did not pray.* I simply lay there, passive, waiting to see what would happen. Then there was a disturbance. People at the window were saying that *they* had come. The sounds of horses' hoofs were heard below. The worker of miracles snatched off his stole and commanded me in a voice of thunder to walk across the floor. I walked. It was not comfortable but I did it. 'Get her a pair of shoes,' he ordered and then he vanished. He fled. Somebody was sent for shoes. I was fitted with a pair of patent-leather slippers and my crutches and the shoe with the patten were packed into a parcel.

When Father saw me he said: 'You could have walked all the time.' Grandmother was very angry with him. Mary O'Connell said that he was an incorrigible man and they both agreed that he should be prevented from influencing me. As though she were bribing me to give up my father Mary O'Connell said that she would take me on a pilgrimage. She would take me to Saint Columcille's Well at Gartan. It was a holy place, where he had been reared. Gartan was in Tyrconnel which Mary O'Connell assured me was O'Donnell land. Saint Columcille was an O'Donnell. She, herself, came from Tyrconnel. Although the saint was an O'Donnell and she was an O'Connell she endeavoured to convince me that in *his* time, she and he, through their families were one and the same tribe. They were made one by territory. I resented her claim to relationship with Saint Columcille because I had always regarded him as a minor appendage to my great-grandfather who had built the Long Tower Church upon one of the saint's sites. Every time I was taken to the church I was shown the stone worn by the saint's knees. As the church was much larger than the stone I judged the relative importance of the saint and my great-grandfather accordingly.

Grandmother showed me a picture of Saint Brigid with a cathedral in the palm of her hand. She told me that Saint Brigid had influenced Columcille when he was a young man, that he was to her what Saint John de Yepes had been to Teresa of Ávila. As I did not know what John was to Teresa of Ávila and she seemed unable to explain it to me I had a vague and hazy notion that he was her son. Saint Augustine was always shown black against his white mother. These were delicate matters and could not be urged. There were tentative pieces of knowledge which had to be stored and found out about later.

On an early morning Mary O'Connell and I set forth upon our pilgrimage. We arrived at a very desolate place at nightfall. An old woman was bent over a turf fire, stirring a mixture in a hanging pot. I had to sleep in the same bed as Mary O'Connell. I was prevented from going to sleep for she was picking her corns. I was compelled to listen. We arose at dawn and said our prayers, kneeling on the earthen hearth with the old woman. Everything was clean but poor and bare, a table and a stool and the little unadorned window with a flower in a jam pot. The earth outside consisted of low stretching fields, full of mists. Larks rose and little shy things twittered and broke in flight over the grassy pattern. We had to walk to the Well in our bare feet. The sky was very low. It was coming in like a tide, breaking into ripples that were edged with gold. It was not pleasant having to walk in bare feet but Mary led and I was obliged to follow. There was no sign of the shrine. We came upon it suddenly, blossoming like a white rosebush at the end of the fields.

The roses turned out to be pilgrim rags and when we got there we found that the bushes were hung with old shoes and sticks and crutches. Mary had brought my crutches. She laid them down solemnly upon a path of stones. We prayed together. Then she dipped into the Well and gave me the water to sip. It tasted of salt and soda and I wanted to spit it out but did not dare. Mary prayed loudly in ups and downs like the priest who performed miracles. I did not pray. I was in that state of grace when the peace of a place falls upon you like a mantle. We were alone at the shrine. We were alone in the sharp misty morning — in our bare feet. I could smell the heather. I could smell the dark moist earth. I was abroad in the country space, untroubled by any demand for favours. It was sufficient to be there — and to get rid of my crutches. It was quite a relief to see the end of them. Mary O'Connell was painfully in earnest — painfully because I was able to see her objectively. I was not sharing her fervour. She groaned and moaned and very watery tears trickled upon her cheeks. She fumbled at the buttons on her bosom and brought out her brown scapulars and dipped them into the Well and put them back, dripping wet, into her bodice. I always felt horribly superior about Mary O'Connell. I do not know where the superiority came from but it was not pleasant to me. It made me more uncomfortable than it made her. She was oblivious of my feelings and unconscious of me, but she was obnoxious to me in several ways and I was most terribly conscious of her. I hated to have to sit on her knee and have my back unbuttoned. I was always pushed off by her curved and very formidable ridge of little jet buttons. She was obliged to grip me back so that I was held and pushed at the same time. I felt *crushed*.

And yet, in spite of my antipathy, I have remained linked to her by many things — especially by that cold and sunny morning and our bare feet upon the wet grass. We came back to the old peasant woman across the fields. She was standing on her threshold, shading her eyes with her hand. It was strangely peaceful in the little kitchen — the fire blazing and the crooked hand-patterned bowls on the table, with iron spoons. There was the smell of the night-washed earth, drying out from its dews; the smell of *distance* — of untraversed space. I was too young then to analyse it, but I had a distinct feeling of holiness, of oneness, of what was unbroken. I was content — a child with two old women in the wilderness.

Chapter Four

There was a terrible scene once when Elizabeth swallowed a hammer. She maintained so persistently that she had swallowed it that nobody could convince her otherwise. She screamed and screamed with terror because the hammer was inside her.

Mary O'Connell was undressing her when James dropped the hammer down her back between her chemise and her scarlet stay-bodice. It was a small hammer with a slender yellow handle, out of his toy carpentry set. For some peculiar reason when Elizabeth made the fuss the hammer failed to reappear. It could not be found. Her drawers were unbuttoned, taken off and shaken before her eyes but the hammer did not drop out, so she remained absolutely certain that it was inside her. And as the habitual manner of getting things inside was to swallow them she maintained against all argument that she had swallowed it. It was such an awful thought that she should have a whole hammer in her interior that she had hysterics. She sobbed and shrieked and kicked and was utterly and entirely comfortless. Grandmother was sent for. Mother was sent for. They both failed to pacify her. Father was sent for in the hope that a male voice would establish authority. Every time a new person appeared the hammer had to be searched for all over again. Elizabeth's garments were almost shaken to ribbons. Nobody thought of searching James. The only gaps in Elizabeth's panic were when her bright black eyes, opaque with tears, watched out to see if the hammer were appearing from the tormented garments. Finally the doctor came. He gave Elizabeth something on a spoon and brought the hammer out of his pocket. It was not the same hammer. It did not have a yellow shaft, but by then Elizabeth was so exhausted that it sufficed that it was a hammer.

I remember making an awful scene myself about a dress that had been given to the washerwoman's daughter. I remember nothing at all about the dress until it was given away. I was then apparently seized with a tremendous and exaggerated fondness for it. Mother reasoned with me that it was a very ordinary dress, worthless and even ugly. It was only a cotton dress. It was pink. It had checked pockets. When it was laundered it stood out as stiffly as boards, so starched that parts of it had to be torn asunder and I had this wild and uncontrollable affection for it. Nothing that could be said against the dress could console me against its loss. I wanted that dress with the strong will of the young and undefeated. A search was made for it. Masses of things that needed washing appeared on the octagonal landing. People went in and out of doors — but I was not cheated. I *knew* that it had been given away. I have not the faintest memory of its return. All that I have carried forward was this passionate desire for its recovery. It was mine. I possessed it. Nobody had the right to take it from me. That was the first time in my life that I had any sense of possession. What happened then immunised me for life against the value of personal belongings. I never again rebelled.

Perhaps I loved this dress because it was a simple dress. Mother had curious and extravagant notions about how she dressed us. She never shopped for anything at any time. She wrote a note — and presently bandboxes would begin to arrive. We children were not exposed to any caprice on her part. She had a system. Our clothes, and the servants' clothes were bought twice yearly, in the spring and autumn. All the children's things came from a Mrs Galbraith who had a shop in the Town Square, known as the Diamond. They would arrive in great bandboxes which rustled with silver tissue paper when unstrapped. Grandmother always stole sheets of the tissue paper. She said it was excellent for the complexion because it contained arsenic. The secret of some lady who was a mayor's wife was that she always wiped her face with tissue paper. She never used towels.

It was exciting to see the things come out: sailor suits for James with varieties of collars and whistles; blue and white suits with short and long pants. He abhorred having to try them on but he adored blowing the whistles. I remember lawn sunbonnets, corded and fluted and delicate as pale roses, cashmere smocks and pastel-tinted paletôts with exquisite embroideries. I remember a brown velvet bonnet with a blue satin lining. I remember furniture draped with paper-wrapped wonders and Elizabeth and I parading on soft creamy carpets and Mother glowing and she and Grandmother arguing about guineas. I remember also an awful time when I was taken to some ceremony in a dress I hated. It was a salmon-pink dress with a pale sea-green velvet bolero and a hat to match. It was one of Mother's favourites. Obviously we had not similar tastes for I could not bear to wear it. It was slightly tight under my arms and also it made people stare at us. I think now that Mother indulged in a deep delight in making us look different. It was a very individualistic age. There was a family of blonde little girls who were always dressed as though they belonged to the theatre. As Elizabeth and I were as dark as Spanish gypsies I think Mother enjoyed glorifying us accordingly.

It must have been about this time that I became shoe-conscious. The aftermath of miracle, if it had taken away my crutches, had not lengthened my leg. Instead of a steel patten I was promised a special shoe. Mary O'Connell tried to prepare me for this shoe by telling me what a marvel it was going to be and that it would enable me to walk like other people. Until that moment I was not at all conscious of the fact that I was not walking like other people. Speed was the sole essential. So long as I could keep up with Major there was nothing to worry about. My attitude towards the new shoe, for which I had been fitted by a shoemaker who measured me and tickled my feet, was the normal attitude of anybody towards a new pair of shoes. Anything new is exciting.

When the shoe, with a three-inch cork-sole adjustment, appeared it was so clumsy and ugly that it was a pure offence.

That time I was a very naughty little girl. I flung the awful thing across the nursery floor and refused absolutely to put it on. There was a fearful battle in which nobody won. Nobody could win against my spirit — but I was deeply injured. I came out with scars which have never disappeared. It was then that the 'slow stain of life' began to get me.

As this is a chapter of afflictions I may as well put the loss of the turquoise rosary in here. Grandmother had been away and returned — I think she went to Rome. She brought me a present with a special blessing. Every time I used it I acquired indulgences in heaven. I loved that rosary not because of what it did for my soul but simply because it was a thing of beauty in itself. The turquoise matrix stones were linked by a silver chain — a perfect combination. I carried the rosary in my pocket during the day and at night I put it under my pillow. One morning it was not there. It was never found. I made no scene about it. I did not cry. I mourned it drily and burningly. Grandmother tried to comfort me with the offer of a mother-of-pearl rosary in a mother-of-pearl egg. The egg had a clasp like a piece of lace. I refused it politely. I did not wish another rosary. I desired only the one which I had worshipped instead of worshipping on. I had loved it too much — and it was taken from me.

Its loss became part of the Divine negativeness that had not answered passionate prayer, had given the simple pink dress away — and had provided the awful and insulting shoe.

The wound was cumulative. It struck deep. It created denial in the wild heart of a young being to whom life was, by instinct, a pure sublimation. It took away something for which the only word I can find is faith.

Chapter Five

My seventh birthday was celebrated in Mother's bedroom. Mother was in bed, sitting up against white pillows in a cambric nightgown with frills on her bosom and at her wrists, and her dark hair in thick, long plaits — winding down her shoulders and over upon the turned-down sheet like velvet serpents.

Everything was glowing — the fire on the hearth, the yellow eiderdown, the shining windows. Everything had the bright glory of the princess within and without. There was a sensation of well-being, of all at its best. It was a large room. Our low table was set on the hearth rug where Mother could see us from the bed. She had Montessorian principles perhaps before Madame Montessori had them. She provided us with furniture according to our size. It was moved from room to room when we needed it. Even the china teaset was specially ordered. It was larger than a doll's teaset and smaller than that used by adults, exactly in between the two — pure white china with golden rims to the plates and saucers and golden handles to the cups which had a bird in the bottom. You drank to the last drop to see the bird fly out.

There were an iced cake with my name on it decorated with angelica leaves. Elizabeth poured the tea and I cut the cake. We both served James who was there in his sailor suit with the whistle cord looped into his pocket. His mouth was open. The only guests were Mother in the bed and Major on the hearth rug. Major was given his wedge of cake on a plate, not in the usual surreptitious fashion when he got my porridge in the morning under the table with my dress held out in a fan to screen him from discovery. I never ate a taste of porridge that I could escape from. When Major was absent I disposed of it spoonful by spoonful between the brass flutes of the ashpan beneath the grate. It baked all day into a cement that must have caused some housemaid a good deal of trouble.

People kept coming to the door to take a peep at us. The parish priest was in the room. When he had finished blessing Mother he laid his hand upon my head and said, loading me with weights: 'Now, you have attained the age of reason.' And just as a cactus or a thought of Mr Cherry attached me backwards to the jungle and primal forms of life, Father MacMenamin's words attached me, later, to the Encyclopaedists.

The doctor came in. He held Mother's hand droopingly so that the rings slid down her thin fingers, and he watched the hands going round on his watch. Then he insisted upon putting Elizabeth upon the bedside table while she read Gladstone's speech out of the newspaper. It was no trouble at all to her, including all the big words, but she cast her eye occasionally towards the tea table to see how fast the cake was vanishing. Elizabeth and I never had any difficulties with spelling. James, on the contrary, never mastered words of one syllable. He performed incredible variations on the definite article. There was nothing the matter with James, except his sisters. He was squeezed between us — one to the north and one to the south; or east or west, no matter which way he turned. If he had had us both on top or both below he might have escaped. But with one who was older and one who was younger he had no chance at all.

Elizabeth read the speech to the very end. The doctor was enchanted with her, standing up like a politician in her décolleté dress with the large bows of ribbon on her shoulders. He wished to take her home with him, although he had ten boys and girls of his own. At this moment Elizabeth was exactly three years and one month old.

There was a distinct understanding between Elizabeth and me just then. We were linked by our absolute indifference to a new sister who had appeared and who seemed to be entirely Mary O'Connell's baby. She was always in

Mary's O'Connell's arms — being shown to Mother — or on Mary O'Connell's lap having safety pins taken out. We were prejudiced against her for she brought the perambulator out again. We all much preferred the mail cart with which we could run races. There was a way of balancing the weight that enabled the one in the shafts to run downhill in a state of suspension that was as good as wings.

The new baby wasn't invited to the party. We had it all to ourselves. Afterwards I was allowed to sit upon Mother's bed. It was a shining occasion. I could see James and Elizabeth sitting like grandaunts on either side of the little table by the fire.

Everything about that house had this glow to it. I think the glow came from Mother. I remember returning there from a summer at the seaside and being made intensely aware of shining floors and gay rugs and flowers that were reflected in mirrors. Mother always had flowers. She always had a garden. There it was a rose garden, nothing but roses. It was in this garden that I discovered the meaning of treachery. I was introduced to deceit. Mother had taken me into the garden. We stood together in the pinkness. All the roses were small and pink, the only ones that would, perhaps, grow in that particular soil. Suddenly, in the very centre of the pinkness, a bright orange tulip shot up. In those harsh northern springs summer comes suddenly. This accounted for the presence of tulips and roses in the same bed. It did not account for any tulip among Mother's roses. This one was such an awful colour, a raging orange. It afflicted me like a blow from an enemy. It *was* an enemy. I did not understand it at the time, but this flower filled me with betrayal — as though somebody you trusted had suddenly deserted you and left you an enemy badge to prove it. Mother explained nothing. She did not pull up the tulip. You couldn't punish a flower. She left it there and ever afterwards when I saw it I had a miserable feeling.

On occasions Mary O'Connell took James and Elizabeth and me to visit our grandaunts. They lived in a wide steep street that went up to the new cathedral. We nearly always visited the cathedral first. It was new and windy and full of sunshine up there. The stones were clean and washed and what grew in them grew sideways, as at the seaside.

Grandaunt Ahn and Grandaunt Brigid lived in a perfect little house. Everything in it, including the furniture, had been made by hand, by their father. In the summer time you went right through the hall from the street to the garden, where there was a damson tree and a view of the river. Grandaunt Ahn told us that her father had built the house for her mother because of the damson tree. Grandaunt Brigid told us he had built the house because of the view of the river. They always argued about it, this against that and that against this until the impoliteness began to show. It always ended by each of them saying that the other could have it her way.

Grandaunt Ahn was in her early twenties when Grandmother was born. This, according to Father, made them all great-grandmothers. Ahn was a little shell of a woman who consisted chiefly of clothes. She resembled one of those wooden dolls that could be peeled to the bone. She wore a black lace cap with lappets that lay against her cheekbones like shutters. Her eyes were large and deep and dark, and when she smiled the sadness went out of them and you *knew* she was happy. Grandaunt Brigid was tall and stately and although she was not fat she was puffy. She had long hands and feet with little cushions on the insteps and on her fingers. Her cheeks were full of little red veins. When she spoke the words were puffed from her lips. She was the younger but she domineered over Ahn. She contradicted everything that Ahn said. Her clothes did not billow away from her the way Ahn's did. They clung to her in satiny folds or were clamped down with bands of velvet. And her cap had no lappets. It stayed well perched above her ears. Each of them wore a black silk satchel attached to the waist. Ahn's was always having to be searched for. It would emerge from the folds of her skirts like a kitten. Brigid's was never lost. It always jumped onto her lap when she wanted it.

They always offered us tea but when the tea came they

had it and we got the cake and the biscuits, and Mary O'Connell always told us to 'catch the crumbs'. Whenever we approached the table both Ahn and Brigid shot their hands out tremblingly as though they had to save the china.

They sat on opposite sides of the fireplace. They always had a fire. In summer it was a mere flame but in winter it was a burning core of warmth. Ahn sat on a low armchair against a wall cupboard with blue glass goblets in it. Brigid's chair was taller and harder with a bright wool antimacassar folded in two at the back. When either of them left the room they put on fleecy Shetland shawls over their shoulders. Mother sent them the shawls.

When Grandaunt Ahn and I were alone in her bedroom she always put the miniature chest of drawers into my hands and allowed me to look at her earrings. The miniature chest of drawers was an exact replica of the real chest of drawers in her room. She told me every time that the same person had made them and that either of them could be taken to pieces and packed as flat as a pancake. When we were about to leave the room and go downstairs again she always whispered into my ear: 'Give my dear love to Katie.' Katie was my mother.

Brigid never sent her love to anybody, but she always asked Mary O'Connell about Father. 'What is he up to now?' she asked, then she would look quickly at me or James and say that my hair ought to be cut or James ought to have a horse. He had a rocking horse with real piebald skin but this did not satisfy her because it 'wasn't as good as a circus'.

Brigid was triumphant because the new baby was given the name of Brigid. 'They have two Katherines and two Elizabeths and two Brigids,' she remarked and looked hard at Ahn. It made me wish my name were Ahn. I was glad nobody had ever made me a Brigid. Mary O'Connell said that 'next time', she would bring the baby. Neither Ahn nor Brigid said a word. They did not like babies.

When the time came for us to go home they always began to fumble in their satchels. Ahn would take out a crisply new Bank of Ireland note for five pounds and give it to me.

Brigid took one out and gave it to James. They took turns over Elizabeth. We never saw these notes afterwards. As soon as we were out in the street and around the corner Mary O'Connell took them from us and gave us peppermints or bull's-eyes instead. We preferred the bull's-eyes. They lasted a long while and no matter how much you licked them the pattern never came off.

Mary O'Connell took James and Major and me to see the burning of a traitor. His name was Lundy. In the time of King James and King William of Orange, Lundy had very grievously offended the City Apprentices. They were never able to forget it. Every year they hung him out from the high Walker Monument and burned him. Walker was the governor of the city at the time of Lundy — so his statue must have got a good deal of pleasure out of the destruction of Lundy's effigy.

At the time of the afternoon when we were accustomed to return from our walk, Mary O'Connell took us out. She turned down the little side street past the grocery shop, which had an uncle who was a monsignor, and instead of going through Bishop's Gate we went directly upon the City Walls, at their widest place, where the Monument was. It was twilight and the cold air was sharpened for frost. There was a great crowd packed around the monument railings. Mary O'Connell put me upon one of the obsolete cannon which always kept their noses out of the gaps, waiting, as black as boars, to snort at the invader. Major got upon the cannon too, behind James who kept telling Mary O'Connell that he wanted to see. Major and I had no desire to see. It got worse and worse, darker and darker, and there was something in the atmosphere that filled you with terror. It was an hour of gloom and doom. When it was almost dark enough for the moon to come out, the people crushed in together and let out an awful roar. They wanted Lundy — the way another crowd had wanted Barabbas. It was so dark that you could hardly see when one person ended and another began. And then, high up in space where the poor stuffed man swung on his gibbet, a star appeared. It stayed poised, waiting for the wind to swing Lundy towards it. As soon as his feet touched it it went off like a meteor and the blaze began. The traitor hung in the heavens like a lantern. He burned from his feet upwards. All his joints went off with cracks and explosions, and rags and tatters fell down in awful, ghostly wisps upon our faces. The more he burned, the more he exploded. It was pure terror to hear and wonder what part of him it was. Everybody cheered, except Major and I. Everybody seemed delighted, but we were delighted when it was all over, when the sparkle stopped and the night was as black as pitch. It was a relief when we got off the Walls, down into the streets where lamps were lit and all was in its customary position.

James pestered Mary to tell him more and more about Lundy. All that she would say was that: 'Lundy had opened the Gates and that he was actually a hero.' He was certainly a hero when he was upon the gibbet. You forgot all about Mr Walker who had the Monument. Father wished to take us up the Monument by the spiral staircase which wound and wound inside it. Mother forbade him to do it. I told him quite politely that I had no wish at all to go up so far to see the view over the city. It was quite enough to peep over the noses of the cannon or, at the worst, over Waterloo Gate or down over Shipquay Gate where you saw the Guildhall and the river and the Ferry Landing. The Gate I liked best was Ferryquay Gate where you could see right down into the pastry cook's where Mother bought buns and chocolates. The cook looked as small as James when you saw him from the top of the Gate.

Chapter Six

We were sent into the country that year, and not to our customary summer home. A cottage was rented for the season. It belonged to the golf links and was surrounded by them — except at the back where, when you opened the door, you stepped right out upon a sandy beach. This was very convenient and saved dressing in the morning. You arose from bed and walked into the sea. Major enjoyed this but Elizabeth hated it. She hated the coldness of the water.

Every weekend Father played golf. He often played on other days. He and Major played golf. This took Major from me but, as it gave him to Father, the loss was balanced. Father always brought something home with him after the game, and Major nearly always had a golf ball. Father found watches and odd earrings and bangles and endless gloves and picnic forks and pieces of newspapers and magazines. He was a finder. He was always bringing something out of his pocket to show you or saying: 'Listen to this!' It was nearly always a murder story — about grandmothers smothered under featherbeds by wicked sons-in-law, or misers drowned in pots of scalding water. Mother forbade him to tell me about murders but he said they did not equal those in the *Arabian Nights*. The ones in the *Arabian Nights* did not interest me but his did. He told me not to take Mother too seriously and that every time we had chicken for dinner a murder had been committed somewhere. This put me off eating chicken and involved me in arguments with Mary O'Connell. She did her utmost to prove to me that chickens had no capacity for suffering, that they were entirely subject to the will of man or woman. She proved it to me. She asserted that she could make any hen or rooster in the world walk a straight line like a trapeze. She took

James and me into the kitchen one morning and demonstrated it. A large white rooster was tied to the table. She took a piece of white chalk and drew a line across the flagged floor. She then untied the rooster and held him in a certain fashion by the wings which seemed pleasant to him. He made no complaint, but his eyes looked wild. She stroked his head and called him a pretty birdie in tones of affection. Then she began to whirl him in circles. When she had whirled him enough she put him down upon the floor, with his beak on the white line — and it was perfectly true. That bird walked the chalked line to the very end. After that I was able to eat chicken again. But, although I believed Mary O'Connell, I did not disbelieve Father.

One day Father held me up over a thorn hedge to see a madman. According to Father he was stark naked and stark mad. He was certainly naked. All he had was his own hair. He looked fascinating to me in the cornfield. He was waving his arms and swimming through the corn so that you could see the red poppies and the blue cornflowers. He was followed by a collie and Father told me that the collie was mad too.

One Sunday morning when the church bells were ringing a terrible thing happened. Father was playing golf with somebody who had a lady attached to him. It was a cold morning and the lady had a muff. It was either too early or too late for muffs, and the lady only had the muff because she had a baby Belgian griffon. When the sun came out she put the griffon on the ground. It attached itself to Major. Major ignored it. It was such a small creature that he wasn't quite sure about it. It was like a spider — you couldn't tell whether it was an animal or an insect. It worked itself into a panic trying to make Major pay attention. It was exasperating. Just to put it into its proper place Major decided to take one snap at it. He snapped at the wrong moment for as he snapped the little beast gave a leap and Major swallowed it. It almost choked him and when they got it out it was dead. The lady made a scene. She attacked Father and Father told her plainly that if Major had been choked it would have been a major and not a minor affair. He and Major were very perturbed when they came home and were in great need of sympathy. Of course we all sympathised also with the lady and the baby griffon but a dog which had to be kept in a muff should never have been exposed to golf links. Father wrote a cheque and sent it to the lady, beseeching her to get a new griffon and keep him where he belonged.

Mother wished us to go away from that place because of the madman and his collie. But they caught the madman. And the next thing was that Elizabeth had hives and had to have bran baths. Mary O'Connell was very busy with Elizabeth, and James and I and Major lived on the beach. Father stopped playing golf and was absent again. Everybody wondered where Grandmother was.

Chapter Seven

I was awakened in the middle of the night. My throat was dry and my eyes stung and somebody was pounding out great knocks into the darkness. Our nursery was at the top of the house. Mary O'Connell slept in a smaller room at the far end of it. The door between was always left open. I called to her but she did not answer. My voice was too hoarse and muted to reach her. I climbed out of bed and made my way to her and succeeded in rousing her. The house was on fire and the knocks were coming from the street!

I was carried down a ladder in the arms of a fireman who smelt of tarpaulin. The world was illuminated magnificently and far below, in a circle like a circus, I saw my mother in her dressing-gown, the new baby brother in her arms. The baby was two weeks old. When the fireman took me to her she begged him to rescue Major who was shut in the yard at the back of the house. The fireman absolutely refused to risk his life for 'a brute like that!' Mother pleaded eloquently and with the desperation of those who offer diamond necklaces for loaves of bread in starvation emergencies. The knowledge that Major was in danger was an affliction to me. I willed the man with all my petitional powers to do what Mother wished. Finally, after much persuasion, he assented. He gave in because Mother and I pleaded so eloquently. We assured him that Major would not harm him. Major was a gentleman. I discovered then, in the middle of a November night with the house burning down, that Major had acquired a perfectly awful reputation for vindictiveness against all men in uniforms. During a muzzling period he had been caught in an open street with a bare face and been arrested by a member of the local Constabulary and brought home in disgrace. He never recovered from the ignominy. From that moment onwards he either avoided men with queer hats and too many buttons or he chased them for their lives. The poor brave fireman who would go through flames to rescue a human being was scared to death at the thought of rescuing Major. I prayed for Major. And presently there he was — in the arms of the fireman who told Mother that he had leapt into his arms and clung to him like a little child. Ever afterwards Major showed his devotion. He became a visitor at the fireman's home and took an interest in his children. If he could he would have taken them presents or put money in the bank for them. Whenever he met the fireman in the street he flung himself into his arms and embraced him on both cheeks.

The house burned upwards into the skies. It shone towards the stars like a new planet that kept going off in meteors. The dome of Grandmother's chapel resembled one of those large glass marbles that has a pattern inside; then it split open, rose like a fountain, and came down in fireworks. All about us voices were saying that Father had done it. Something was revealed to me about Father as something had been revealed to me about Major. I could accept no fault in my father that was unjustifiable just as I could accept no fault in Major that could not be traced to a *reason*. Father was nowhere visible. He was so often absent that it was not noticeable.

We three children were put into the hotel with the dangerous wine cellar. I was prejudiced against this hotel so I kept slipping out of it to my mother. I preferred to be with her in the circus. It was a most exciting and spectacular night and it would have been a pity not to be in it. But I was, finally, put back into the hotel. Grandmother was there and she said, also, that 'Father had done it'.

The next day when I saw him I asked him quite simply if he had done it. He looked at me with his jet-black eyes. 'Don't ask me,' he said; 'I spent the night on the sofa. I was the last to be rescued.' The fact that I had been the first to be rescued and he the last seemed to put our importance on the same level. But it disturbed me frightfully that he had almost been forgotten. That put him into the class with Major. It made me love him more passionately than ever.

The house was burned to the ground. It was not insured. Salvage men were hired to clear away the wreckage. On a December day, in a biting wind, Father and Major and I and the salvage men went over the ruins. I wore a bonnet and scarlet mittens and I kept slipping into holes. Father and Major always waited for me like gentlemen and helped me out, but the salvage men were in a hurry. Father and Major and I were against the salvage men. We were combined against them. Major would have preferred to have done the job himself. He was always picking something up and showing what it must have been. Father told the men that diamonds were indestructible but that you might as well look for needles in haystacks. High above us a gable wall was exposed. A piece of familiar but faded French wallpaper kept flapping in the wind and then being slapped again upon the wall. Birds were flying as though frightened. It was cold and dismal and the charred smell got into your throat and the salvage men continued trying to make Father obedient to them. But Father did not give in. When they went away he fastened my gaiters. He went down on his knees on the blackened wreckage. 'Dearest lady,' he said to me, 'there are two things that you must never tell anybody — your income and your religion!'

We went back into the hotel. I hated the hotel smell. When you entered you had to pass a bar where a lady with very frizzy hair was always tinkling glasses. Mary O'Connell always hurried us past her to the stairs and every time the voice of the lady in the bar said we were not to take Major. But Major always took himself. He was upstairs before any of us. It was his duty to see us safely out of our coats.

There was a day when we did not go out. It was afternoon all day, a dim twilight. It was going to snow. Mary O'Connell was crying and Mother's door was locked and nobody seemed to know where the key was and whether she was inside or outside. Mary O'Connell asked me suddenly if I would like to see my little new brother. She said I ought to see him — that he 'resembled wax'.

She took me upstairs and downstairs and along corridors where nothing was as bright as the brightness of our own house before the burning. We came to a place with candles. The new baby was lying in a little box with a very white fluted lining that made me think of Mother's cambric night-gowns. He was very still and yellow and Mary O'Connell said that that was the jaundice and that he was exactly a month old. Nobody told me that he was dead and I was never sure about it. He was only slightly more unreal to me than he had been alive. It was only very much later that his significance reached me. He has remained with me in the nature of a seraph who descended from heaven solely to participate in the burning of a house.

Chapter Eight

Mother had transformed an old farmhouse into a summer home on the shores of the Swilly — that inlet of the Atlantic that is known as the Bay of Shadows. Its waters are so lucid that clouds are reflected in their depths. So many summers of my childhood were spent in this place that I cannot remember them by dates. I can only recall what happened there.

I had to lie in that place in a splint with a weight attached to my foot by a strong cord on a pulley. I had a daybed by the window in the sitting room which looked out directly upon the garden which was a forest of hollyhocks — messy flowers which always seemed, to me, to need washing. Green linnets clustered and fluttered on the sandy paths. Three gates led out of the garden. One, to the right, from the path below my window, went into the lane which took you to the farm about a mile up towards the hills behind the house. The front gate at the bottom of the garden also led into the lane, but where the lane had abandoned its hedges and run out by itself onto a rocky bridge over a stream. Beyond the little bridge it was all marshland, full of purple irises and creamy with meadowsweet. The lane ended at the road — on which school children passed in the mornings and afternoons. The girls always walked properly upon the road but the boys danced and gesticulated upon the dyke like demons. On the other side of the road were the sand dunes which we crossed when we went to the shore.

The long days were so quiet. A little speckled hen habitually came in by the open window to lay her egg on a cushion. It was a bright blue silk cushion and when she squeezed out the egg it trembled for the fraction of a second, lucent as a pearl on the blueness, before it hardened. She had very lustrous black and white feathers and a very *soignée* appearance. Everything about her was sleek and absolutely in its place. She wore her red chillers like a locket and her tiny white ears were carved like pieces of ivory. She only stayed to lay her egg. We never became intimate. She always managed to keep just out of touch. And when she was on the cushion — as fastened down as I was although for a different reason — her round and beautiful pebbly eye gave me more *méfiance* than tenderness.

It was during the splint periods that I read a vast number of little red books containing morals on temperance. Most pitiful tales of the 'Come home, Father' variety stirred me horrifically. I have not the faintest notion how these books were acquired. They occupied a shelf in the sitting room. They were published by an Episcopal Society and must have been purchased as a pure act of charity. I am certain that I got past Mary O'Connell with them simply because she never read anything but her prayer book, where all the places were marked with lace-edged pictures of the saints. I think they escaped my grandmother because they were so obviously intended for youthful consumption. They introduced me to drunkards.

Grandmother would sit and sew and talk. She sat by my shoulders on a chair with a very high back. I heard when she creaked and when her silks made a swishy sound. I could see her hands. On one finger she had three wedding rings: her own and the thin one that had belonged to her mother and the ring that had belonged to Grandaunt Waters. On the third finger of her right hand she wore a ring that resembled three. It was a golden serpent with emerald eyes and it wound round and round her finger from head to tail. Her workbox was open, its fat satin lining nipped well in with buttons. When she pressed in a needle or pin you always expected the satin to burst. It made a little crack like seaweed.

Her beautiful face would lean forward between me and the fire of faggots and turf burning upon the hearth. She wore a Mary Stuart white lace cap, its peak edged with tiny pearls. Her dark curls billowed from it. She was my darling companion. She was there when Major was not there. She was my gateway to the World. She always had something to say. She told me that Abraham Lincoln never wore buttons when he was young. His mother had invented a system of small twigs and holes by which his clothes were held fast to his body. Grandmother adored Lincoln. She had been in love with one of his young men and had remained permanently in love with him. On her deathbed she insisted upon looking into a mirror to see if all was in order as she went to heaven to meet him. She prejudiced me against Grandaunt Waters who was 'for the South'. Grandmother told me how she had dreamed, on her first night in New York, of soldiers lying with bandaged heads against the kerbstones. A year later her dream had come true. She was the sort of person who dreamed dreams that came true.

Mary O'Connell was devoted to her. But they had a quarrel. Mary O'Connell accused her of being a traitor. She said that anybody who would dance with the British Fleet was a traitor. Grandmother said that she had received an invitation and that the only reason why she could not go would have been if she had *not* received an invitation. She would wear her lace dress over the violet *moiré* foundation, and no jewellery.

Mary O'Connell was horrified. 'Excuse me, Ma'am, it doesn't matter what you wear. I don't care if you go in a petticoat.'

Grandmother said to me when Mary O'Connell had left the room: 'You can't argue with servants. It is a bad principle.' She described the wonder to me: battleships at the mouth of the moonlit bay, illuminated like Christmas trees, and the most enchanting music — nothing at all in it but the purest delight.

The quarrel did not diminish. It dried into a curious tension. Mary O'Connell went about with a face that seemed to be paralysed. Whenever she had occasion to speak to Grandmother clouds rolled between them and nothing was quite as clear as it ought to have been.

The windows were kept open in the summer. Even when it rained nobody shut them. There was a fixed belief that summer rain was a blessing, that nothing but good could come of it. Somebody was always coming in with wild marguerites or gillyflowers or dying poppies. Desolate and perishing wildflowers would be pressed on the seats of chairs or upon the floor where there was always a scrunch of sand.

On an afternoon full of white butterflies and the scent of southernwood there was the sort of stillness that belongs to summer afternoons. A linnet was asleep on the path, its wing stretched out with abandon. Grandmother was sewing. She told me that Catherine of Siena never wasted a thread. She always bit them off right at the needle. Suddenly, in a pause, we both heard the thud of hoofs. Grandmother stood up so quickly that her work fell off her lap. She listened. I listened too. It was nothing. It might have been the baker's cart or the paraffin man. But there was a clutch at my heart, a sharp spurt of something that frightened me. The thuds came galloping on. At that time the hollyhocks were so tall that I could not see any vehicle arriving at the coach house. I was unable to see who it was, but the galloping came right up to the very door of the coach house and I heard Corney's voice. He was scolding. He was shouting and a horse kept snorting and blowing and all the time Grandmother stood there as though the world had become a phantom.

Then Mary O'Connell came and stood on the threshold. Grandmother looked round at her. 'What is it now?' she asked.

'Corney says he's foundered the mare. Her legs are stiffening like telegraph poles.'

'Send for the vet.'

I lay there, wondering in a sort of rigidity. I knew who it was before Grandmother said it. 'Your father . . .' she began, and did not finish it. She picked up her sewing and held it as though she did not know where to put it. She wrung her hands with the material in them. 'Oh, dear! He's . . . he's beyond the beyond . . . .'

Father stood on the threshold where Mary O'Connell had stood. 'Dear Lady,' he began but I did not know which of us it was meant for. Grandmother was staring at him. I saw Mary O'Connell behind him. 'Come in,' Grandmother said; 'allow Mary O'Connell to pass you.' Her voice had the sound of reconciliation to Mary O'Connell in it. She was so much against my father that she was on Mary O'Connell's side.

'I have ordered dinner,' he remarked mockingly, 'if it is not too late.'

'It is the middle of the afternoon.' Grandmother sat down. She smoothed out the piece of sewing.

Mary O'Connell began to spread a cloth on the table and lay down knives and forks.

'Cold mutton as usual, decorated with mint sauce,' Father said very lordly and haughtily. Then he beamed at me and added: 'Like ducks on the pond. They go together. You would no more drink the pond without the ducks than you would drink mint sauce without mutton.' He made a grimace.

'John!' Grandmother pleaded with him as though he were breaking one of the Commandments.

'John!' he repeated, mimicking her perfectly.

'I hear you have foundered the mare,' Grandmother said sternly.

'So they tell me. That fool Corney got her from me with her legs going. He should have walked her up and down and given her brandy.' He glared at Mary O'Connell. 'Tale-teller,' he mocked.

'John!' Grandmother was drawing him off Mary.

'John!' he mocked, slightly higher. He made a little sign with his forefinger on his forehead, pretending to fix a peaked cap into place.

Mary O'Connell asked, in a perfectly awful voice, if there was anything else he wished for.

'Bring me cheese and bring me bread and bring me butter for my bread.' He beamed at me again, dark and glancing as a devil. He came towards me, stopping when he got to the chair with the pulley to pick up my weight. 'How much does this weigh?' he roared in a voice of thunder. Nobody answered him. 'A good two pounds, I should say.' He put it down. 'All a pack of nonsense.'

Grandmother rose brusquely and stretched down the daybed as though she intended to put the weight back into position. All she did was to snatch the speckled hen's white egg off the cushion. She put the egg into her workbox. She began to sew again, measuring a thread off a spool at arm's length.

'Not a strip of good to you,' Father said to me. 'That doctor goes by guesswork.'

Grandmother stopped threading her needle. 'Don't put lies into her head,' she said. There was a burning rivalry between her and my father about me for some reason. They fought over my body as they fought over my soul.

'Lies!' He sat down upon the edge of my bed. 'I never give you anything but the truth.'

I believed him. Mary O'Connell came in with a tray full of dishes. 'There's practically a full leg of mutton,' she said sternly. 'Would you sit over to the table, sir?'

Father stood up. His beard was coal-black. His eyes were sparks. 'Don't *sir* me,' he said.

'John,' Grandmother began again, 'I implore you!'

Father danced over to the table like a goat. He was really an incorrigible man, as Mary O'Connell said. He couldn't be put down. He was quite gay and easy when he asked where the carving tools were.

'In their place,' Mary O'Connell answered.

'Are they functioning?' he demanded.

'If the knife is not sharp enough I'll ask Corney,' she began.

He interrupted her. 'Oh, no, you don't. It's bad enough what he has allowed to happen to the mare.' Father seized the long thin-bladed carving knife and began to switch it into the air like a scimitar. Mary O'Connell let out a scream and Grandmother cried 'John!' again, but differently.

When Mary O'Connell screamed Father whirled the knife more than ever. He only stopped whirling it to point it at her as though they were having a fencing match. She backed away from him and when she moved round the table he moved after her. When she turned he made such a tempestuous dash that he landed almost face to face with her, the knife up in the air. Grandmother was standing up now. Her face was pale. She went out of the room quickly and came back almost at once. Father was still chasing Mary O'Connell round the table. He was letting out war whoops. When Mary O'Connell got a chair between them he lifted the chair with the carving knife and got clear at her again. He was not in earnest but Mary O'Connell was. She was scared to death. I wanted him to stop. I wanted to catch him when he came by but he never came close enough. There seemed suddenly to be a great deal of noise. Grandmother was ordering him to put down the knife and 'eat his dinner before it got cold'.

'Cold before cold,' he sang out, 'it couldn't be colder.' He laughed the most awful laughter and I heard Mary O'Connell praying. She was saying the litany. The cloth began to move off the table. The chairs all seemed to be where they had never been before. There was a dreadful sense of something about to become real.

Then, without warning, two policemen came into the room. They were members of the Royal Irish Constabulary. They had harps on their uniforms. They took hold of Father firmly and removed the carving knife from him. Mary O'Connell sank down upon a chair, her white apron flying up like the wind over her face. Father said, mocking at the policemen as he had mocked at Mary O'Connell: 'Allow me, at least, to say farewell to my daughter!' It was so strange when he said it. It made me realise that I was a daughter. When he came to the bed they still held him by the arms. When he put his head down I flung my arms round his neck and would not let him go. I clung to him like mad. They asked me, please, to let him go. They told me to let him go in a voice of authority. I did not let go. When one of them put his hand on my arm I bit him. Grandmother began to implore me the way she had implored Father. Mary O'Connell took her head out of the apron and groaned when she saw what was happening. In the end, of course, the policemen won. They were stronger than I was. We were torn asunder. They took Father out between them. They took him away. The silence was awful, black as pitch. I turned over and put my face into the pillow. I refused to listen, to hear. What did it matter what they said to me now? This had happened. It let in upon my subconsciousness all the defeats that had ever happened to me. It was a moment when the blow struck. No misery was greater. I was beyond reach of anything ameliorative, untouchable. I would not eat. I would not sleep. I would not talk.

Grandmother stood there, as miserable as I was power-less. She said: 'Now I cannot possibly go to the Fleet Dance.'

I did not ask why. I hated Mary O'Connell as a deadly enemy, one aided by Satan. She won — and all the rest of us were destroyed. Father was not to blame. He was no more to blame than Major, to whom accidents occurred. What had happened with Father was not an accident. It had mounted, stroke by stroke, frantic as music, before my eyes. He hadn't had a chance.

But, the next morning, surprisingly, he was back. I was held, safe, in his strong arms. 'What did they do to you?' I asked. 'Where did they put you?'

'In a dungeon, with chains, the Prisoner of Chillon! The worst thing of all was the thought of all that uneaten mutton.'

It was easier when he mentioned food. I smiled through my tears. He had bacon and eggs for breakfast. I asked for the egg in the workbox for him. Grandmother was absent. She had gone to town by the early train with the market people. 'What a mess!' Father exclaimed in the middle of eating. 'It's too bad you are a woman, Kathie. They are the very mischief.'

I had not known that I was a woman. I told him that I was on his side. I was consoled when he said that that saved him, saved us both. He made me promise to stay on his side no matter what occurred in the future. Together we should be strong. I promised. He left after breakfast. He went back to town. He said that it was a perfectly ridiculous situation 'bound to cost, at least, half a crown'.

All day I lay there thinking about it, then putting it away. I hated it when James and Elizabeth ran round the table and laughed. I hated the peace when they weren't there, when I heard their screams coming in by the back windows from the cornfield.

Mother came. She had a present for me — a bassinet and a donkey. It was one of those invalid carriages on which I could lie flat. It was to be drawn by the donkey and we were all to go on a picnic to the bogs. When the day came to go Mother stayed at home. Mary O'Connell took James and Elizabeth and Grandmother in the governess cart with the pony. Grandmother held the donkey by the reins and my carriage was drawn behind, with Major in train. It was quite a cavalcade. we bumped up over the rocky lane and visited the farm. The farmer's wife was a Mrs Patch. Her real name was O'Doherty but as everybody in that place had the name of O'Doherty they were all known by their nicknames. You never heard the name O'Doherty mentioned. There was a great midden in front of the farm, as large as a lake. It was brown and hairy with straws and smelt of cowsheds so badly that you had to hold your nose when you passed.

Grandmother told us about princesses who had been pushed into the bog in the twelfth century and were still as good as new if they could be got out. She said that on the splendid occasions when turf-diggers had found one of them they came out looking as beautiful as ever. We hoped for a princess. The bogs looked like middens but they had no odour. All you smelt was the wind. They were brushed with cotton rushes. Wild orchids lay upon them in patches of amethysts. It was beautiful up there, remote and swept with exhilaration, 'the next step to heaven,' Mary O'Connell said.

James and Elizabeth were allowed to ride home on top of the turf carts. We had to go slowly — on account of the donkey. Grandmother and Mary O'Connell had more room in the governess cart and James wasn't getting twined up with the reins.

We had to pass a pig which belonged to a little house set far back in some fields. There was nobody about and the pig was out on the boreen watching the world go by. He wished to have a conversation with Major but Major did not wish to have one with him. Major went politely to one side. The instant he tried to get past, the pig prevented him. He and Major had a little game of darts across the road, then they both suddenly lost their tempers and became locked in a real combat. Major could have jumped into the bog but he must have had no wish to emulate princesses, or perhaps he did not know that you can swim in bogs. Grandmother and Mary O'Connell commanded Major to leave the pig and get into the governess cart. It was too late for Major to obey them. He was too much engaged. He and the pig fought as though they were in an arena. It resembled the pictures of bullfights and early Christians and lions. You did not want to look but you had to. It got worse and worse. Then the pig lay down. Grandmother was in a fearful state. She said that ladies should never visit bogs alone and she wished Father were there.

A man and a woman came across the fields. They were not in a hurry. It took them ages to come. Major was exhausted. His tongue was hanging out and he was panting for breath. The man and the woman made an awful fuss. They insisted that the pig was dead and could not be used for bacon. Grandmother said she was dreadfully sorry the pig was dead and she scolded Major. Mary O'Connell stopped her from scolding Major. She said it was cash and not sympathy that was needed. Then Grandmother invited the man to visit Father. She assured him that Father would be furious when he learned that Major's life had been in danger. She said, in her haughtiest manner, that pigs such as that one should be kept at home and not allowed on broadways.

Father had to give the man a cheque but he praised Major. He said it wasn't every dog that could kill a pig. 'Just imagine,' he remarked to Grandmother, 'how very much worse it would have been if Major had not been there. The pig might have attacked you!' He made her realise that Major had saved her life.

The Cheetah we had there — all Mother's cats were named Cheetah — had kittens. She kept them under the American stove in the kitchen. The kitchen was directly opposite the sitting room, separated by a flagged passage which led directly to the porch. Major kept a bone on the porch. On a very hot day he brought his bone into the flagged passage. One of the kittens peeped out at him and made a dash across to the sitting room. He put out his paw to stop her, to send her back to her mother. But when he put his paw upon her she never rose again. Mary O'Connell brought her limp body in to show to Grandmother. She said: 'Can you conceive of it? It is a perfect scandal. He's a brute and no mistake.'

Anybody could see that Major did not mean to do it. He was not that sort of person. He and Cheetah were friends. She sometimes washed his ears when he was sound asleep. She continued to be friends with him so it was clear that she did not blame him. She had more justice in her than Mary O'Connell.

When Father was told he said that Mary O'Connell was making a mountain out of a molehill as usual and that no manslaughter charge could be brought against Major. He said that the worst that could be said about Major was that he was unlucky.

From that time on the porch door was kept closed and whenever Major reached for his bone there was always a fuss to see if all the kittens were under the stove.

Chapter Nine

There was a time without splints when I, too, went to the shore in the mornings. The sand was as dry as sawdust and the waves came in with lacy edges and there was nobody there but ourselves. After we bathed, Mary O'Connell made hot Van Houten chocolate on a spirit stove which was shut into a tiny tin screen, or in a hole in the sand. Sometimes we had bites at the crackers while we were still in the towels and our teeth chattering. When Grandmother was not there to help, Corney brought everything in a basket, including Cleopatra, the rubber doll with a whistle in her back. Cleopatra really belonged to Major but Corney kept her on the toolshed window and declared to everybody who remarked upon her nakedness, that she was *his* lady. Cleopatra was a very exciting creature. When she was thrown into the sea she swelled up as large as a good-sized infant and Major was sent out to rescue her. He did it nobly. When the seas were rough and roarers rising it was very dangerous for Cleopatra and often looked as though Major would not return. But back he came, with the life-sized infant in his mouth.

There was one summer when an obnoxious little pug dog fell in love with Major. The affair afflicted the entire summer. She belonged to a family of women who had never been there before. They were not our sort of family for we would never have possessed a dog with its tail in a permanent curl and a broad silk ribbon tied over the creases on its shoulders. This creature — which was a mixture of a dog and a cat and a workbox — attached herself to Major upon a Ruth and Boaz basis: 'Whither thou goest I shall go and thy people shall be my people!'

Major was obliged to suffer her. She was too large to swallow and she couldn't be fought like a pig because there was no fight in her. She was as full of honey as a beehive, ready to kiss anybody or anything upon the slightest provocation. Grandmother told us that the ladies, to whom she belonged, had informed her that she would only approach water if it were in a saucer. Yet when Major went into the sea after Cleopatra she was either so jealous or so genuinely perturbed about Major that she went in after him. Instead of taking the waves, the waves took her. When it was evident that she was being carried out to the Atlantic Ocean we had to cry out to Major to save her. He was bringing in Cleopatra as nobly as ever but he dropped her, trusting that the whistle in her back would keep her floating, and he went after the pug. He brought the pug in. She had to be wrapped in towels and given Van Houten and every bit of her chattered. Major quietly went back to the sea for Cleopatra who had sea wrack all over her as though she had grown hair in the interval. Corney said that Major should be given a medal or mentioned in the daily newspapers like the lifeboat squad.

I remember sitting in the little dippy field behind the stable on a day without a sound in it. There were too many rocks in this field for it to be ploughed. Nobody, not even Mother, could make a garden of it. It had its own decorations — a nutmeg tree and gorse bushes and tall spiny whins. I was sitting on a rock in the sunshine, quiet as a lizard. Suddenly I was aware of a weasel on the rock opposite. Mary O'Connell said that they were worse than rats and more spiteful than Beelzebub. But somehow I was not in the least *afraid*. It was not fear. Nothing chilled through me. The little creature and I were fused into the quietness by the sunshine; we existed there together — in the same climate. But I knew all the time that he was an enemy, that he could kill me. I, on the contrary, could never have killed him. I was aware of him with a burning intensity. All the wits in my body were gathered into consciousness of his presence. All of his were gathered about me. We had no weapons but our eyes. His eyes and mine were held fast together, put up like shields. I was introduced to weasel. I became weasel — aware of his senses. He became me. We became friends. We became more than friends. The identification was as strong as love. I do not know how long it lasted or what broke it but whenever I see a small weasel-like creature moving anywhere I recall him. I go back to his place in nature, the rocks and the sunshine and the *peace*, and the beautiful sweetness of the nutmeg tree upon the air.

I climbed a mountain in that place with Father. Height was a new experience. It enabled one to possess the earth. The Bay lay far below us like blue water in a basin and Father and I owned it. We owned the wind and the heather and the wild-rose bushes hung with the fleece of sheep. Father said that he would take me across the Bay to Port Salon where there were pink caves full of flying gulls.

We had a friend, a shepherd, a boy in bare feet who taught us to make rush crosses. He always had a sheaf of rushes in his brown hands. Out on the close-cropped grass, starred with yarrow, listening to the munching sheep, he weaved Maltese crosses as evenly, neatly and significantly as illuminated letters. He taught me how to snare blackbirds. It was quite simple. You could catch one anytime you wished. He dug a sod out of the ground on three sides, cutting it with a knife and bending it back on the fourth side as if on hinges. Then he scraped out the earth and put fat wriggling worms into the hole and put the sod back, but holding it up with a twig so that the hole was just open enough for the blackbird to see the worms. The twig was attached to a cord and we were attached to the cord at a distance, behind briar bushes, or with our backs to the hole so that we seemed disconnected. But one of us kept the corner of an eye on it and immediately the blackbird went in, we jerked the cord, the sod fell — and we had the bird. We took him home and shut him up in the coach house. One day we had five blackbirds with their bright orange beaks flying about in the coach house and eating their fill of corn. We always let them go home at bedtime.

On Sundays this shepherd played cards during Mass. He was no more religious than I was. When there was no horse of our own in the stable Grandmother was driven on the

O'Doherty car to Cock Hill Chapel. She and I sat on one side and Mrs Patch and the shepherd sat on the other, with Mr Patch on the dickey. Grandmother wore her best clothes when she went to the midday Mass. She was all silks and flounces. Whenever Mr Patch offered to put the horse's blanket over our knees Grandmother had to be very strong-willed against him. When we drove fast her skirts fluttered like a flag and it all, somehow, had a great gaiety about it. The Chapel was on a hill where I never heard or saw a cock crowing but during the week whenever a cock crew Mary O'Connell always said that it was the cock on Cock Hill. He was a phantom bird.

Grandmother always sat in the first seat, next to the altar rail, where you could see the priest and the acolytes dressing through the door into the sacristy. You could see how the acolytes behaved on the altar, pinching the one who was changing the missal; or screwing up their faces at the one who was holding the little crisscross cruet when the priest was washing his hands like Pilate. Grandmother said that they were a disgrace and that sometime she really would have to tell about them, but she never did. I always hoped she wouldn't.

One Sunday Major came to church by himself. He came by a different road from the one we had taken. As soon as the Mass began and the organ was rising he walked up the aisle and sat down outside the pew, without a cushion. He was very polite and reverent but Grandmother whispered to me, with her face squeezed tight into her prayer book and the aigrette in her bonnet shaking and her whisper coming out like a hiss, to take him out. I walked down the aisle, smelling the turfy smell of the Sunday clothes. When I got out to where the fonts were there was Aloysius, the shepherd, on the curly stairs which went up to the organ. He and three other boys were playing spoil-five. I did not feel that it was right. I could understand his not praying — but not cards, especially the way they slapped them down on the piece of stairs.

Major and I waited out by the graveyard wall where

there was nobody but horses, tied to stakes and trees. We heard the sound of the people rising for the Last Gospel and then they all poured out from the chapel. Everybody was laughing. They were laughing at the weather and at each other and the horses whinnied and the chapel bells rang their maddest. People hopped up on to cars and carts or walked off, trotting like donkeys, the women in their best shawls. The horse went home, as Mr Patch said, like a runaway. Every time I looked at Aloysius he seemed to be quite a different person.

One year we had the Lenten Stations at home. Mary O'Connell arranged it. Mass was said in our sitting room. The cheesy sideboard was cleared out and decorated with lace and candlesticks. The priest from Cock Hill brought the altar stone. Mary O'Connell said that our place was consecrated. Confessions were heard in the bedroom and everybody was forbidden to listen at the window or trample the wallflowers. Everybody on the mountain side came to the Station. They overflowed from the house into the garden, kneeling on the paths with the hollyhocks nodding above them. They confessed their sins and received the sacrament and there was a sermon about there being no excuse for anybody to live in a state deprived of absolution. If they lived at too great a distance from the Church, then the Church, as on this occasion, would come within their reach.

Mary O'Connell was very happy that day. It was a great event to her. She said it was one of the things that could never have happened at Mrs Dysart's.

We went out with the O'Doherty harvesters. Mrs Patch packed a basket with enormous soda breads and pats of butter between cabbage blades. She gave each of us a differently patterned pat of butter — a star or a dolphin or a daisy or the Prince of Wales' feathers. The scythes rasped through the corn at its ankles. It staggered and fell over in long slow waves, with the poppies coming out in tiny red drops. The stubble was as harsh as toenails. A man brought me a nest. There was nothing in it. He said the rats were running like an exodus.

The cornfield was at the back of our house. It rose steeply on the mountain side. When you stood at the upper end of it all you could see of our place was the bright golden thatch of the roof. And when you got to the bottom it stopped at a trench, where the field had been dug out for the house to be built.

Every afternoon regularly, Mrs Patch came down the upper lane from her own house and stood at the top of the cornfield to watch the sunset fall upon the Bay. She spoke to nobody. She kept her eyes out upon the glory and when it was over she turned and went home. Once I was there when she came in. She went over to the hearth and stood upon her tiptoes to kiss her husband. She smiled at me. 'You see,' she said, 'I have no children. I only have a husband.' Aloysius' dog, Sancho Panza, was lying in the warmth.

It was after the corn was cut that the rats came when Corney called the chickens to their peppery mash. The rats ate out of the trough with the chickens. Corney said 'Bad cess!' to them. They were not afraid of him. Once when I was sitting on the porch step a rat slipped by me as quick as lightning. Whenever I was left in bed at night I could not sleep. I was certain that if I went to sleep rats would sit on my head. I was unable to keep my feet stretched to the end of the cot lest they should enter by the bottom, so I sat straight up on the pillow, waiting and waiting for somebody to come. It took hours for anybody to come. I was in the back bedroom with James but James was always sound asleep. I could not wake him up to tell him that I was afraid of rats. James and Aloysius were not the sort of persons to whom you could confess fear.

The word 'cess' troubled me. Men came with a load of faggots and Mary O'Connell said they were to empty the cesspool; then she took us to the shore and when we got back the men were gone. They were very old men, in their seventies, and they referred to each other as boys. One of them would knock at the door and say that the 'boy' was outside. When you went outside to look at the 'boy' there was only an old man with a beard like Abraham's

I asked Father what cess meant. It was a rainy day.
Leaves were blowing and there was an air of misery. Somebody had been crying. I was on a swing and he was pushing
me. He said cess was a tax and, somehow, it did not serve as
an answer.

Margaret, the cook, allowed me to bake a cake. She told
me the exact measure of everything. I stood on a stool at the
kitchen table in one of her white aprons which reached
down over the stool to the floor. I did everything she told
me. When I repeated what she said about the cream of tartar
she had a fit of hysterics. She collapsed onto a chair in a fit
of uncontrollable laughter. Corney stood on the threshold
and gazed at her. We both gazed at her. Presently she recovered. She told Corney that I would be the death of her. I had
a sense of injury, of a vague unfairness that was beyond
either interpretation or explanation. I was glad that Corney
did not laugh. He just smiled a wry, slow smile at Margaret,
a little contemptuous.

Nobody liked Margaret. She made wonderful cakes and
everybody liked her cakes and she liked you to like them,
but she almost snapped your head off if you went into the
kitchen without asking her permission. She sometimes
made mistakes. She once made pancakes with yeast.
Grandmother took them on the plate right into the kitchen
and told her, in no uncertain tones, that when yeast was
used pancakes were not the result. Margaret resented
Grandmother but she could not argue with her the way she
argued with Mary O'Connell. On another occasion we had a
fish sauce with sugar in it instead of salt, and this upset
Father terribly. He said that, even if she were colour blind,
there was no excuse. He said she should be dismissed and
that he would take over the kitchen. Immediately he said
this Grandmother came out on Margaret's side and she went
into the kitchen and locked the door. She was shut in with
Margaret for a long while. Father invited me to go for a
walk. He confided to me that Margaret was probably telling
fortunes and that for anybody with Grandmother's principles the whole business was nothing short of a crime.

Chapter Ten

A new house was built upon the ground of the one that had been burned. I have no recollection of it beyond a hazy registration of rooms with unpapered walls and the odour of paint. We must have lived in it for part of one winter for it was decidedly there that a doll was given to me for Christmas. Mother had brought it from London. It lay in a box, decorated like the little brother's coffin, with its eyes closed. When it was taken out the eyelids opened stiffly and the real eyelashes went upwards into the painted waxen eyebrows. If you pushed a finger into its stomach it said, 'Pa, Pa' one minute and 'Ma, Ma' the next, in a very squealy voice that bore no resemblance whatever to anything human or in the animal kingdom. I had no affection for it. The crystallised fruit in the enormous box in which handkerchiefs were to be kept later was much more absorbing, and the balloons were more exciting, except when they sighed and sank and James and Mary O'Connell blew them up until they burst. That sent me and Major into the corner. It was too remindful of the explosion of Lundy upon the Walker Monument. And it made Elizabeth cry, which was never a pure pleasure. It absorbed all your attention until she was able to stop.

That must have been the winter in which we had a brief spell of morning lessons at the Mercy Convent in Pump Street. Pump Street was where Valetta, the doctor's daughter lived. For some reason I was always exceptionally interested in this red-haired girl. The doctor's house was opposite the Convent. You saw it when you went in and when you came out. Valetta was always either going in or coming out or leaning out of the upper oriel window.

I do not remember *what* I was taught at the Convent. I remember a nun's coarse black serge skirt being used as a pen-wiper and violet ink spilling out into iridescent splashes upon the broad rims of white inkwells. I remember gigantic parchment-like sheets of paper hung on rolls which were whipped over like sheets and blankets when the lessons changed.

It was Mother who drove us to the seaside that spring. There was a new pony and a new governess cart, both black and both larger. The cart was wider and deeper and the wheels were so tall that we were obliged to descend by the door. That was the first spring in which everything had a definite recognition and *renewal*, the significance of a re-gained Paradise from the moment we emerged from the city area. When we moved through the Pennyburn trees — where you could still see the broad Foyle River — we began to follow the little Donegal railway. The road and the rail-way ran parallel as far as Burnside, a tiny station which stood out in the barest condition. It had no trees at all, nothing to decorate it but a truck against the wall and the arm of the signal box. From there the road began to climb the mountain and presently we were high above the first edges of the Bay, at a place named Inch. Mother explained that there was only an inch of land or an inch of water there at any time. When it was dry you could walk across to Rathmullen and Rameltown and the Coast Guard Station. When it was wet you took the little steamboat from Fahan, the next station. Fahan was a wonder. It was where the seaside rally began, where the waves came in. The tiny seaside houses were perched aslant the mountain so peril-ously that they were only held from slipping, it appeared, by the strokes of their white fences or low white walls crusted with shells. The hedges were thick with fuchsias and honeysuckle and the field marguerites had become so tame and civilised that you could see they were the sunflowers' white daughters. They had the same eyes. There was one place on the narrow ledge of road where tea roses caught in your hair as you passed. You had to drive close to the hedge because of the danger on the other side where you might go over into the ravine. Far down below the black crawling train puffed into Fahan Station. People buzzed from it like flies, one stream going up the stairs and coming over the bridge to the mountain side, and the other stream trickling out through the railings to catch the toy steamer at the end of the toy pier.

From Fahan we went down again into the safer road, past the golf links, where Mother drove fast because of the madman. We never saw him but we always saw his collie. Then we came to the road where the O'Dohertys began. Every O'Doherty house had an orchard. People came out to see us go by. We could hardly wait to get out of the governess cart so as to pick everything up again and belong to it.

The shore was the last miracle. The rocks stood up, dripping with sea wrack, the sea breaking against them in fountains; then it lowered its steps and slippered in upon the white, pure sands. There was a high ridge of shells banked against the spiny sea grass.

Happiness is a state. It is immeasurable. It cannot be counted out like Time in an hourglass. It is irrecoverable in its forms. All you ever know is that you have had it. That is the remnant of childhood, the what we had. I had it in that place, on that shore, passionate as all awakenments. Pure, and wild, and true.

It was not Father who took me to Port Salon. It was my grandmother and Mary O'Connell. All was as he had said it was: gulls flying out of the arches and the caves as pink as salmon in the sunlight, plus the element of danger; the awful subjection to the will of the tides, the knowing that if you were caught in there when the waters came you would have to float to the ceiling and be fished out in a shrimp net. Another thing that squeezed the heart was the way the boat sank into the water. The more people who went aboard the deeper she sank until it was almost certain that it would be as much as she could manage to get there. She panted and puffed and groaned all the way. Major wished to swim after the boat but the man with the tickets insisted that either he did not come at all or he came as a paid passenger. Grandmother bought him a saloon ticket.

We had a French governess. She arrived at seven in the morning by the first train, the one that came to collect the market people. The next train would have brought her at noon, too late for morning lessons. We always wished that she would miss the first train and catch the second but she never failed to appear in time for breakfast. On the hottest days she had *chocolat à la crème*. She sipped it with a spoon. She skimmed off the froth which gave her a moustache, then she skimmed off the moustache — with the same spoon — and bared her teeth to bite at the biscuit. She always gave me an impression of waving either the cup or the saucer or the biscuit at you when she had to say something. From the moment she came until she departed at the close of the day we were forbidden to speak English, except at mealtimes. We invented a way out of the difficulty, a form of de-Anglicisation: 'Havez-voo an am mare?' said as quickly as possible. This was certainly not English, but it served to drive in the nails. We should, of course, also have been forbidden to speak anything but French. The non-English let us out without loss of honour.

Mademoiselle went with us everywhere. She went everywhere that Mary O'Connell went — Mary O'Connell's lamb. She replaced Grandmother, but we never accepted the replacement. She never did anything plainly so that you did not notice it. You seemed to know far more about her than you wished to know — that she had ribbons in the flounces of her white petticoat, that she had so many buttons to her gloves and that her parasol came out in the same folds, and that she changed her *guimpe* every second day. Every now and then she showed us the *Bon Marché* catalogue with all the things that little French girls wore. She told us that Paris was the most polite place on earth. Whenever you left a door open she always said, in French: 'One can see that you have never been to Paris.' Paris became a place signalised by closed doors.

She saved me from drowning. It was one of those days when we went up to the bogs. We had walked to the bogs over the fields of the upper farm. She and I were behind the others. We were out on the heathery patches. The whole earth was a shade of blue — the amethystine heather at our feet, the deep blueness of the mountain air, the deep blue of the sky. We walked in blueness. The air was darkening and of the clarity and awareness that goes before rain. Birds were flying low. We came to a place where we had to climb through the heather on the edge of the bog. Suddenly, out of the deep tranquil silence, thunder boomed with the roar of guns. I was so startled that I jumped forward into the bog. I was sinking into the dark peaty water when Mademoiselle grabbed me and got me back onto the heather. Her face was as pale as death. It was her fright that frightened me. She became real, and of a substance that prevented me ever afterwards from mimicking her. It was such a temptation to eat and drink as she did and spread a handkerchief when you sat down, and wipe out the creases from your behind when you stood up.

She provided us with numerous story books, bound in bright red cloth with gilt-edged pages, published by Hachette. These stories never emerged freely from the French into my imagination. For some reason they remained stilted. They lacked the real-life quality of the little red temperance books, although they were actually better stories. We had, of course, all the Aesop fables. It was not then, but when we were much older, that these came back to us. At the time they bored us a little. Let me confess that all fairy tales bored me. I wanted what was *true*. For this reason I was much more interested in the lives of the saints. I was far more thrilled by the story of Margaret Mary Alacoque who had Our Lord come to visit her with his heart exposed outside his shirt like a badge, than I was in the *Water Babies*. The episodes that reached me most out of the *Arabian Nights* were those which told of thieves being boiled in oil, or somebody's head being slashed off with a scimitar. Except pictures. Pictures of anything were absorbing — even Grand Viziers could be endured to be *looked* at.

Father and Mother came to visit us. There were lots of strawberries. Father said that Major was becoming old. I was utterly unable to believe that anything could touch Major that did not touch me. We were the same age. If I were still young then so was he. But Father relieved the impression of evil by confining it to a single issue: it was time for Major to have a son. Major's son would, in due course, be presented to us. None of us welcomed the idea because of the subtle undercurrent that he was, in some fashion or another, to usurp Major. But when the puppy actually came we all adored him. He was a chocolate lamb, not jet-black like Major but the spit of Major in shape and form. He had darling shaky legs that sprawled, and he played with everybody and everything. You just could not help loving him. He played with our toys, with the kittens, with anything in the hat-stand, from shoes to taffeta parasols. He ate Elizabeth's cane-handled white silk parasol with the prinked-out frills which she always took to Cock Hill on Sundays. I had to give her mine. I didn't wish to give it and she did not wish to have it, but it was still something to hold open over her Leghorn hat, or poke into her shoes when it was closed. Major's son shook the kittens and chased them and they never died. They spat like mad and that made both him and Major wag their tails with great flaps on the flagged floor. Major taught him to catch rats — field rats and water rats. They were always in the stream, battering the water cress and giving little squeals.

Major always was there the first thing in the morning when you woke up and the last thing at night when you went to bed, but Mary O'Connell always made him go out after we had said our prayers. James and I combined to keep Major's son behind, either in his bed or mine while we galloped through the prayers. But Mary O'Connell found out about this one morning when she found James' head and the head of the chocolate lamb on the same pillow. Afterwards he and Major were locked up in the coach house.

One morning only Major appeared. The coach-house door was locked. We were forbidden to open it. When we discovered that Major's son was locked up in the coach house we mutinied. James and Elizabeth and I began to dig him out under the coach-house door. But Corney found us. He and Margaret were furious. Margaret wrote a letter about it to our parents. Corney took the letter to the post office. All that Mary O'Connell would say was that it was out of her province. Margaret forbade us to go near the coach house. Whenever we did, Corney was there to shoo us off with a pitchfork. I wrote a letter to Father and our three signatures were attached to it. The letter told him that Major's son had been taken prisoner and that Margaret was the archenemy. Before any responses came, one morning the coach-house door was wide open. When we rushed towards it Corney was there, without a weapon. He made a sign to us to come quietly, as though we were in church. Major was the first to go. It was Major who found his son. He was lying still and quiet on the earthen floor. He had scraped out a perfect oblong space and laid himself in it — to die. We knelt down and mourned him with breaking hearts. We loved him. We would have given the blood out of our bodies to save him — and they had allowed him to die! It was useless for them to apologise, to explain that they didn't know that he was going to die. He had known. He had made his preparations. I was stabbed with the wonder of his prescience, the miracle of his conscious return to eternity.

Corney tried to make us realise that we had been separated from him because he had had a sort of measles. We were utterly beyond the reach of any justification at that stage. We knew that we could have given him love. If love were not a remedy it had, when all was said and done, the faculty of love.

We went about with black faces, enemies to the hilts of our spirits — of Margaret in particular. She had always been a sort of natural enemy in the household; now she became a particular one as well.

Next to her we hated Mademoiselle. We were not good at lessons. Instead of having them in the garden, under the tall hollyhocks where a petal or two always floated down when you were thinking deeply, we were brought into the house

and seated at a table where there was much more authority.
Mademoiselle had a black ebony ruler. It was quite heavy.
You could see where it was rolled at the ends. She had a way
of clattering this down when you were inattentive. Although this made you give the answer sharply, it was never
the answer to anything you wished to remember. Syntax
was merely a queer word that sounded like *sin tax*.

It was associated with punishment that I had to embroi-
der red poppies on a doily for Mother's return. Embroidery
was not my sort of activity. James was let off. Elizabeth had
a piece of canvas netting into which she stuck bright wools. I
never knew what Elizabeth's thoughts were. I only knew my
own, and it always seemed to me that Mademoiselle had
made a mistake.

The days shortened. The flowers fell on the paths. The
wind came in with a great blow from the sea and we began
to have baths in the kitchen at night instead of going to the
shore in the mornings.

Father and Mother came and Mademoiselle ceased to
come. We went to the orchards with clothes baskets, and
James and Elizabeth and I climbed into the trees and shook
down plums and apples. There was one cherry tree, a white-
heart cherry tree. Elizabeth and Mother had the cherry tree.

Father took James away for the day to visit the Coast
Guard Station. James was insufferable about it. He had the
air of a man going with another man *to a place where only men
could go*. Elizabeth and I were reduced to little girls. In the
afternoon it rained. Mother read to us and kept the fire
stacked with faggots. We had pancakes for tea. First of all
we waited for Father and James with the pancakes on the
fender-bars, stiffening. Then we ate them. And the waiting
lengthened out so that the clock was watched for the quarters. When the lamp was lit the storm began to beat at the
windows. Every now and then Mother stopped reading,
listened, and said that she wished they were here. Mary
O'Connell kept coming to the door, plucking at her apron.
Whenever she wished Elizabeth to have her bath Mother
said: 'Not yet.' Finally Mary O'Connell won. Elizabeth was

bathed, fed, and put to bed in Mary O'Connell's room.

It was dark night when Father and James came home. They were both soaking wet. Mother stood up when she saw them. She let out a little moan. Mary O'Connell stood on the threshold behind Father, waiting. Mother went over and took James away from Father. She began to undress him before the blazing fire. Mary O'Connell brought in the sitz bath and towels and kettles of water and the enamel jug full of rain water. Father kept repeating to Mother: 'You understand, Katie, I missed the boat.' Or 'We missed the boat. We swam across after the steamer which was nowhere to be seen. When we got to Fahan the steamer was blind asleep. It was a tough swim. James enjoyed it. Didn't you, James?' When he spoke to James, James never answered. His mouth was tightly shut. His hair was clamped in patches upon his forehead. Mother laid her cheek against his head. She held him when he was wrapped in the fat Turkish towel and Mary O'Connell fed him with a spoon as though he were a baby. Father left pools on the floor wherever he stood. Mother begged him to change his clothes. He said he was waiting for the bath. He wanted Mother to give him a bath too. When Corney came in and carried off the bath with the water in it Father said he needed solid food rather than water and would they please bring in the ham and mustard. He stood on the hearth and steamed. Mother implored him to take off his wet clothes and put on dry ones. He was angry with her. 'You give your attention to your son,' he told her, 'I can damn well take care of myself.' He ate slices of ham in his fingers, then he ate the bread. He forgot the mustard. Mother cried. She tried to tell James a story about a boy in Sparta and then she cried. James' hair dried out into a tuft over the Turkish towel. Mary O'Connell took away the towel and wrapped him in a blanket instead. She asked: 'Will you keep him, ma'am, or shall I?' Father made fun of her. He asked her how her cornelian brooch was. He asked me if I had ever remarked that on no occasion did Mary O'Connell forget to fasten in her starched collar with her cornelian brooch? James didn't cry. He didn't

say a word. Mary O'Connell said he had lost his tongue. He
put it out at her.

Mother said: 'John, you are quite mad.'

'Now, now,' he stopped her, 'if we had both been
drowned you might say that, but here we are!'

Mother wouldn't look at him. She kept her face towards
the fire. Her thin fingers were pressed up against James' ear
and the stones in her rings shone in the blaze.

Mary O'Connell took James from Mother. She made me
go with her. I didn't want to go. I looked back into the bright
room with Mother in the firelight and Father in the lamplight. His beard moved up and down when he munched.
Neither of them said good night.

Chapter Eleven

Another time in that place Grandmother took us to visit a Mrs McIntyre. She was an old lady about the size of Grandaunt Ahn. Her son was a captain in the Enniskillen Fusiliers. She was going away somewhere for the winter and she asked Grandmother if we could take her cat, Dot. She explained that Dot was quite an aged cat but an excellent mouser. Grandmother said we already had several cats and that all our cats were named Cheetah. Mrs McIntyre was firmly convinced that Dot should remain Dot. To change her home was bad enough but to change her name too would be too much for any cat. So we broke the law and took Dot home with us. She was one of those ordinary cats with a tabby-cat saddle and cap which took in her ears, and a tabby tail. The rest of her was snow white. She refused to stay in the kitchen. She adopted the speckled hen's cushion as her permanent home. She was very nice about the hen and always moved off the cushion when the egg had to be laid. She was a most understanding cat. She seemed to know by instinct what was the right thing to do. She was no bother at all.

Mother drove away by herself in the governess cart and came back with a young girl in her bare feet. The girl's name was Sarah. She waited on the table in her bare feet. When her shoes came it was quite a business to get her to wear them permanently. She kept them on the door mat and only stepped into them when she entered a room with a tray. Mother said it was a hard business civilising her. She was always going into the kitchen to reason with her. Sarah was great at games. We played a most exciting Castle Rampant game with her. It began in the upper regions of the cornfield at the back. It was always called a cornfield even when it was growing turnips. Armed with peeled sally-rods one half of us chased the other half back to the Castle. You had to slither like mad down the cornfield and when you came to the deep ditch behind the house Sarah always held you tightly and then raised you up and pushed you through the back window, where the fort was held. Father played this game too. It was an absolutely breathless affair. The heart used to pound out of your body as you catapulted the rods out of the window.

One day I was very hungry. I longed for my dinner. It was codfish with a white sauce. It looked perfectly heavenly on the dish on the table but when I came to eat it it tasted like wood. I could no more have eaten it than I could have eaten a piece of turf. The next thing that I remember after that was that I was singing a 'Glory! Glory!' song right out at the top of my voice *in my mind*, and the doctor was there with a thermometer and Mother had her hands clasped and water was being boiled. I had diphtheria. The next thing I remember was lying on the day bed in a state of bliss. It was peaceful and happy and there were green grapes, like Christmas-tree decorations, upon a plate. It was all over and I was being spoiled.

Mother and Grandmother were both there. Grandmother had her workbox open, the blue as bright and bursting as ever. Mother had a book on her lap. Something awful had occurred about Sarah. Sarah had committed a heinous crime. Mother said it was the limit. Grandmother said: 'It was bad enough about her shoes, but I always knew you would never make anything of her. It's hopeless.'

I listened with all my ears. I didn't wish anything to happen to Sarah. All I discovered was that Sarah had been found with a pudding dish under her bed. 'Imagine,' Grandmother shuddered, 'a custard in it one day and the next . . . It's too horrible! Oh, my dear, you are wise. She must go.' I opened my eyes. I asked if Sarah were going away. Mother turned the page in her book before she said: 'Kathie, if you had a wild rabbit and it wished to go home you'd have to let it go. No matter how much you cared, if it were unhappy with your way of doing things you wouldn't keep it?' It was a question but I did not answer. I would keep Sarah. Sarah, I was told, was a wild rabbit.

Grandmother said that she was a very disobedient girl. She told Mother that '*They* preferred a life without shoes to their feet, and a piece of ling drying out salty on their thatch. A china plate meant nothing at all to *them* and *they* preferred pails to basins. *They* were neither fish nor fowl. . . .'

Mother was shocked. She maintained that there was no reason why they should be allowed to remain that way. Grandmother said she agreed but 'it was too much trouble'. She looked at me very steadily. 'Do you know, darling, that you have been ill? You have been away from us. It's nice to have you back.' She ate a grape and put the plate on the bed for me.

Another time I awoke and they were there, in the same places. But Mother was not reading. She was crying and Grandmother was scolding her. The fire was roaring in great tongues of flame up the chimney. Grandmother was talking about diamonds. She was saying that diamonds should always be kept. All other things went up and down or vanished but diamonds always stayed their own shining selves.

Mother said: 'I knew nothing about it. They were in the bank. How was I to know that he would take them out without asking me?'

'He is capable of anything, *anything.*'

'I blame his mother.'

'My dear, blaming his mother is a sheer waste of time.'

'She drove him.'

'He shouldn't have been driven.'

Mother sighed. She said in a faraway voice, entirely deprived of argument: 'I wish he had consented to become a barrister. *That* was what I wished. He would have been better as a barrister. You see what luck he has. Everything he touches turns to money and then. . . .'

'He loses it as fast as he makes it. I don't feel so bad about the money. Money, as you say, can always be made. But diamonds! Jane wished so strongly for you to have those diamonds, to *keep* them. I remember the last time she wore them, at the opening of the cathedral. I can see her.' She shut her eyes and opened them, staring straight ahead. 'I can see the crowd pushing her against the pillar, and then pushing her into the seat. That was when it happened. She was so stout. Her whalebones were always splitting.'

Mother was silent. She was sad. It was Grandaunt Ahn who had said that Jane was a very wilful woman. None of them could ever master her. Jane was Aunt Waters. She was Mother's Aunt Waters. Mother was Grandmother's daughter but it was Aunt Waters who had brought her up. Grandmother's name was Elizabeth and Grandaunt Brigid said that 'Elizabeth was never at home so how could she bring up a child?'

'Well,' Mother said suddenly and with great determination, 'that happened six months after we were married. I am only finding it out now, but it happened *then*.'

'It's villainous.' Grandmother stopped sewing. She told me to eat the grapes. She said in a louder voice: 'Better be careful. Walls have ears.'

Mother cried again. Tears rolled out of her eyes slowly and fell upon the pages of the book. Grandmother watched her. She tidied her workbox, took the ivory bodkin out of the wrong place and put it into the right place. 'Crying never helps,' she said in a different voice, not scolding. 'There it is, the house has been sold over your head, lock, stock and barrel. It's a marvel there are any sheets.'

'This house?' I asked.

Mother said gently: 'No, Kathie. We're safe here. The new house. It was a very ugly house anyhow. Now we are going to spend the winter here.'

'I'm not,' Grandmother said quickly; 'winter at the seaside is more than I could bear.'

Mother smiled at me. 'We won't mind it,' she said in a voice that made me support her. To me it was the best place on earth.

I didn't know then what the winter was going to be. Mother was not always there. On one occasion she set out in

the dusk to drive to the railway station. Mary O'Connell
tried to persuade her not to go. It was raining. A gale was
blustering. The mist over the iris marshes hid the road. But
Mother said that she had to go. She had to be in the lawyer's
at nine o'clock in the morning. I was still sleeping in the day
bed. Mary O'Connell slept on the couch. First she put Elizabeth and James and the baby to bed; then Margaret went to
bed; then Mary O'Connell knelt on the hearth and said her
prayers while she undressed. She crossed herself and unbuttoned her bodice; then she began the Hail Marys and untied
her tapes; then she finished the Rosary, all loosened up.
When she got to the Amen she stood up and things began to
drop off her, but she always kept her chemise. It came down
over her knees. She was not yet at the chemise, one evening,
when Major scraped to get out. It was not the first time he
had asked that evening but Mary O'Connell either had her
hands full or her lap full and she had paid no attention to
him. She had locked the front door after Mother. She said
'Bad Scran' to him but she let him out. She came back and
put on her dress. She was shivering because she had left the
door open for him. He did not return to his rug in the porch.
Mary whistled and whistled. She heard him barking far
down the lane. She came in and told me she did not like it.
There was something queer in the way Major was barking.
She got Margaret out of bed and she made Margaret light
the lantern and stay with me while she took the lantern and
went after Major. I was to look out of the window and if she
flashed the lantern three times Margaret was to come. Margaret said it was all nonsense and she was sure Major was
only catching rats but Mary O'Connell said she had to go.
Margaret and I both kept our eyes glued to the window. The
rain was slashing down and it was impossible to see clearly.
But there were no three flashes. Then, presently, we saw the
headlights of a vehicle coming up the lane.

Mary O'Connell carried Mother into the room. She had
fallen when driving over the narrow bridge into the stream
and her ankle had been sprained. The pony had scrambled
out into the marsh and waited for her. It was Major who

found them. If it had not been for Major, Mother might have spent the night in the marsh. Her ankle was swollen. Mary O'Connell bathed it and patted it but the swelling stayed. In spite of this, Mother insisted that she had still to be at the lawyer's at nine o'clock. So she and Mary O'Connell went off at daybreak when the air was a sheet of dampness and cobwebs were spun in the garden in little nets of pearls.

After that I developed an anxiety complex when Mother was absent. I could not bear when the wind whined and she was not at home. I was certain that when she was out there, exposed to the elements, she was always in danger. I began to pray for her safety, to ask God to take care of her.

Chapter Twelve

We were living in a grandaunt sort of house in a tiny street, Kennedy Place. It ended in a cul-de-sac against a wall. The houses were very fine and quiet. Everybody who lived in the street was fine and quiet. They walked with grace towards the doors and when they knocked or rang bells they waited with the utmost politeness for the doors to open. And even when the doors opened they were in no hurry to enter. They waited until they were told to enter. Nothing ever happened in a hurry. The single exception was the house opposite ours, against the wall. That house had seven boys and they had no patience at all. They never waited for the maid to open. They rang and rang again and brought their mother. She had curly hair. When she opened the door the boys darted past her like flashes of lightning and the door was clapped shut before you had time to see the wall-paper.

James and I lay in the room that should have been the drawing room but was made into Mother's bedroom My bed was by the window and James' was on the other side of the fireplace. Mother's bed was in the middle of the room. It was always made up and tidy and I never saw her in it.

There was a strong iodoform smell. A nurse came every morning after Mary O'Connell had swept and dusted; then the doctor came. I was given bandages to roll. I was kept in bed but I was not ill. I was simply forbidden to walk. James was the one who was ill, for whom the doctor and nurse came. He was in very great pain. Every now and then great screams of agony burst from him. Mother would come. Mary O'Connell would come. But nothing stopped the pain. I think I must have been in a splint again. I do not remember anything about it except that I never seemed to get out of

the bed. All my attention was absorbed by the presence of
James. Everything that happened in that room was focused
upon James. It was terrible to have to listen when he had the
pain. I had to lie there, knowing this awful suffering. Pity for
James swelled through me in gushes. I wanted to stop it, to
stop his screaming, and I could do nothing. He had been
'chilled to the bone', the doctor said. His hip bone was
breaking off in chips. He actually had an acute form of
ankylosis. When the pain was very bad he was given drops
of laudanum and the doctor said that 'another chip of bone
was coming through'. The doctor put glass tubes into his hip
and the nurse took them out and held them. I was told to
look out of the window. The nurse always asked me what
was happening in the street. That was when I counted the
seven boys. I learned which of them was Alexander and
which was Eric and which was Jack — and all their differences. Hugh was the youngest. He wore petticoats. They
only had one maid and she did not wear an apron with
bows. She wore a real apron that covered her all round.

The nurse made our beds very tidy. It was more peaceful
when she went away and James and I could speak. James
did not always answer. Mother would make a sign to me
and the silence would begin to last. I had to wait until
Mother said, 'Darling'. She said it to James. Sometimes the
silence went on again. I was unable to turn, or move, or
break it.

Mary O'Connell brought us our meals on trays. It was
always made to look so that you wished to eat it but you
were disappointed afterwards. When James' pain was in the
room it was impossible to eat. Mother tried not to give him
the laudanum. She always did it against her will because
she 'couldn't help it'.

In the long afternoons if James slept nobody made a
light. The twilight came and Mother faded into a ghost. We
waited for the nurse. I longed for her to come so that it
would be over, but sometimes I longed for her not to come,
when James was quiet.

Daylight disappeared and took everything with it. I

could see the firelight in the rooms opposite. The house of
the seven boys had its firelight in the downstairs parlour.
The house next to it always put its blinds down while it was
still daylight. The house next to that was where the editor of
the *Sentinel* lived. It had windows without blinds and nobody was there except in the mornings. But the fourth house
was my treasure. It had the firelight in the drawing room, a
room with silver walls that always made me remember
when Margaret sang: 'I arise from dreams of Time'. The
curtains were rose-coloured and so were the lamp shades
and cushions, and every day when the banks closed a young
man appeared on the threshold. He stood at the drawing-
room door and a very pretty lady arose from the region of
the firelight and floated over to him as wispy as a moth and
he clasped her in his arms. Her moth-like arms went up
about him and he kissed her for a long while and then,
together, they floated back to the hearth. You could *see* their
laughter. The pretty lady made tea at a low table. Their maid
had an apron the size of a pocket handkerchief that was tied
behind like a sash. She wore a cap with streamers which
flew out when she left the room. They were the last thing to
get through the door. When she brought in the silver tray
you could see that it was too heavy for her. You had to wait
for the silver teapot to slide off, but the pretty lady always
put up her hands and caught it in time. The young man ate
all that was on the plates. He popped this and that into his
mouth as though he were starving. Then he kissed the pretty
lady again and gave her his cup for a second cup of tea or a
third or fourth. He never seemed to end. It took her a long
time to pour the tea. It was such a tall pour. I never saw the
tea, only the pour. Mary O'Connell said it was the bride's
house and that all brides were ridiculous.

Father came to visit us. He changed his shirt. Whiteness
shot up over his head in a mountain and he disappeared;
then his black head came out with the beard squeezed into a
curl. His arms waggled into the sleeves and the deep dent in
his back became visible. He held his sleeve links in his
mouth without swallowing them while he cracked his cuffs

into place. He looked into the mirror and said that James and I were 'a nice pair'. He said we should absolutely put a stop to it. 'This house is a hospital,' he remarked to Mary O'Connell. She went out of the room without answering.

When Father was there everything seemed to quicken and move. Drawers shot out and in and there was no question about the noise. He used both of Mother's silver hairbrushes at once. The furniture seemed to move forward so that there was not enough room to pass. When Mary O'Connell came to the door with the tray she took it away again.

Father looked around when the door closed. 'Ghosts!' He sat down upon my bed. He said he was a haunted man. 'You know, Kathie, once you commit a mortal sin or even a venial one it puts you into their clutches.' Then he sat upon Mother's bed, facing James and he told James to cast 'all this' from him. 'My son,' he said, 'you must get out of it, stand up and become a man.'

James asked when the doctor was going to let him out of bed. 'I can't play trains on the bed,' he said.

Father was grand. He encouraged him. He said he would invent a train that would go on beds. All that was needed was a large wooden tray with grooves in it. James would only have to tip the tray to start the train.

James argued that it would fall onto the floor, where he would not be able to get it. Father said that that could be overcome as a problem. All that would be necessary would be a paling around the bed. Flower pots could be stuck on the corners, and flowers could be grown so as to spell out names like the floral names of country stations. Change the flowers with the seasons. Tickets could be passed through the rails and the first-class ticket-holders could go through first. He had James quite excited. His mouth was open again. You could hold up the third-class passengers, Father said. That would teach them a lesson. They would find out it paid to go first class. All fortunes were made by those who went first. It stood to reason that if they went second or third that was bound to fix them permanently. He told James he could become rich simply by holding up the traffic.

James said he would buy more trains with the money.

Father said that was the spirit.

Mary O'Connell brought the tray back. She wanted to know why Father had pulled out the drawers.

He was most reasonable with her. 'Looking for shirts,' he answered. She pulled a shirt out of a drawer. It was a very crumpled shirt and she said that she was certain that he had put it there. Father said to me that you could never argue with a woman who was a friend of the family.

Mother came. It was a relief when she came in and Mary O'Connell went out. She had a teapot full of crystallised ginger for James. It was a Chinese teapot. The lid was fastened down with straw and it had cane on the handle. Father asked to have a taste of the ginger. Mary O'Connell was there again but when she heard Father ask for the ginger she went out in disgust.

As soon as the door closed upon her Father said: 'Now, Katie, there is no use in your belonging to the opposition. You must give me time to recover.'

Mother said sorrowfully: 'Would you?' She would not look at Father, even when he commanded her to do so. She kept her eyes fastened upon the piece of ginger that James was nibbling out of her fingers.

I was aware of a darkness within that was more depressing than any darkness without. It blotted out more. Mother was sad. She was unhappy. There was a rope pulled tight between her and Father and neither of them got any nearer. I did not understand it. I was only conscious of the misery, the torment. There was a great, peaceless urgency in the air. It was as bad as James' pain. I was impotent against it. I asked God to wipe it away, to make Father and Mother happy. This was not the galloping hasty prayer to 'God bless Father and Mother' on your knees at bedtime. This was an approach to God, an appeal to the *power* of God.

Father stood up. There was no wildness in him any more. He hadn't had the piece of ginger. He brushed his hair again, with one brush this time. I saw that he had two white horns of hair over his temples. They seemed to shine out, reflected from the flames that were reflected in the mirror. He lit the incandescent gas on either side of the dressing table. The burners flared with a puff. The cold unshaded light made me tired of being in bed. I wanted to play — not with trains on beds — but real games, jumping games, over and under the bed, hiding behind the curtain and screaming at the top of one's voice when somebody began to grope. I wanted Major. It came down to that. I wanted to play games with Major. Major was the mask on the frustration. I was so miserable that the behaviour of the 'Brides' did not make me wish to see them. It was their hour and I was indifferent. I didn't care if their fire went out. I was black inside.

Mother told Father that James still ran a temperature on the slightest provocation.

Father said he wouldn't upset him for worlds. 'Why, Katie, I love my children. *And they know it!*' He came towards me. His eyes were not dancing. They were still. He blamed the doctor. 'Let us go away and live where there are proper surgeons,' he said. He beamed at me until the beam got inside me and I could feel the voyage beginning.

Mother put me back into the darkness. It was too late, she said. We ought never to have settled here. There was nothing wrong with the doctor. It was James' hip. The pain was in the heart of the bone where nobody could reach it.

Father argued. He said: 'He isn't any good as a surgeon,' very argumentatively.

Mother called him John in the same tone as Grandmother.

Father stood up. He looked as though he wished to stay, but he kissed me and went away. The room was terribly empty and when I looked out of the window at the Brides they had put down their blinds.

In the morning, when Mary O'Connell had finished with the room and the windows were still open, Mother put the flowers back on the dressing table which the nurse put out at night. She put the vase on the very corner so that I could see every bit of it. Nearly always she had her hat on. In winter she put her muff on my bed. When she stroked it or said it was sealskin she always blew the fur so that you saw that it was bronze at the roots. It was as slippery as water inside the muff and always warm, like a bath. The purse part was very hard to open. She never used the handkerchief she kept there. There were gold and silver coins in a sealskin purse. There were lots of little pieces of paper. One day she made me smell the snowdrops. They were pinned where she usually kept the violets. When she held them out to me she asked if they didn't make me wish to go to Buncrana, to the house at the seaside. When she asked that I wanted to crush the snowdrops, but I didn't. I stopped. It was exactly like holding a kitten that doesn't wish to stay. You have to squeeze.

The day Mother put a great sheaf of daffodils into the vase she said that we *were* going to the shore. First of all, Mary O'Connell would go and take the nails out of the shuttered doors and windows with Corney and air the sheets and blankets. Then Mother would go and sow the hardy annuals and sleep in the beds to see if they were dry; then she would come back for James and me.

That summer it was James who had the invalid bassinet. He had it without the donkey. Mother or Mary O'Connell or Corney or Margaret took turns at being his donkey. It was less bumpy with them. It took a long time to get him anywhere. Stones had to be lifted out of his way on the roads. Mother's favourite place for him was on the high dunes, not the low ones we crossed when we went to the shore, but the higher ones where the sheep cropped. It took two to get James up there but once he was up it was worthwhile for he could see the sea and the road and the schoolhouse and the railway with the train going into the station. He saw when the Ballantyne girls got bicycles. There were three of them and each of them had a pigtail and wore a pleated serge gym suit over a white blouse. They used to race like mad to the schoolhouse. They lived in a place called the Crescent. The Crescent was set in a curve before a half-moon lawn. It consisted of three houses and the middle one was haunted.

A Canon Newland had died in it the previous summer and since his death he allowed nobody to stay in the house. He was always interfering with them, running up the front steps to pull the bell before they could reach it; or stretching his arm out for the salt in the cupboard. Every cook they had, Mary O'Connell said, left on the second day. Tenants only lasted three weeks. Canon Newland had been very fond of his house. He had built it and he wished to take it with him when he left but he had departed in a hurry. Mary O'Connell said that he was revenging himself because of having had to go at such a short notice. He was wrong — but there it was. The Ballantyne girls didn't seem to trouble about it. They were always occupied with their bicycles.

Instead of going to Port Salon or to the bogs for excursions we had to go where James could come with us. We went with him into the town to mail the letters and see the passengers start off on the Long Car for Carndonagh. It was a bus turned inside out Mother said. The people sat back to back under an awning with their luggage stacked in the well between them.

Another walk was up the wide road past the schoolhouse to a place where a lady lived with a colony of crows. All you could see was the gate into the avenue. The trees were spotted black with crows. Mary O'Connell told us that the house had a curse on it. It was condemned to crows. Within a mile of the house all you could hear was the cawing of the crows. It was a parliament of crows. They passed judgments there. The lady's father, according to Mary O'Connell, had been turned into a crow and these were his children. Whenever you saw a crow flying anywhere else it was always making for the parliament. It was deafening when you were among them, cawing out their laws. They positively swooped at us like policemen. They spoke about us from the moment we turned the curve on the road. It appeared to be true when Mary O'Connell said that it was as much as your life was worth to pick a leaf in that place.

Misery always seemed to attach itself to the weather. The weather went with your feeling, like a picture to a story. You saw the picture and you remembered the story.

The garden poppies were shaken in the wind. Their metallic purple petals lay scattered on the path. The clouds were the same colour, stacked like battlements in the sky. I went into the house. A door slammed somewhere. Mother screamed. She cried out the way James screamed when the pain got him. I tore at the door handle. It was loose. It turned both ways but it did not open the door. I screamed too. It came out of me because I wanted nothing to happen to Mother. She opened the door and put her arms about me. 'It's nothing, Kathie,' she said. How could it not be something when she had screamed in that way? Father was there. His eyes had darts in them. It was not nothing. It was Father. I was finding out. When he was there somebody always cried or was angry or sad. I asked him what he had done. He laughed at me. He roared out the most awful, shattering laughter. All he said was: 'I can see you are being educated.'

Somehow I could not plead with him before Mother. The words would not come out. I waited. She was holding me so tightly that I could hear her heart ticking under her soft dress. But all that day I thought. I made a plan about Father. When the opportunity came I was ready. 'What did you do to Mother?' I asked boldly, showing that I knew he was guilty.

This time he did not laugh but he said that he could see that the family had got me.

We were standing under the tree where I had asked him the meaning of the word 'cess'.

Nobody had got me, I argued, baffled because it was not coming to anything. I had no right to judge him until I knew what he had done. If he would not tell me nobody else would. 'Father,' I pleaded, 'I love you . . . more than anybody . . . .'

'So! What could be better?' He was happy again, not mocking.

I had to let him down. I was forced into action. 'But, if you go on making Mother cry and everybody miserable I won't allow myself to love you.'

'So. Put me out of your life — like that!' He waved his hand. Birds flew out of the bushes in a cluster, twittering. I nodded. I was unable to say 'Yes'.

'Well, that's all right,' he said gaily, as though it were all settled and done for and never going to happen again.

He defeated me. The 'yes' that would not emerge was so strong inside me. It was upright like a sword with two blades. Nothing came clear between us. The meaning was withheld. I wished him to know, to take in that I was offering him all I had to give in return for all that he had the power to withhold. I was utterly unable to communicate to him, beneath the spoken word, the passionate urgency of my requisition. It was a child's cry to the Father for peace and security and a stabilised spirit, a cry to the Source.

We scrunched through the gravel in the lane; it was strangely whitened, bleached in some curious fashion by the stormy skies. The skeletons of the hedges were beginning to show. There were red haws on the bucky rosebushes and sloes in the privets. Something came to an end; a sort of sleep or patience lapped over its threshold in that instant in Time and my heart was filled with a foreboding wildness for the man at my side. I desired that nothing should change or become slow in him, yet at the same time I wished him transformed; so my desire split him in two and split me in two. I turned from him then with a child's terrible gravity.

Chapter Thirteen

The child's consciousness spreads itself out upon the canvas of Life in a pointillist system, a dot here and a dot there. Cumulatively the blur takes on its pattern, subject to vision as matter is subject to light. We begin in darkness, a state that resembles blindness. Our first years are a pure process of forgetting. We put the danger from us. We refuse Life. This is why whatever gets through our defences is so important to the psychologist. It is all he has to go on — what has robbed us of Paradise. We begin to function as individuals upon planes of resistance. We do not wish to see or hear or have *it* explained or pointed out to us. The dream is so much better. The freshness of our innate design is so much stronger. It has to be withdrawn from us in the nature of a hypnosis, in the strain of some little Kafka animal that is compelled to contribute its individual mechanism to a universe so completely outside its powers to conceive of it that no God is necessary. No Third Party is necessary for the fulfilment of its logic. But, unlike the animal, we are obliged to seek God. Our logic has a different condemnation.

So the scaffolding goes up on us as surely as the shell on the terrapin. We have no choice. We are conditioned by the tegument of our single personality. The autonomy is set and, washerwomen or kings, the game has to be played out.

Why, at the end of life, we return so insistently to the mould of our childhood is simply because it is only at the end that we are capable of comprehending the beginning. When Death becomes the event, the full significance of our limit when Life was the event is laid clear. The boundaries are clarified as well as the brotherhood of our kind. We become universal. The love from the soul is infinitely more passionate than that of the heart, because it includes it.

Places come back to us like trysts with destiny. Our sensations have always wrought the wonder upon us and, as a bloodstream, they carry it to the end. They disguise behind the eyes of Age the full vision. Nothing grows cold, not even Winter.

It was one of those northern twilights: the air was a sweep; the light pared itself in sheets out of the rising calm of the darkness. All form was folded in it, or loosened from it, with an abnormal intimacy such as the flight of a bird or the shapes of cedars or a horse travelling or a bridge spun across a river.

We were being driven to a new home. Mother had discovered a house which possessed the advantages of summer as well as the advantages of winter. We were never to live in the city again. It was situated on that side of the river known as Waterside, some miles out on the other side of the hill. Sometime in the late autumn afternoon we were driven over the Carlisle Bridge and through the narrow Waterside streets, out along the highway to Glendermott. I hated the bridge. It was always the most extravagant peril to me to be spun above any volume of water. Even a jetty with the water *plonk-plonking* beneath the boards took me to a core of danger. But, apart from the menace of the strong-flowing river beneath me, there was the grandeur of the riverside, the woods packed in dark density, with the luxury of a garment, upon the rising land. The cold, stony houses set with the gems of firelight and lamplight; the flying, chasing clouds; the music of a horn blowing over distance; or a dog making argument, or some solitary bird screaming its lonely sentence between the day and night. 'Good-bye Brother,' it seemed to be saying to the vanishing world.

We came out above the dim Glendermott Valley, its darkness whitened by its two Presbyterian churches holding up their towers like indices above a patch of graveyard. We turned sharply to the right above them into a road that was fittingly named the Trench Road. It had the dug, indented quality of all Celtic roads, made for escape. Birds chirped at us from the hedges as though we had disturbed them in their first slumber. We drove through to a shabby gateway with tall rusty iron gates into an avenue of beeches. They were unkempt. Not only did their branches meet above but they met across. In places their crisp dry leaves were rustled out upon us as though we were the Babes in the Woods. Major followed us. He was happy. He had the swing of music to him, his tail up and, when he came close, his eyes were seen to be smiling. There was the smell of the forest.

We were swept to a doorstep in the centre of a square white house which lay blocked in the dusk. Something about that place embraced us from the beginning. It had an air of greeting, of waiting for us, of having expected us for a long time. The door was opened. All was exciting and mysterious within. Lamps moved about in upheld arms. The voices of men and women came out of shadows and remained disembodied. Somebody was hammering and whistling at the same time. Mary O'Connell lured us into a large strange room where a fire was blazing. Mother said it was a furnace and hoped that the chimney would not catch fire. Mary O'Connell assured her that the house had been built to stand a siege. We sat on rolls of carpet or on bundles that had to be pressed to make sure that they would support us. Elizabeth was given a tiny camp stool which was planted in the very centre of the hearth before the fire. There was furniture, but it appeared to wish to keep apart from us. Tables and chairs were all pushed against a wall as though they were undergoing punishment. Mary O'Connell made tea on top of the piano which had one foot up as though it had caught a thorn. She delved into baskets and paper bags and gave us muffins to toast on long extensible forks. James kept putting his in and out and showing Elizabeth how to do it. Elizabeth only did it once. She held her muffin out at the longest distance and got it done perfectly. The kettle boiled every few minutes and Mary O'Connell had to keep putting it back and forward on the hob. James' muffin fell into the ashes. Mary O'Connell could not find the tea pot. She kept rummaging and scraping and swearing in Gaelic that she had packed it in one of the baskets. It was Mother who found it. It was in the first basket. The muffins were buttered on both sides, by accident. Everybody was hungry, but Major was the one with the largest appetite. All the cats were in that room, parading round the walls with their tails up and their eyes as round as brandy balls. Everybody who came in or went out was told not to let the cats out until the cage with the canaries was hung up in the dining room. Mother kept going in and out because of the canaries or because the men had stopped hammering. Major always went with her. He knew his duty. Mary O'Connell said she would scourge the life out of the first one of us who ventured to go into any room but the sitting room until she gave us permission. When we asked her where the sitting room was she said we were in it.

After tea she decorated the place with blankets. She hung them about like banners. Sheets were folded over chair backs and the air became roastier and roastier. She opened a door on the far side of the piano. It was not the door we had entered by from the hall. It was a door into a room where she was trying to light a fire that absolutely refused to kindle. It wouldn't 'draw'. She knelt before it and rammed it with shavings and sticks repeatedly and it would go off like gunpowder with a lot of smoke and sputtering. Then it stopped dead. She disappeared somewhere and returned with a thin, gaunt young giant in shabby clothes. He moved behind her like a spectre. When he lit the fire it burned like magic. And when he leaned forward to it upon the hearth it became clear that he was not a poor young man at all but a prince in disguise. He had hair as bright as new sovereigns. When he went too near to the blaze the bright and precious metal of his forelock was lifted magnetically and one waited for the gold to pour.

The grate was the shape of an hourglass or one of those chairs that are the same right side up as upside down and are only to be found at photographers'. When the fire burned itself free of gusts and spurts it settled into a steady core that made it seem like a body sitting in the chair without arms or legs.

Elizabeth and I were put to bed in that room, between hot blankets and sheets. It was delicious. It provisioned you against ghosts and burglars and supported you with a comfort that was the equivalent of courage. James was put into the bed in the room beyond. We had peeps at it which showed only the fluttering area confined to the light thrown by the waxen candle. The candle had a flame that licked the darkness like a tongue. It took it off in sips. James kept asking what we had. He had the green enamel linen press and Grandmother's table. The candlestick was also out of Grandmother's room. We had nothing but chairs on which to put our clothes, and the new wallpaper, patterned with garlands or white myrtle tied against blue ribbons with bows or cupids, which went bright and dark according to when a cinder fell.

The next morning resembled Christmas morning. We were awake with the first slit of daylight. The forest smell was there, the chirp of birds. We heard the horse whinnying in the courtyard. Major was barking out the reveille.

The house hung over the valley but our immediate view as children was blocked by our beeches. Some perfectly mad being, according to Mother, had had the idea of cutting down part of these trees to hedge the lawn. They were espaliered against space. They had their own beauty — the artificial beauty of branches twined on the margin of a missal. As trees they were deformed. The land on the other side sloped steeply down into the Trench Road. When you stood plainly in this field you could see the fertile valley, ribboned with a river and populated with woods. These were plantation lands. They had been ploughed in the deadliest antagonisms. They were at peace now, the feud only rising occasionally. You could see the estates, garrisoned with trees. The names of the people were Scottish. The place names were Irish. Picts and Scots. The age-old division. Stevensons and Maxwells and Thompsons and Beresfords and Cunninghams. Ardmore and Glendermott and our own townland, Altnagalvin.

We had become Altnagalvinists Father said, when he came. Grandmother objected to a red dining room. They were the fashion but they were abominable. She rejoiced that the fireplace had been left alone for she had a friend, a perfectly intelligent woman, who had painted a white marble fireplace red. Mother said: 'What could she do? The hall was green, the drawing room was grey. One was ruled and governed by the paper-hanger.'

We had a new gardener, MacGuinness. We were strictly forbidden to hold conversation with him because he was inordinately blasphemous. It took a little while to discover his vices. It was very had to resist his allurements, to stand and watch while he hoed the purple cabbages and spat safely over them out of reach of them and us, and told us that he knew the history of every father and son, lock, stock and barrel, in Ulster. He knew the bad blood to the bottom and the good ones to the top and by Christ there wasn't a ha'p'orth of justice to choose between them. Mankind, according to him, was conceived in sin and fore-doomed to darkness. The only place where you were safe was a limbo that was the dead image of a scullery, a place where the dishes were washed. He was always telling us that he was a master baker by trade. His work was night work — like his mother's. She had been a midwife. I asked Father what a midwife was and was told that it was 'just one of those words that are pronounced hussif'. I thought of 'hussif' for years as the feminine of hassock. Midwife remained, for me, in the category of 'misled' which I always *saw* and pronounced 'mizzled'. It meant nothing to me except this man's mother.

MacGuinness remains a form bent over rows of cactus-cabbages, furrowing the brown earth with a sort of vengeance, and spitting out his Voltairean spite against the behaviour of mankind. When he saw one of the Thompson boys in our company he went by, wheeling a wheelbarrow with a force that stamped itself upon my susceptibilities with the definiteness of an Egyptian frieze. He awoke the feuds of the world upon me against a background of the weather. That day there was a wind. It whipped the garment upon his breast. He was exposed as a man stabbed by Time and the most eternal disaster. His gaunt profile was moulded in for me for always against what was elemental and in- eradicable. He was the disinherited, the man from whom all prices had been washed. He had nothing but his spirit and this awful sensibility. He was tattooed with history upon the place in which it had been made. It was as he said it was. Every leaf in the tree, every blade in the field bore out his testimony. He was the peasant fruit, the bitter ruined kernel of destruction. All over the universe his like are to be found. Their pride is the pride of kings. They are the wild and abandoned seed of those who made the sacrifices.

When he got me alone he asked me what I was doing with 'that whelp'? Jack Thompson was not a whelp to me. He was a boy from one of the Presbyterian manses who wished to become acquainted with us. MacGuinness tried to shake me with the knowledge that 'he and such as he had priest-running in the blood'.

And the curious thing was that neither MacGuinness nor his sister Margot could be persuaded to go to church. They had a record for abstinence from the sacraments. MacGuin- ness gave as his excuse that he was out all night in the bakery and could never get up in the morning. His hours as our gardener were arbitrary. As we had Margot for a cook he escaped his duties. She could never refuse to collect the vegetables which he should have delivered to the kitchen. She was as gaunt as he was and if she did not blaspheme she had the strongest principles. Nothing could shake her from an idea, once she had it. She had a fibrinous spot on her right cheek as large as a five-shilling piece. When Mother urged her to allow the doctor to see it she refused absolutely. She was positive that 'when it was ripe', it would fall from her like a walnut. This actually happened. She appeared one day with her face completely undecorated and assured Mother that the walnut coin had 'come off the branch', as she had said it would. It had fallen at her feet when she was sweeping the floor and she had, quite simply, picked it up and buried it in the garden. As part of her for a period of many months it had merited internment.

It was Margot who told us that the little house in which she had lived with her brother had once been at the other end of the garden, upon the roadside. As we knew, it was now at the top of the garden. You had to walk up a path to it. It had been built originally by her father with the garden behind it. One night when her mother came home late and was undressing to go to bed she heard a very gentle tap at the door. She was a fearless woman by nature. She had just walked up the road in the darkness and was accustomed to it. If she had nothing to be afraid of out in the middle of the night alone she had nothing to be afraid of in her own house with the fire burning and her husband snoring in the bed. She opened the door. Nothing was visible to her but the stars. She smelt the southernwood that grew on the doorstep and when she looked down in that direction she felt something step over her foot and run by her into the house. She returned to the kitchen. In the middle of the floor there stood a complete little woman no higher than a hand's span. She was dressed very distinctively in a scarlet petticoat with a spotless white apron. She wore a shawl crossed on her bosom and her hair was tied down with a tiny handkerchief. She curtsied to Margot's mother: 'If you please, Ma'am, and by your gracious mercy I have been enjoined to present to you a petition. Ever since this house was built it has caused us a great deal of grievous mortality. Every time you throw a basin of water out of doors one of us is drowned. We are so tired of bewailing our dead that we are obliged to ask you to have the courtesy to remove your house from where you have planted it. This earth has always housed our colony. We have no malice in our hearts towards you. We have forborne until we can forbear no longer. These deaths afflict us. They must end. Will you please have the charity of heart to set the house back half an acre? If you do this no harm shall ever touch you. You will die by moonlight, with no enemies about.'

Margot's mother promised her that the house would be

moved. And moved it was, for the whole world to witness. So it stood as she told us — out of the boundaries in which harm could be committed.

When we asked her brother about this he spat and swore by Jesus and all the Angels that it was Gospel truth. As a child he had sown seeds in the garden when the house was on the roadside. He remembered it with the accuracy of the five fingers on each of his hands.

The spell MacGuinness cast upon us was too great to keep us from him. This was how we came to have a change of gardeners. The new man's name was MacDaid. He won us like a Greek, with a gift. He brought us an Irish terrier puppy. The room off the dining room had been turned into a library. All the books were there. The walls were lined from floor to ceiling. It was where we had our lessons. MacDaid walked in upon us in the middle of a Latin declension and put the fluffy, tobacco-coloured creature down upon the table. Instantly the small and woolly object absorbed the ink out of the inkstand like a piece of blotting paper. He lapped it in black, dripping licks which drove Mademoiselle into a fluster. She made a snatch at him as though he were a piece of toast that had begun to burn, and dropped him upon the carpet. Major told him not to mind. We were indignant. MacDaid stood, listening to what Mademoiselle had to say to him. He was a tall, trembly sort of man with an habitual innocence about him that probably always got him into trouble. He did not attempt to reason with Mademoiselle who had bounced from the course of *mensa* into his behaviour. He left the room. We left with him. Outside he assured us that the puppy was purebred and that he had got him for us from the Stevensons. Major was very pleased, but he examined the puppy to show MacDaid that he really knew more about it than he did. We knew nothing at all about it. We were satisfied with the puppy. As he was Irish he had to have an Irish name, so we inscribed him in an exercise book as Rory O'Moore. At that time we were producing a journal and, as editors, were obliged to devour history. The name of the journal was *Liberty*. It had a wild Shetland pony drawn

on the cover as our symbol of perfect freedom. All important facts were entered in an exercise book. The puppy was
put down with the notes on the Irish chieftain. Father
wished his name to be Malachy so that he could have a
collar of gold to distinguish him from Major who had a
collar with silver studs. We refused the name of Malachy
because we did not wish him to have a collar of more value
than Major's. Major was first, and none could precede him.

Father appeared one day with a very strange dog, a
Pomeranian that ate oranges. Mother said: 'Oh, he's very
pretty *but* a Pomeranian!'

Whether he was Pomeranian or not we liked him.
Mademoiselle told us where Pomerania was. He was far
from home. Father said he had attached himself to him in a
tram and simply would not leave him. He said he clung like
Clementine and his boots were not number nine.

Mother said that Father was losing his mind.

Father said: 'Probably. It is due to too much exaltation.'

They had an argument as to whether the Pomeranian
was to be kept indoors or outdoors. Father said he could be
worked out on the same plan as the canaries. Mother said:
'Indoors, that settles it!' in a tone of voice that unsettled it
completely. Father argued that every time the windows
were open the canaries were outdoors and that, definitely,
the dog was a dog and not a canary. I think it was Major
who settled the matter. He took charge of the Pomeranian as
he had taken charge of the puppy. They were dogs in the
forest and he was the lion. They had to obey him. Dogs
seemed to rain upon us. A black pointer appeared. He
walked up the avenue, over the threshold, and stayed. He
stayed as you stay in a hotel, because it suited him to stay.
He was very aloof. Our ways were not his ways. He was a
man with a profession who was, either by force or accident,
obliged to take a holiday. Father suggested that he was
probably writing a book and had to keep his thoughts to
himself. He was uncommunicative. Mother gave him the
name of Ponto. She was for him and not against because he
was jet-black and carried anything from pansy roots to Mrs

Henry Woods' novels. Father said this was a degradation for Ponto, and he took him away from Mother by simply shooting off a gun. Ponto ran to Father when he heard the gun.

Our next dog brought her name with her. The moment we saw her she was a Minna. She was nut brown and gentle and had a girl's waist. All the dogs smiled at her as though she was coming through the rye. She was a mixture of greyhound and spaniel with a touch of sheep dog. She was good with sheep. She kept cows out of our hired fields. The land on either side of our avenue belonged to us but Mother rented it by auction every autumn. Although we always knew that it was ours and that we could walk on it we were always surprised at what we found there. We had no cows of our own. The doctor had ordered goats' milk for James. We had a nanny goat that was kept tethered in the pasture.

Minna seemed to have her own profession as distinctively as Ponto but she was not quite so rigid about it. She was more outgoing than Ponto. But we never belonged to either of them as we belonged to Major. Minna took a great fancy to the china closet. It was a small room off the dining room, lit by a pane of glass in the wall that overlooked the back hall. Minna liked it because it was dark. It was a place to go to when she wished to have a moment to herself in peace. At times the company of others was a little too much for her. It was all very well, Mother declared, provided she paid no attention to the china. 'I hope to goodness that if she takes it into her head to break anything she'll go for the Limoges.' The Limoges was a white and yellow breakfast set that nobody wanted. For some reason it was intensely detested. Every now and then efforts would be made to put it into circulation in the hope that use would do something to it. But, preserved by hate, it was apparently immunised against breakages. It possessed the miracle of the unwanted. It endured.

It was at this period that Mary O'Connell and Mother went in for poultry. Mother bought black Dorkings. The hens were peacock black on top and in front, but underneath and behind they wore chocolate-coloured feathers. The cock

was as proud as Lucifer. There was no chocolate about him
in any place. He and Major were rival rulers. They governed
the courtyard with sceptres of iron. Nothing could go in and
out of the gate without their consent. Unlike Major, nobody
loved the cock except his silly hens, and even they sometimes ran away from him.

Mary O'Connell suddenly left us. Grandmother and I
walked through the meadow to the road. The air was so still
that you could hear the pollen in the flowers, the sort of
stillness when what you smell has movement. It rustles in
your ears. There was going to be a storm. The clouds were
all banked into a fortress. I asked if Grandaunt Ahn were
going to die. I did not make it a question. I said into the
stillness: 'Grandaunt Ahn is going to die.' Grandmother
said, 'Child!' very sharply. She stopped and stared at the sky.
Her beautiful face was clouded. The little golden shells in
her ears trembled. 'Child,' she said again, 'we must hurry in.
It is going to rain.' Death became part of the stillness. It did
not rain. We hurried and the menace followed us like a
hound. Mary O'Connell and Grandmother drove away.

Mother cried at breakfast when Grandaunt Ahn died.
Ahn was her darling. She did not wish her to die but to stay
immortal. She stood in the dining-room window underneath the cage with the canaries and not a word was said in
the room. One walked and pushed the chairs without
speaking.

Mother drove away too. She gave me three exercise
books of her own, the ones she had written when she was a
girl. They contained stories which she had *copied*. I loved the
exercise books in their embroidered covers. I loved the sight
of her fine purple handwriting, but I was not at all interested in what she had copied. It astonished me that she
should have taken all that trouble to *copy* anything. When
you wrote you wrote what came out of yourself.

We were alone with Margot and MacDaid. Father was on
one of his absences. Margot gave us our meals in the
kitchen. She never once asked us where we had been when

we came in. She had no patience when the pony put his head in at the kitchen door. She tried to put him out but he was strong because we were there. Our presence supported him. We stopped Margot from interfering with him. He knew how to turn the wooden button on the wall cupboard. He knew where the sugar was and always took just one lump. After he had the sugar he was willing to go. He went with a scamper, his tail in a wild flicker that sent the chickens flying. Margot made a stew with yellow lentils and carrots and parsley. When we and the dogs entered the kitchen we all felt that the smell of the stew was a marvel. It was elemental. It had powers over us. It was the sort of spell that would declare your guidance in heaven or hell. If you smelt *that* smell you would know how to find your way back.

We raced snails on the wall behind the kitchen table. Margot never said yes or no to the snails and this was a weakness on her part. It lessened her authority. We then took them into other rooms. Their iridescent trails were to be found in decorative patterns upon walls and furniture and curtains.

Father came one day and scared Margot to death by demanding a beefsteak. 'Sir,' she said, 'they do not grow on bushes. I can't pick you one like a blackberry.' He then amazed us by producing the beefsteak. He had brought it with him. He told Margot that all that was wrong with her was her grammar.

The most awful thing about Father in that place was that he came so often in the middle of the night. I was awakened by the barking of the dogs. This began at the bottom of the avenue, and all the way up to the house this barking proclaimed his arrival. It broke the night like an army, tore it open with a sort of terror and confusion that generated shame. We were exposed by it as people and a place to rest of the universe. We became known in silence — which is the worst sort of knowledge. Its response is secret. In the morning this shame would still be in us. But, according to the seasons, all upon the surface of life remained indifferent to it. Fires burned or flowers blossomed and birds sang and

nobody commented. It lay within us as a shadow, a forecast-
ing of a grasp that would one day, perhaps, overtake us.

Father took us to fish in the valley. We stood knee-deep in
waders in the brown water and MacDaid showed James and
me how to cast our lines. He and Father cast their threads in
continual arches across the running river. The wet stones
shone like basaltic mirrors and the brown *diminished* fish
leapt with curled tails upon the banks until Father put them
into the basket as though he were posting a letter. They
looked enormous under the water and when they were
taken out they were only half the size. I never caught a fish
because I was always slipping. MacDaid never caught me
until the last moment. It was agonising. Major wasn't there.
He and Rory were doing their own catching. All I got of
them were flashes in the brushwood or their voices coming
out from trees or bushes with a terrible alive necessity. I was
glad when the fishing ended, when we climbed into the tall
trap and went homewards. I had a special feeling against
water, an emotion deprived of love, haunted with a sensation that always mounted in tempo to pure terror.

The sunset was in the valley. The trees breathed and
exhaled their breath so that we breathed their essence. All
the time the sound of the river was in our ears. Every now
and then we saw the water, the colour of a dog's eyes,
shining and pursuing. The new pony was going well. His
name was Mulligatawny. He had been bought at an Antrim
Fair, a Cushendall pony that had never had a bit between his
teeth. He was as wild as a feather in a gale. MacDaid said he
could break him easily, but he was no good at all. He neither
tamed nor broke him. I was the first to get him to eat oats.
He didn't know what they were and had no more intention
towards them when you offered them than he would have
had towards a bead necklace. I mixed the oats with sugar
and when the mixture brushed his velvet nozzle the sugar
entranced him. He always expected sugar with his oats. He
was of the genre of persons who eat strawberries with
pepper or take mustard with cake.

He was a beauty, a dappled beige with black nostrils and hocks and hooves. His tail was camel-cream and it had an arch like an Arabian stallion. He defied anybody to touch him. The sight of a bridle made him mad, and if you so much as touched him with the loop of the crupper his hind legs shot to heaven. He snorted wind every time he was harnessed, and it took four men to hold him the first time he was taken to the blacksmith's. Mother had to get the Stevensons' coachman to train him. But, even when he was trained, he had the strong curve of defiance in all his movements. He yielded his strength by sufferance, as though every step he took in harness bled his substance from him.

We had to pass the white Presbyterian churches. The two white spires rose like antennae in the sunset. When we came close to the graveyard we saw a battalion of soldiers packed as dense and bright as poppies in the graveyard space. There was a strange music loosening itself in a challenge upon the air. It asked a question, a long persistent music that took the distance and bore our hearts in its flight. The men were carrying their rifles in reverse. And then the drums beat and beat and you knew that a soldier had died. You knew that death came to them who marched with music, and that the sun was setting in the valley, its thin gold as sweet as lips upon the hillsides. Father and MacDaid took off their hats. The pony was the only one who escaped the wonder. None but his own magic could inform him. He dashed up the hill as though he had wings to his feet, and yet he was not irreverent. What he did was curiously fitting. It put triumph into the ending. His gesture was a flourish upon what had ceased to be. Father understood. 'Fine,' he said, 'fine!' The reins were drawn as tightly as rails and the trap was going so smoothly upon its springs that you knew it was balanced to the edge of a hair. One was spun out high in the glowing atmosphere, still feeling the echo of the drums.

We had two donkeys: Frances, who had been with us to the shore, and Garryowen. We were allowed to ride and drive the donkeys ourselves. Garryowen had a short black

mane like a starched fringe. When we took Frances in the
donkey cart she was slow but reliable. She went where you
led her even if it took hours. Garryowen often refused to go
anywhere. You could get him into the shafts and as far as the
middle of the avenue or the road; and there, when he took
the notion, he would stop. He would neither go forward nor
turn. He was struck with a profound meditation in which
nothing reached him. At other times he would tear off at a
gallop and get you there much sooner than you had expected. Once on the Glendermott Road, when we were
almost home, with the Thompsons behind us in their trap
returning from school, Garryowen turned suddenly and
flew back to the town in a wild gallop. He regretted it, of
course, especially when he saw the bridge, but he did not
regret it more than we did. He was so out of breath by then
that he was obliged to walk all the way home. When he
bolted, the Thompsons stood up and cheered. Not because
of any indication from MacGuinness but simply because this
family was much older than we were, we never became very
intimate. The youngest boy was older than I was, and James
was never allowed to play games with him because James
had to be careful. The Corkerys who lived in the other
manse were all entirely grown up. Mrs Corkery visited
Mother and they discussed the Psalms.

It was about this time that Elizabeth's name appeared in
the morning newspaper. It was preceded by Miss and had her
surname attached. It was announced that she was the proud
possessor of a polo cart. Father thought it was a forgery, but
Mother said: 'What on earth shall we do with a polo cart?'

James said: 'Roly-poly, pudding and pie, kissed the girls
and made them cry.' Elizabeth said she didn't wish to cry,
and everybody laughed. Everybody was happy about it.

Father went into town and returned with the polo cart
and a hotel horse. It was a black cart with silver lamps and
fittings and cerise-red plush cushions. Father declared that
he had ordered a black and silver harness and a black horse
to go with it.

Grandaunt Brigid had been asked to buy a bazaar ticket

and she had bought four, one for each of us. She had wished
Brigid, her namesake, to win the prize but Brigid hadn't. She
was utterly indifferent to it when it was won. Elizabeth was
very excited because it was such a large and magnificent
present. Her eyes glowed with possession every time Father
asked her permission to use the polo cart. He always added
that he might as well keep it occupied until she was ready to
use it herself.

This was one of those periods when none of us was fully
occupied. There were no lessons for the simple reason that
there was no governess. In some remote place dividends
had failed and the natural consequence was that Mother,
faced with the problem of going without a cook or education for us, had chosen to teach us herself. This left her with
the kitchen running as usual but it did not, by any means,
keep us controlled. Her lessons were run on the principle of
Magnall's Questions, upon a sort of IQ basis. So long as we
answered the questions her conscience was absolved — and
we were free. It was on these occasions that Father asserted
himself. Mother's failures were, automatically, his opportunities. He — who never gave us a lesson of any sort and
never had us upon his conscience — now took up the problem of our education like a crusade. He declared that it was
disgraceful the way in which we were being *wasted*. We were
running to seed, no better than cabbage stalks. The argument began at the breakfast table and was continued
apparently whenever one of us was present. He used it as a
deliberate paternal testimony for the future, as proof of his
concern for our development. Mother's invariable reply was
that James' health entitled him to a holiday and that, for this
term, it was her intention to teach us herself.

Father was scathing. He remarked that this meant nothing more or less than the catechism plus Wilkie Collins. If
James could run about he could stand discipline. Discipline
would be *good for his health*.

A nanny goat had been bought for James as the doctor
had recommended goat's milk for him. She was a wonderful
nanny goat with two delightful kids and two perfectly

wonderful udders but they were always dry. It was quite a mystery. Her kids could not be blamed because she was tethered in a pasture out of their reach. Major was blamed. He was blamed because of what had happened to him upon a previous Shrove Tuesday when Margaret, the cook, had asked Grandmother for a wedding ring to put into the pancake batter. Grandmother had three wedding rings, only one of which was her own. She gave the cook a very thin ring that had belonged to her mother, on the strict understanding that it was to be returned to her after the party was over. She then went into town for the day. Upon her return the first thing she did was to ask for her ring. It then transpired that nobody had got the ring. James, my brother, had got the thimble and was destined for an old maid, but none of us had the ring. We had been called from the table in haste for some reason or other. No pancakes were left. Where then was the ring? Major had been given his share of the pancakes. As he was the only one not likely to know what a ring was when he had it, he was locked up in the stable and given a powder. He was both angry and depressed about it. In the morning the ring was there — and Major was let out of the stable. It was Grandmother who blamed him about Nanny. 'Major,' she said, 'I do not trust you.' Father saved him. Father hid behind a hedge for hours and never took his eyes off Nanny. He entered the house and told Grandmother that she was, once more, mistaken. It was not Major. It was Rory. Rory, who had begun with ink as a puppy, had simply changed from black to white. Rory was Nanny's milker and Nanny approved of him. She never butted him when he took the milk, the way she butted the cook who came when there was no milk left to take.

James now had quarts of goat's milk daily and Father returned to the argument about our education. We were, he said, running to seed. He persisted until the entire question became a torment to Mother. In exasperation she asked him why he did not teach us himself. Father looked utterly confounded. He resembled James when he had his mouth open. It was at this moment that he came down in favour of the village school. He had only suggested it previously, now he was entirely for it. Why on earth should we be exposed to waste, or inefficiency, when there was a national system of instruction practically upon our doorstep? He became so eloquent that either from conviction or sheer exhaustion Mother gave in about it. Both she and Grandmother regarded us as victims. They pitied us. They treated us as innocent persons who were forced to expose ourselves to all sorts of vices or temptations.

We, on the contrary, did not feel punished at all. The adventure excited us.

When the day came for us to go to the Ardmore School, Father was absent and Mother and Grandmother stayed in bed for breakfast. We were told to deliver ourselves in the governess cart to the schoolmaster. We were given our lunches, wrapped in silky tissue papers. What everybody seemed to forget was that we never went abroad without a cavalcade. Not only did we have an animal in the shafts, we had all the dogs and cats as well as the two kids. The cats, as usual, draped themselves upon the branches of trees at the end of our first mile. We arrived at the schoolhouse with nine animals. We arrived late. The pupils were all in their places. We settled into our places. No places were offered to the dogs. They just stood around, sniffing, with an air of bright vigilance. Major was inclined to ask questions. Rory kept his eye on Major, waiting for the signal. The darling kids kept scampering across the threshold and leaping on and off the low stone window-sills where there were pots of scarlet geraniums. There was a strong smell of apples and bread and butter.

The schoolmaster said that he had heard that Elizabeth read political speeches. This was not quite fair to Elizabeth. It was part of her past. At the age of three she had been put upon a table and given a newspaper containing an address by Mr Gladstone. It was only natural that she should resent having it brought up as a permanent introduction to her mentality. The schoolmaster saw that he had made a mistake. He then declared that his intention towards us was mathematical. He approached the blackboard and wrote a problem upon it in white, chalked figures. Then he took up a long cane and pointed with it at the problem. But immediately he took up the cane Major and Rory told him to put it down. They did not go to him. They stayed with us but they protested strongly against the use of swords. Instead of yielding to their protests he began also to protest against them. This was fatal. The tone of his voice exposed him for what he was. There was a terrible and instant argument in which all the dogs joined, standing up to do it. The kids quickened upon the window-sills. The geraniums trembled. The atmosphere sharpened and filled with threats. All the pupils, including us, became tense and stirred, our wits on edge. For a schoolmaster he was very stupid. He was quite deficient in psychology. Instead of putting down his gun he flourished it in order to emphasise his authority. There was such a racket that it was impossible to hear what he was saying.

When the matter had gone as far as was reasonable it became unreasonable and Major had to deal with it. With Rory at his heels like a henchman he stalked the schoolmaster. When he saw Major's *intention* the poor man fell back against the wall and begged us to *preserve* him. He clung to his cane. His voice was piteous. Major was jet-black and the schoolmaster was as pale as death. Rory's hair stood up on his shoulders so that he resembled a boar. It was quite a scene, and the curious effect that it had upon the pupils was not to make them feel sorry for the schoolmaster but to make them clap and cheer Major. They were on our side. Boys clapped as though they were at a circus. Little girls screamed. The dogs were right up against the blackboard and the problem upon it and the schoolmaster became flatter and flatter against the wall. Suddenly he let out a most awful roar: 'Class dismissed!' he yelled. 'Everybody go out into the field.'

Instantaneously the pupils rose from the benches and all together, as one man, we pressed through the doorway and out into the air and the dogs came with us. The schoolroom and the schoolmaster were left to themselves. It took the unfortunate man some time to appear. By the time he did we were all deep in our lunches, sharing nuts and sweets. Major was being treated as a hero and we were acquiring friends. It was one of our most popular occasions. All things were being offered to us.

The schoolmaster seemed to possess no potency at all in the open air. Major and Rory watched him but did not bark at him. He was caneless and solitary. He came towards us slowly and as dignifiedly as possible. He announced that it would be advisable if we went home and 'took our troop with us'.

That was the beginning and end of our village schooling.

Our single day at the Ardmore school introduced us to the Orrs. They were a delight to us. There were seven of them, each of them extraordinarily alike. They only differed in degree and volume. They had straight black hair like Spaniards and opaque prune-like eyes. They lived in the last of a row of tiny cottages which belonged to the Stevenson estate. The first cottage was occupied by our gardener MacDaid and his bedridden mother. This little row of grey cottages, raised above a narrow river and a strip of roadside, set back with flower gardens, always made me think of the Lourdes Grotto. It was all in a place by itself. It had the withheld air of its special purpose against a background of wild hills and woods. It had an isolated perfection with its bright flowers and the running water. They were such small little houses, containing their families as the shrine under the glass globe maintained its saint.

The Orrs invited us to play games with them. With a family of seven, where even the baby played, any game was possible. Jack Orr invented a game that included the donkeys. He produced a coil of thick cord. He and I mounted the first donkey, and his brother and James followed on the second. We trotted down the tiny path to the MacDaid cottage where he tied the cord firmly to the handle of the door and flung the cord to James and his brother who tied the handle of the second door and so on until all the doors of the cottages were tied up so that they could not be opened from within. As soon as the deed was accomplished we galloped back to the road. But when we got to the road we saw a vehicle coming over the crest of the hill in the distance and by the scarlet gleam of its cushions we knew that it was Father. The only place we could hide was under the stone bridge. On top of the donkeys we were pressed so close to the arch of the bridge that when Father rattled over us it felt as though he were driving upon our heads. It was unimaginably exciting. We had the thrill of outlaws and pioneers all in one breath. We did not dare to emerge from the bridge until it was certain that Father was not turning upon his course to seek us. For all we knew he may have been sent out as a scout. We stayed there with Time lengthened out upon us and our heads holding up the archway. Jack Orr gave us all sorts of unusual information — that the donkey which MacDaid kept in the shed behind his cottage was eternal. It was as old as Adam and refused either to work or die. MacDaid met every day with a spade and preparation for a funeral but the donkey did not die. Donkeys never died. None on this earth had ever *seen* a donkey die. They were blessed animals. Every Christmas Eve, at midnight, donkeys in anybody's stable, Christian or heretic, went down on their knees because the Lord had been born in their manger.

When it became too late to stay we had to go out and make ourselves visible. Jack filled us with courage. There was nothing to be afraid of. Nobody had seen us tie the door handles. At that hour of the day women were asleep or in the fields; old Mrs MacDaid was the single exception and she could not move unless she brought her bed with her. We had heard her voice, a thin whistling voice like a weasel's, and were certainly glad that she was tied to the bed.

James and I rode home as fast as the donkeys consented. Father was there. He was drinking tea with Mother. James and I exercised the utmost discretion. We precipitated nothing. We waited for the storm to burst. We watched

MacDaid go past the windows when his work was finished and we had our very definite thoughts about what he would find at home.

The next morning James and I were strung from the absence of the night into the presence of the day and crisis. But no crisis came. Nothing was said. The storm burst beyond us. It burst elsewhere. The atmosphere was black and even thick with it, but not *on us*. James and I suffered astonishment of heart. Although we had no visible proof it seemed to us that the one who got the blame was Father. Father was strangely chastened. That was all there was — the effect upon Father.

It was days later when Grandmother was there and Father not there that dim reverberations reached us. Grandmother had us all by the fireside, cracking nuts. She was putting fresh lace on one of her caps with lilac velvet bows. She was very sweet. She said that her grandmother was the image of Martha Washington. They had the same profiles. She took off the cap she was wearing and tried on the unmade one. James asked her why she wore a cap and she said to keep her hair tidy. She could never wear her hair in James' fashion with the bush in the centre. Then she said she was glad she had brought the dining-room furniture from America. It was Spanish mahogany, a deep yellow wood carved in acorns and pineapples and upholstered with black horsehair. Grandmother adored the rocking chair. The horsehair was buttoned firmly into the seat and back and up over the arms, and she gave us pennies every time we rocked her. James sat astride one arm of the chair and I sat sideways on the other arm and we rocked her like wild horses in a circus. The faster we rocked the more she loved it.

'Do you know,' she said suddenly, 'it is quite surprising that there are so many little Orrs! It is disgraceful. There are far too many of them to be fed properly. Orr, the coachman, was your mother's groom before she married your father. If I were you, dear children, I would avoid the Orrs. They are all right to begin with. I know all about that. But, let them in upon you, and you'll see you'll regret it.'

There was something so subtle about this that it made us ponder. We were stirred by the *mystery*, by the unspoken intention. It never occurred to us that a law had been emitted which prohibited us from contact with the Orrs. Our relationship to them was our business. We were too independent for it to be otherwise. They were our neighbours — several miles away, just as the Stevensons and the manses were our neighbours. We were even closer to the Orrs, because MacDaid lived in their row of cottages and we saw him daily.

When Christmas Eve came again James and I went to bed with Father's chronometer watch. Father could never wear it. Every watch he put on stopped the moment it touched his body. When the house was quiet and it was close to midnight James and I got up and sneaked out to the donkey's stable with candles and matches. We climbed into the hayloft and lit the candles and watched. We were breathless for the miracle. It was warm in the hay. The air was biting cold, ready for snow. There was one of those travelling moons, racing through clouds like a railway train. We heard the church bells very faintly. We heard the clock in the hall rattling its chain. Midnight began to strike and nothing happened to the donkeys. Memory failed them utterly while we were there to witness. They stood upon their feet with their tall rabbit ears falling down with laziness.

The miracle was that we did not set fire to the hayloft and the stables and ourselves. James and I never told anybody that we had found out about donkeys. We kept it to ourselves. We had investigated, and this left our consciences curiously satisfied.

Chapter Fourteen

We had a tutor, a tall thin dark young man with a beaked nose and a pink face. Mother had chosen him because of his qualifications. From the first moment we regarded him as a natural enemy. Governesses were bad but use had accustomed us to them as a second nature. A man governess was unnatural. When our first lesson was due, and we knew that it was due, we were out in the fields. James was mounted on Garryowen and Elizabeth on Frances and I was on Mulligatawny. When Mr Carey appeared in the meadow, waving his arms and beckoning to us to come, we did not lend him our ears. We faced the opposite direction. In the excitement of escape I must have urged Mulligatawny with an argument that might have been applied to Frances with good results. Its effect upon Mulligatawny was beyond all logic. He simply sailed off at full strength across the landscape. His speed was so smooth that I was able to hold on. I was balanced upon him with the lightness of a jockey. With Mr Carey behind me to give testimony I could not allow an accident to occur. It would have been a sin to let anything happen. The principles of freedom were involved. My flight with Mulligatawny became an instantaneous Act of Faith. I was both terrified and exalted. I began to dread the time when the pace would slacken and the bumps begin. I prayed to the angels, to the archangels, to Gabriel who had made the annunciation to Mary, to the angels who had visited Abraham, all the angels, my own special angels, to preserve me. This prayer had it own language. It was a wordless force rising from me like flames from a fire. I belonged in that ride to my angels. It was an angelic flight.

And then, suddenly, somewhere, Mulligatawny stopped dead. I went straight over his head into the hedge. The hedge saved me. It held me up like bedsprings. There was an awful arrest in the world. Not a bird sang. The earth was touched with the intake that withdraws expression when the gong strikes. Mulligatawny was the gong. His breath was blazing from him in funnels and his sides were heaving like a pair of bellows. We were a pair of fools there in the bright morning and I was sinking with a horrible crackle deeper into the thorny hedge.

In spite of this bad beginning Mr Carey was devoted to me. He told Mother he would teach me anything I wished to learn; any extra lessons I wished were mine for the asking. I refused to ask. I wished not one extra-curricular moment with him. Mother tried to tempt me with drawing lessons. She said: 'You should, Kathleen.' Little phrases stand out upon us. They remain. I hated it when they called me Kathleen. I would not consent. It was all very well for Mother to draw. Her Irish ruins hung on the drawing-room walls and in Grandmother's bedroom. I was not urged or moved to draw these *morne* landscapes.

Mr Carey gave us Latin in a more interesting fashion than Mademoiselle. He made us smell the wars, the Gallic and Punic Wars, and the wars of Catiline. He invoked for us the full stress of the Roman meaning, of conquest abroad and prisons at home, of a power which was driven by its ultimate dereliction of soul to commit cruelty. It happens when nations and vast groups of people attain the integration of individuals, when all their organs have settled down to their proper functions. The judgment is focused then to its purest and impurest worth. Friendlessness attacks in this hour when this unit has to stand absolutely alone. This is the hour when the swords swing — when they have to go either backwards or forwards, to the right or to the left. It is the hour of balance. This was the hour in which, Mr Carey told us, the Romans were afraid of mice.

When an entire nation is afraid of mice it is done for. It is grave when soldiers have to be paid to fight. Death can never be faced for money. It has to be faced for Life. It has to be faced with redemption when it is massed for war. Faith must be there to wipe out the bloodshed, to bleach the scarlet from the sins and crystallise the evil out upon the consciousness of history. Time waits and none escapes the judgment. They may destroy the traces but always, somewhere, the broken statues will tell. When pillars fall, they lie. This is enough.

Mr Carey introduced us to Shakespeare. He imbued us with the impersonal attitude — that we were not to think of Shakespeare as a man but as a theatre. He sent me to Bacon. But he kept us reined. Although he cast controversy upon us he did not set any bias in our minds. The play became the thing. These actors on the board were all that mattered. Our journal, *Liberty*, bore Mr Carey's traces. And yet, insistently, we were never in his flow. We remained in opposition. The thoughts he spurred from us were wildly and wonderfully our own thoughts, not his. They burst from us with a magic that ignored our control. What was written was always never at all what we had planned. It was infused with what we had never considered. It bore traces of our intention just as our work for Mr Carey bore his traces. Tracks would be a better term. 'This is the road, walk in it!' was the law that operated. The fashion of our walking was subject to the inspiration of the moment.

It was in the time of Mr Carey that Mary O'Connell ceased to be there. She had gone away to watch Grandaunt Ahn die and had never truly returned to us. We had waited for her. Father always reappeared. But Mary O'Connell had no resurrection.

Mother walked with the visitor to the door. They talked for a long time. MacDaid was moulding the pansies. They hardly seemed to me to be flowers. They were more like velvet imbedded in parterres. They were not gay as roses were gay or daffodils in a spring wind. They were not blanched from the dark earth like snowdrops. They were the dark earth itself, piled from its softness; little furry flower animals or flower insects. Mother was very proud of them. All the time she talked to the visitor she kept her eyes on the pansies. Major lay on the doorstep, curly as a sheep but with the poise of a lion. Mother did not ask the visitor to stay to lunch. There was nobody to lay the table. Margot never mastered the laws of knives and forks. It was Mother who had to lay the table and she was already occupied, talking to the visitor on the doorstep.

On a day when a trumpet was blowing in the valley Father staggered in upon us with straws upon his shoulders. Mother moaned when she saw him. 'Stealing a pair of boots,' she said to him tragically, '*that* is the bottom of the sea.'

He began to pick the straws from his clothes. He had slept in a rick riddled with rats and as hot as an oven. He tried to appease Mother. He explained. He had needed a pair of boots in a place named Strabane. He had gone, quite naturally, to the shoemaker's to be fitted. The boots fitted him exactly. He refused to take them off. Why unlace them in order to lace them up again? He was in dire need of those boots. He had given his name and address to the shoemaker and told him that he would send him a cheque and the fool of a man had run down the street after him, screaming that his boots had been stolen. Like Cervantes and Villon, Father had been thrown into prison. It was not his fault at all, he tried to convince Mother. It was the fault of the shoemaker who, most evidently, had no understanding of the banking system. A cheque was a cheque.

Mother said it was no use. She said something awful. She said that it was all over the town that he had stolen a pair of boots.

'And now,' he said, taking the last straw out of his hair, 'you must simply add that I pass the nights in haystacks. I am nothing,' he smiled gloriously at me, 'but a troubadour.'

Mother said he was hopeless. She sent me out of the room. I didn't care what he was, even if he were a troubadour. I still loved him. But somehow, when the Thompsons drove past us on the Glendermott Road, I could not bring myself to look at them. I was afraid that if I smiled at them they would not smile at me because their father was not a troubadour. He took the horsewhip to Jack when he was late for meals.

There was a positively awful racket in the night. Major was barking his loudest and Rory was helping him. Indoors the Pomeranian barked back to them. Father was coming home. I lay in the darkness, black with misery. This was Macbeth knocking in the middle of the night. Every night now the shutters were put over on all the windows with iron bars. MacDaid did it before he went home. After prayers were said Mother barred and bolted the front and back doors. We were shut in and Father was shut out. I was in the dining-room side of the house. I heard when Father got into the courtyard. The horse whinnied and the cock crew. Time was telescoped so that dawn and midnight were fused. Even the rooster was cheated. The night was pitch black. It took ages to find the stars, pin-pricked into the curtain.

I heard the tumult going from corner to corner of the courtyard, from the tool shed at the right to the stables at the left. The kids bleated and Nanny answered them. Then I heard the smash and crash of glass. The back window in the little library was made of plate glass. It was the only room without shutters. It had been built on to the house from the vegetable garden. One window looked out upon the vegetables and the raspberry canes and the other window looked out upon the stable gable. Father had broken the window and plunged into the house. I heard him. I did not see him. I heard Mother's voice and I knew that she was crying.

This was wrong. It afflicted the night. I denied him then, at that instant. He was the Father and I turned to the Mother. No matter what his Calvary was, I stood by the women at the Cross. I was Peter. I refused to be registered with him. I went to sleep with the pattern of this resolution upon my being and I awoke with it as potter's earth from a furnace. The shape was taken.

He was there at breakfast, telling me and James about the Boers, the Dutch farmers who were being robbed in Africa. Fused by my inward decision I did not respond to him as usual. Boer was an ugly name for a farmer, and Africans were native. They were in the pictures which Mother forced me to look at when she took out a red volume from the *Ethnological History of Mankind*. I hated having to regard these people with ivory pins through their nostrils and their hair stacked like mountains. The arrangements of their bodies were equally bizarre. I did not understand *why* Mother considered them important. They did not interest me. They were repellent and unutterably alien.

Brigid was provided with a new Mademoiselle all to herself, a governess who knew how to lay a table. I was obliged to give up my room to her but as this bestowed a more wonderful place upon me it was not a sacrifice. Every evening after supper Margot unfolded a folding bed for me in the little library. This was a very pleasant arrangement. It gave me the benefit of the adult world at those hours when I was accustomed to be cut off from it. It also gave me books to read. It was the loveliest joy to put out one's hand at any time and find that the wall was lined with books.

Mother had bought a piano for the dining room, a special little piano with purple fluted silk behind a fretwork screen. The piano was a little hoarse so we were told that we could play on it when and as we wished. This was to encourage us to practise. We sat in the dining room in the winter evenings. In that wild hour of the young, before sleep subdues their spirit, Mother played rakes and marches to which we danced and paraded around the table to our heart's delight. It was a wonderful table. If you lay full length upon it and grasped the ledge with your thumbs under, you could swing yourself underneath it from one end to the other. We were adept at this. Mother played out our energies until time for prayers. By the time she had finished the rosary and her special prayers to Saint Anthony, Our Lady of Good Counsel, and two Litanies we were tame enough for bed. While the others were carted off to other parts of the house I only moved to the next room, with the door kept open a crack. I could hear when they spoke. I could hear when the cinders fell. I was not alone. I heard when Father was there. I heard when Mother and Mademoiselle checked Mr Dawlay's accounts. Mr Dawlay was Mother's agent. She told Mademoiselle that it was disastrous. He used up all the rents to buy new doors and window sashes. It was incredible, she said.

She told Father about it the next day. He was standing with his back to the library fire. Mademoiselle was there. Mr Carey was struggling with arithmetic and James in the drawing room. Mother said she would have to 'sell another street'.

Father was not on Mother's side. He was against her. He was also against Mr Dawlay. He said Dawlay was a blackguard and that women were positive fools and that if he had his way he would blast the entire property and build decent dwellings.

Mother was distressed. She said: 'John, what are you accusing me of?'

'Your aunt's behaviour.'

'You are unjust. She only agreed to have those houses built because the bank advised it. They were needed for the workers in the new shirt factories. She meant them to be good. Now they are falling to pieces.'

Mademoiselle stood up. She wished to get away. Mother told her to stay. Father told her to go. She was glued between them, unable to go but reluctant to stay. She wetted the point of the pencil and began to add up the column of figures from the bottom. When she got halfway up she had to begin again.

Father said Mother was cutting off her capital which was equivalent to cutting off her head.

She begged him to be constructive and not destructive.

'That's just it, my dear wife, I am what I am and you *don't know* it.' He beamed at me. He had recourse to my spirit. He was unaware that it was tightening against him, that I was, for the first time in my life, applying reason to him. I was listening with the probity of a judge. 'Your beloved aunt should have built decent streets. Why Katie, she had the Walls for an example. You can't set up matchboxes in a walled city.'

'*She* didn't build them. She paid for them to be built —

and don't forget the Cathedral and convent.'

'Oh, the Cathedral!' Father mocked. 'That only proves her grandiosity and pomposity.'

'John!'

Mademoiselle stood up. She said Brigid needed to be taken somewhere. She went out.

Father suddenly whacked out one of his legs as though about to dance a jig, but he stood still again at once. 'Well, the Cathedral hasn't fallen down.'

'Neither has Nazareth House nor the College.'

'I won't budge one iota from my argument.'

This time it was Mother who beamed at me. 'He's talking nonsense, Kathie,' she said gently. It was the first time she had ever condemned him to me. In her eyes he had condemned himself before Mademoiselle. I was established between them as a tribune. This is the child's misery, the inadequate honour of a function of difference. I tried not to look at either of them. I saw Dot, Mrs McIntyre's ancient cat. She had abandoned her kittens in the attic. She was sitting independently on the hearth rug, immaculately clean as usual, like a person on a visit. She was the only one of our cats who preferred to live in the house. Father saw me looking at her. She had caught a rat, he told me. She had killed it the way Major had killed the pig, because she had to. She looked so peaceful with her creamy bib tucked up to her ears, not a spot or stain of battle upon her. Father said: 'Get rid of Dawlay. I know you won't because I say it, but you're wrong.' Then he caught my eye and he said wistfully, on another note: 'I count for nothing. I'm nothing but a lamb on the shoulders.'

It was strange that the abstruse lamb upon his shoulder reached my heart more directly than the argument about Mr Dawlay. It shot a pang through me. It reached my heart and the love flowed again, as simple as a river.

Grandmother was on Father's side about Mr Dawlay. She did not give Father the credit. She said: 'I cannot tell you *why* but I have a feeling against him.' Mother said it was all very well but she had to have somebody and she saw no difference between him and anybody else. Grandmother said that was true too.

When Mother left the room James and I rocked her and she sighed deeply. 'My dear children, listen: when I was a very young girl I went to America. I was taken out under the chaperonage of Mrs Gavan Duffy. They would not allow me to go alone after what had happened to Catherine. Catherine was my sister. She went out of her mind. It took us almost three months to get there. You can't imagine. The first night I was in New York I dreamt I saw soldiers sleeping on the kerbstones with bandaged heads. Very shortly that became true. The Civil War broke out. Jane was for the South. She had so many friends in the South. I was for the North because of one man, a young man in Lincoln's army.' She always told us this story in the same words. We knew it by heart. But every time she told it we listened to it with freshness. It was a revelation of tragedy. 'He asked me to marry him and I said yes. I knew that Jane would never consent. So we agreed to elope. He was to come for me with a carriage at midnight. When the night came, I was ready. I stole down the stairs in the darkness and when I got to the last steps a door opened and Jane came out with a candle in her hand. She came to the bottom of the stairs: "Go up to your room, Elizabeth," she said. I went. It was no use. I had to do it. I waited for *him*. He was such a handsome young man, my darlings. I knew that he loved me. I expected him to come.' She actually expected him to burn down the house to get her. 'But he did not come. He never came. I became as one dead. I mourned for him as one dead and all the time I *hoped*.' She cast over us the spell and hypnosis of frustrated love. She always paused when she came to this part. Great, deep sighs broke from her. Often she would lay her cheek against her hand and stare into the fireplace or some world which we could not inhabit. 'So,' she always said, 'it was like that. I was forced to marry. I had many offers. I was very beautiful.' She declared it extravagantly as an inutility, a futility. The beauty was wasted. It belonged only to one man and he had withdrawn from it. 'It was of no consequence. Jane nagged at me to marry. She had come between me and *him*. She wished to atone for it. It was impossible. There was no atonement. She found a husband for me, a man who was twice my age. Oh, he was a very good man, very kind and all that. I was very tired by then. I didn't care. I remember perfectly the day he asked me to marry him. We were returning from a picnic to Staten Island. It was on the boat, coming home. He asked me if I would become his wife. I looked at him. I looked beyond him. I was indifferent. I said: "I—suppose so."' She sighed again. The moment of her desolation repossessed her. We were infused with it. We endured it with her — the awful, swept-away feeling of nothingness held us fast by the heels. 'Go on,' we demanded, knowing that there was more to come.

'Well, the wedding day came. Jane had sent out the invitations. She arranged everything. The church was full of people. I was sitting at my dressing table, being decked out in all my bridal finery and then, suddenly, I went numb. I went numb from head to toe. I said that I could not go on with it. It was impossible. I hadn't the strength to go to the church.' We were conscious of sacrifice. Our breaths were always caught at this crisis; then the lovely voice went on: 'So they brought the priest and the bridegroom to me. Jane sent to the church for them. I was married at my own dressing table with this numbness all through me. I went through it as in a dream. That, my darlings, is how I came to marry the man who was your grandfather.'

The 'man who was our grandfather' was fixed for us as an enemy, a man from the outside who had possessed Grandmother against her will. The marriage, she always added, had mercifully not lasted. 'He gave me everything a woman could ask for and it meant nothing to me. Nothing. The year after the marriage Katie, your mother, was born. The next year Jane was born. She died in infancy. When we had been married for four years your grandfather died. I was not at home. I cannot remember where I was when word reached me that he was in a hospital. I went to see him. He implored me to visit his old aunts in Dublin should it ever happen that I should be in Dublin. He died of the yellow fever. He left me a brownstone house, horses and carriages and a fortune — and what use was it? It has all given me nothing.'

Another time she told us about Mother. 'From the moment she was born she was definitely your grandfather's side of the family. She used to remind me of him. I couldn't bear it. Jane asked to have her, so I consented. That is how your mother was brought up by her Aunt Waters. I had nothing at all to do with her.'

We never had the slightest blame for her because she had deserted Mother. In our eyes she was entirely a woman whose life had been spent upon a quest for the lover who had been taken from her. She never saw him again. She never forgot him. We heard another version when she told us about the Victory Ball. That also was Jane's idea. Jane had suggested it in the process of atonement. She had insisted upon taking Elizabeth to the big Victory Ball in New York in the desperate hope that the young man would appear there. She took good care that Elizabeth would be visible for she made her go as a Goddess of Liberty with twelve little pages. 'I was the belle of the Ball,' Grandmother told us, 'and he wasn't there. I danced every dance as though I danced in Limbo.'

I can see her sitting in the rocking chair in her silk dress with the gold chain and the tiny watch looped into its pocket on her breast. I can see her beautiful face within the shadow of her curls, the peak of the Mary Stuart cap on her forehead and her dark eyes and her restless hands. She was an embodiment of denial; of one whose steps, like those of the Indian mothers who die in childbirth, had been turned backward.

Chapter Fifteen

Winters are more confined than summers. The earth hardens and repulses us and we are driven inwards. Hibernation is a withdrawal. We are taken back to the root.

I remember with Druidic fervour the white core of winters at the solstice, the day when the sun turned again and rebegan its symphysis with the earth. I did not know that the sun was rounding an elliptic. I only knew that there was a point when the death of winter whitened from its source. I stood by stones in a desolate field and *knew* the salvation the way the blades of grass knew it, or the bare trees.

James and Elizabeth and I walked through the snow. I was choked with gaiters and gloves and a scarf. The snow was knee-deep and we were burning hot. We had gone out into it in a wind as sharp as knives. The harshness vanished and Elizabeth's cheeks were as rosy as apples. We glowed with laughter in the lightness. We were upheld by the whiteness, planed by some miracle of light into a new statement of our beings. We were weightless and invalid upon our usual terms. All things stood out with an inconceivable clarity. The conifers became essences of themselves, their green more green, their scent as potent as a syrup upon our tongues. Squirrels became an intimate pattern — taking from us as much as we gave them. Blackbirds with orange beaks, redbreasts with scarlet breasts, and winter berries were bled in drops as significant as blood and tears from the landscape. Even the ploughed fields were covered with the mantle and only stones were bare. From their rounded surfaces the snow vanished with the first touch of sunshine.

We went to Midnight Mass. The world was silvered over with the blue quality of mystery. All was asleep. Only we walked on the crisp roads, our steps like wooden notes. It was a journey of wonder, a voyage in the night. It was not real, and while we walked in it we were unreal. We were with Mother. We were unaware of distance and progress. A cow mooed in a barn as we passed, a dog whined and Major answered and then the stillness waited again to catch our wooden notes. We passed the MacGuinness house, black and back in its garden. We passed the three little houses together where Miss MacLaughlin the dressmaker lived. Grandmother took us there to sit upon her steel fender and see the daisy bowls on her dresser. It was a very small place where we had to be disposed of as in the cabin of a ship. Elizabeth was always put upon the stool behind the door. James and I had to change places with her when we began to cook. We came to the corner where the hill was at its crest. There was a tiny house with tiny windowpanes stacked with red apples and jars of brandy balls. This was where Mary O'Connell visited when we had gone this way with her.

Mother turned down the steep sharp road to the chapel. It was so steep that you were forced to cling to the ground with your heels. There was a tall castle-like wall to the right of the road. The further down we went, the higher the wall rose above us. The chapel yard had little booths in it, twinkling with fairy lights. As soon as we entered, the organ boomed out the warm powerful music and you knew that there were hosts of angels. A great magnification took possession of me, an enlargement within which minimised all things without. The altar seemed smaller. The priest seemed to have shrunk. The acolytes were no larger than dolls. The pageant of the Mass was transposed by distance in the fashion of an Italian landscape; a scene beyond the event. This was only the sign and symbol of what had happened in Bethlehem. We had come to it as the Kings had come to it, because we had followed a star. It had shot through the heavens above the winter fields and perished without a sparkle before we knew. Mistakes could still be made. A great mistake had been made about Jesus. When the Priest washed his hands I knew that he had become Pontius Pilate who hadn't known what to do about it even though his wife had come out upon the staircase with the angel and *warned* him.

We walked home with bells ringing. Mother bought us apples. MacDaid met us with the trap. He was penitent and wanted Mother to forgive him and Mother said, in the voice that always made you do what she wanted: 'We could not be late for Mass.'

It was in the snow that James and I found the wild bull in the spruce grove. He was no longer white, neither was he grey. He was dimmed against the snow, as faulty as a shadow. He was a mad bull and when he saw us he put his head down the way Nanny did. Neither James nor I wished to sit up in his horns. Major was very brave. He turned the bull's attention in his direction. He kept him butting the trees until the men came from the farm. Mother was indignant when we told her, and when Father heard he took us right off to see the farm people. He took Major with us. He had the farmer, so he said, in the palm of his hand from the beginning. His obedience, he said, was puritanical. He submitted to reason. Father spent the whole time proving that the farmer owed him his bull's life because Major had *not* killed him. The farmer said that Major could not kill a bull. 'No,' Father said sharply, 'but your glorious bull could destroy innocent children.' The farmer said again that he was sorry. Major and James and I waited. It was an argument in negatives and if Father won, the victory hardly seemed worth while to us as we walked home. But, as Mother declared, 'there was no more bull in the grove.'

There was snow when Father came again in the middle of the night. There was the approaching tumult, the hordes of sounds coming up the avenue, the battering at the windows and doors. Mother did not let him in. I do not know how he got in but, suddenly, he was there. Lights flashed in the dining room. He was singing. The song had no music to it. It was full of pain. It roused in me an ungovernable pity. I wondered why God could not change him.

His voice went out of the dining room and across the hall and presently Mother screamed. She screamed the way she had screamed in the room at the shore, when the handle turned both ways and would not open the door. And, as I had run to her then, I ran to her now. She was in the hall, trying to turn the key in the front door. It opened as I got to her and she seized my hand and dragged me with her out into the snow. 'Darling,' she kept saying, 'we must hide from him. Oh, dear God, it is dark in the children's room. I hope Mademoiselle doesn't act like a fool.' Then she told me to go back to the house and wait for her. 'Be nice to him,' she implored me, 'until I come.'

I went back to the house. I sought him at once. He was in Mother's room, turning over the bedclothes in a fury. 'Where is she? If only she were here I'd do for her . . . .'

'Father!' My voice was as thin as a pebble thrown over the threshold, but it tamed him. It set the madness down in him. 'Father, you know what I told you!' The words were cried from me. My heart was beating against the ceiling, high as a bird that has been caught. It was not beating from terror but from its own acute discipline, its limit. I was shivering with cold. I heard Mademoiselle stirring and a door being shut. Margot did not sleep in the house. She went home every night. 'Preach,' Father mocked me, 'go on, my lady!' 'Darling' fluttered, a poor stifled word within me. It did not come out. He spurred me to the furthest rendering. I could find no speech to make it veritable to him. I could only stand there, my lips quivering, and know that I was being turned to stone as Lot's wife had been turned to salt.

That is all. It was squeezed out as tiny as a drop of blood upon a grievous wound. I do not know what happened. I think Mademoiselle must have taken me away, or Father went away. The next thing was that Mother was back. She was smiling at me and saying that I could come into her bed and that there were almonds to eat. We ate the almonds between us. Our bodies burned warmth into the soft bed. It was all quite safe again but neither of us mentioned Father.

That was a place where the shutters went down.

In the spring our hired fields were yellow with daffodils. I
went for a walk alone. I went as far as the granite quarry.
There was a tiny lost campion upon the ledge of stone. It
was white in the bottom of the pit where the men had laboured and gone away, leaving nothing but the signal of
their presence. There was nobody. The river came out in
splashes in the landscape, shiny and as blue as satin. The
clouds were cold, and when wild geese rose in the valley
they rose as though the clouds commanded them to return.
They were the same colour. Their wings were pointed
against the daylight in bas-relief, on the surface, a pattern
scraped and defined by its own motion. I was stamped with
a nostalgic, breaking sufferance; bruised from this contact.
The cosmos included me as a trifle. It was so immense that I
was bereft in it, utterly without shelter. I hated the lesson. I
rebelled against the instruction, and I was miserable. My
will rose impotently against the law and the law towered
above my will as extensively as the tall wall on the steep
descent to the chapel. I descended into hell as I descended
towards the chapel. It was a hell illustrated by the swept,
lonely landscape, the wildness, the dereliction of the quar-
ried granite. And then I beheld the little flower that had
such amazing courage to be itself in the midst of vastness. It
had faced the danger. Far away, on the other side of the
valley where the trees climbed in battalions, I realised that
there was another horizon, another valley where lakes were
spun as mirrors. Father had shown me that there were three
of them, all visible at once. When I thought of him he was
linked to the realisation that it was a long time since he had
come to the house. The nights had become quiet, unbroken
by his entry heralded by Major and Rory without and the
Pomeranian within. Peace had fallen almost as a habit upon
our household. It was all right to have it, but it was impossible to thank God for it.

It was a day on which Mother had gone to the auction.
Now that the shops no longer sent her bandboxes she had a
new system of acquisition. She would drive off one morning

by herself, as she had driven off to search for Sarahs, and she would return at dusk with a red chair with fringes or somebody else's music albums or a table that had to have its legs changed before lamps could be put down on it.

Grandmother was about to come. This time, for some inexplicable reason, she had announced that she was coming. She had written from Glasgow where she was stopping for a few days. I went back to the house. The lesson was over. Mr Carey was standing in the hall archway between the busts of Caesar and Scipio. 'Why didn't you come?' he asked. There was no blame in his voice. It was a wash day. There was a smell of soap coming from the offices behind him. 'I missed you,' he said.

I had to stiffen, to shut myself out against him because he was being kind. I was urged by an unholy urgency to ask him *where* Father was? Why did they speak of him so mysteriously? I desired burningly to know and at the same time, cold as ice, I knew that it had nothing at all to do with me. I had put him out of my life. His interest turned over upon me as pages which you have to miss. You do not wish to read what is in them. I was intensely aware of myself as separate. I had to contain what I had to contain. There was no solvency. I had taken up an attitude, raised my hand to testify a resolve. There were none who could melt me from that decision except Father. And he was absent. He did not come.

Mother still insisted upon the *Ethnological History of Mankind*. She seemed obsessed with an idea to make me race-conscious. Her taste was so peculiar that it was a pure severance. Because these square red books with the pictures of natives were her choice I was unable to tell her that I was reading Plutarch or Butler's *Martyrs*. I could not ask her what an immaculate conception was or why the fact that Gautama was found in a rosebush gave him a virgin birth. It was so much easier to ask Mr Carey anything. He explained so beautifully the chance effect of geese upon history and why it was that a cat could look at a king. He made you absolutely clear about the Iron and Stone Ages, the difference between knocking a man down with a stone or battering him with spears. He took the iron bars from behind the shutters to give us an example. When men discovered iron, he explained, women shed the wildest tears, because their men were being destroyed with iron brutalities. The new weapon was always barbaric. It was always the barbaric people who found out how to do it. According to Mr Carey, Rome was an earthly Paradise until barbarism found it. That was why the taxes went up and after that all souls were condemned. It was when things went wrong that people went wrong. We gave Mr Carey a copy of *Liberty*. He was enchanted. Afterwards he told us that he had learned quite a few things from my article on Grattan's Parliament. He asked me if I had a hero. Everybody, he said, had to have a hero. I got out of the answer. I had no hero. I had only Father and I could see that Mr Carey would not admit him as a hero. When he pressed me I gave him the first name that came to me. I said Anaxagoras. Another day when he pressed me, pushed into my mind to find what ruled it, I said: 'Fire and Water.' I do not know why I said it. It was a vague and indefinite response to an urge for first principles. I had no faith at all in his first principles for when I told him once that Father said that the sorbic tree had the blood of lovers and that that was what made its berries red, Mr Carey had not admitted it. He said it was a mythical statement and *not to be taken seriously*. This was a judgment upon Father which I could not accept from a third person. In order not to deny Father I was impelled to deny Mr Carey.

I think that this young man fought for my appreciation and never received it the whole time he was with us. How was he to comprehend that he had been born among us from antagonisms?

Mother allowed us to help MacDaid with the flowers and chickens. We collected the eggs for him. Once a week we drove with him to the city market. The stalls were planted under glass. We drove directly to the florist's. Stacks of daffodils would be handed out, or roses or delphiniums or other flowers, but never pansies. Mother would not allow a pansy to be sold. What MacDaid got for the flowers and

eggs was put into a savings bank for us. We had also first
rights to any five-shilling pieces that appeared. If anybody
gave Mother a five-shilling piece it also went into the savings bank. It was MacDaid who drove us down the first time
in the polo cart to visit Grandaunt Brigid. She no longer
lived in the little handmade house with the damson tree in
the garden. She lived with a lot of orphans and aged people
in Nazareth House where there were nuns with pale blue
edges to their costumes. MacDaid rang the bell for us. It
echoed far away at a great distance and it took ages for steps
to come. When the nun opened the door she said that we
were expected and MacDaid vanished. We were taken down
a long corridor and into an immense room that had to be
traversed like a battlefield. The furniture was massed in it in
different places like troops on the maps of the Punic Wars.
Grandaunt Brigid sat in her old chair before the fire before
the old china. Everything about her was apparently the
same but attached to a remoteness that gave her the air of
sitting upon a throne. The change was that she was *alone*.
She had no Ahn to match her like an ornament on the man-
telpiece. She had no person to dominate and this cut her off
into a state of pure suspension.

She gave most of her attention to Brigid. And Brigid resented it. Brigid did not appreciate that they were
namesakes. She would not utter a word. When Grandaunt
Brigid said that she was sorry that she had not won the polo
cart Brigid looked ready to burst. A nun gave her a piece of
sugar. A nun asked me if I should like to become a nun. 'On
no account,' I said. That made her laugh ridiculously.

When we had eaten the cake and collected the crisp bank
notes we were shown the orphanage, rows and rows of very
tidy little beds with starched cotton covers. We were shown
the old people, walking with sticks on the garden paths. One
of them was blowing wheezes of snuff over the wallflowers.
It was a plain desecration for the flowers were so innocent,
contributing nothing but their gay beauty. Nobody said not
to do it although it was clearly an occasion when a forbid-
dance was due. The garden was on a slope. It was shaved

down towards the river so that the trees had an air of haste, as though they had a boat to catch. They seemed to run forward.

We were shown the little white chapel. It had a *crowned* air. Immediately you entered it you were aware that its difference from the other rooms was that it went upward with a coronet. The robe of the Virgin was very blue. On the altar there were huge bunches of very vulgar roses with white, coagulated petals. We knelt on *prie-dieus* which cut our shins. Brigid had been taken from us. It was a relief when we were returned to MacDaid. Brigid was with him. He had her by the hand and they were walking up and down like sentries. James and I hoped we would never become orphans — even if there were gingerbread on Sundays.

Grandmother was in the house again and everything was brighter. She had a new craze — making dresses for Elizabeth and me. Brigid wore Elizabeth's clothes, the clothes she had worn when she was Brigid's age. Mother said that she had not dared to do it alone, and Grandmother, with her mouth full of pins, commended her for her wisdom. The worst of having clothes made at home was that you were subject to fittings. At any moment you would be called upon to submit to encasement in a garment that resembled nothing except a sort of shield or poultice. You trembled for what it was going to become. It went over your head like an alb, with the sides open; then it was pinned upon you and unpinned and you were mercifully dismissed.

The doctor came again. His car with the coachman on the dickey wheeled its circle upon the gravel and all the time he was there the horse pawed to escape. One of the doctor's little girls was perched on the seat. We were told that she was deaf and dumb or otherwise he would have brought her into the house with him. Grandmother said, after he had gone: 'That beautiful child! She will be as lovely as her mother.' She was about to say more when she caught my eye. 'Three of them, or is it four, are deaf and dumb. It shows you how careful you have to be after measles.' All of us were ordered to take Parrish's Syrup because of the phosphates. We had to take it after every meal and then brush our teeth immediately. The question became monotonous.

Father came on a visit. Something had happened to him. When I saw him suddenly in the doorway he looked nailed to the floor. The dance had gone out of him. He said: 'I have been ill, Kathie, with erysipelas. See, it has changed my hair. I am no longer a dark horse.'

He asked me what I was reading now. I could not think of all the questions that were stored in me immediately; and when I said nothing, he said: 'That's right. Keep your mind to yourself. Your thoughts remain your own. Nobody can steal them from you.'

Grandmother asked him if he intended to stay. He could only remain, he answered her, so long as he had leave. She looked at him long and gravely and with pity. We were in the grey drawing room. A fire was burning and all the windows were open. The curtains were blowing gently.

Father and I stood on the lawn, beneath the laburnum tree. He said it was a pity that Major's son had died. 'He's such a grand fellow, isn't he, Kathie?' I wanted to cry when he said Major was grand. Major understood. His tail slapped in great beats of love against Father's legs. There we were — a man, a dog and a little girl — bound by the most passionate drive of love. We were one entity in that chemistry. The tree had black pods on it. The bark was mottled, as dappled as a pony's back or a pond in which a stone was flung. This was the man I had denied. He was undeniable. The air was cold and clear. The purple blossoms on the rhododendrons burned as wild as frosty flames.

We went back to the house. In the little library there was no fire in the grate, nothing but a piece of pink blotting paper. Father put his hands down upon the green baize on the table, darkened by inkspots. 'And now,' he said mysteriously, apart from me, 'to action.'

He stood on the folding ladder and took books down from the top shelves. He flapped them and whistled the leaves by sharply so that the dust floated from them. 'The

worst of your mother is that she only reads novels. There's
nothing wrong, mind you, about reading novels — only you
can't live on nothing but soup. Read Keating, Kathie. A man
who does not know the history of his own country is only
three quarters of a man.'

It was then that I told him I had been reading about virgin births and Paestum. These were my instant problems. I
trusted that he would explain to me, that he would launch
forth into the understanding. But all he said was that that
was fine and that he would 'tell Grandmother'. There was
something in him that failed me; or something in myself
that had not a long enough reach. My Chinese pride could
only strive to ask when I knew definitely *what* to ask.

He was taking all the best books and stacking them upon
the table. When he caught my eye he said: 'I have read
nothing intelligent for a long while.'

He was going away again. I wished he would stay but I
was unable to ask him to stay because I was governed by the
uncertainty of his behaviour and the ruin of his shortcom-
ings. I was handicapped in my power to persuade him
because our worlds were different. I only stood upon the
fringes of his as he stood upon the fringes of mine.

And then he went away. I was not there and I did not see
him go. I only knew that he was gone and that Mother was
crying. I hated it when she cried and anger against him got
me again. He *spoiled* everything. Didn't he care? I asked
myself savagely. There was simply no answer. He was so
entirely himself. The peace without him made you long for
him and then, when he was there, the peacelessness became
an agony.

Mother took me with her to the attic. It was full of
Saratoga trunks and packing cases — and Dot's kittens. Dot
was always in a state of having kittens or abandoning
kittens. The attic was her kingdom. She lay in furry luxury
in her special trunk purring like an orchestra and the kittens,
which were extraordinarily clean, crawled over her like
detached pieces of herself. She was delighted when you took
out a kitten but she was more delighted when you put it

back. Mother always went to the attic when she needed a piece of material. There were trunks full of all sorts of materials, silks and satins and wools and cottons. She loved to examine them, to stroke them, to make you smell the printed smell of the sprigged cottons or feel how smooth the satins were. She would lay the silk against your cheek and caress you with it. There was one roll she had an affection for: yards and yards of thick grosgrain white silk with emerald-green satin stripes. The white and the green were of identical widths. Mother would stand up with the roll in her arms and whip the silk out upon you like a waterfall or a magnificent curtain in which milk and forests flowed. 'Isn't it a marvel?' she always asked. 'But nothing can be done with it now. Nobody would *wear* it.' There were rolls of taffetas with eyelet embroideries, silks with tiny baskets of flowers. There was a piece of the material that Mary O'Connell wore. Twice yearly Mother had given her enough for two dresses. 'Where is she?' I asked, and was told that she was with Mrs Dysart in her beloved Gartan. Mrs Dysart had sent for her as Grandaunt Ahn had sent for her. Presently she would return.

Mother dived into the trunk and groped and felt and did not find what she sought. She brought out the red felt roll tied with crimson tapes which contained her five spoons. Each spoon was wrapped in tissue paper. The spoons were as thin as the paper. They looked as though you could *bite* through them, but when they were in your hands they were as strong as other spoons. Mother told me that they were Irish hall-marked and that *her* grandmother had worn them in her bosom. When she said that, Mother held the spoons against her heart. They were very precious to her. I adored when she opened the domed trunks and exposed the bright clarity of the pictured lady within. She knew at once by the lady what was in the trunk. If it was not the right lady she shut the trunk.

She showed me the dress she had worn on her wedding day. It was a fawn cashmere with an Alexandra bustle. It was trimmed with tiny carved buttons and bands of silk on the bias. With it she had worn a bonnet of violets. The violets were all crushed together in one place, as lively as though they had just been taken out of the garden.

Sometimes Mother hung things out on the rafters to air. She hung up the Stars and Stripes with the signatures. It was a flag that had been presented by Aunt Waters and a group of Southern ladies to some Irish regiment when their own standard was lost. Afterwards the standard was found and this flag was returned to Aunt Waters. We always used it when it was *out*. We made a tent of it or used it for the roof when we played Uncle Tom's Cabin. Grandmother said that we were committing a sacrilege against the dead — that Aunt Waters would turn in her grave if she knew. It only added to the thrill of the game to realise that it was causing Aunt Waters to turn. We had never met her so we could afford to indulge in independent thoughts about her.

Our most exciting game was Christian Martyrs. This could only be played in the hall. It required darkness and the cavities of the shuttered and curtained windows to provide us with the reality of catacombs. It was a very long hall with two tall windows on either side of the entrance. At one end of it was the door opening into the drawing room and directly opposite, at the other end, was the door into the dining room. Facing the windows were doors. All these doors and windows were deeply embrasured. Opposite the main entrance was an archway into a passage which led directly to the kitchen and offices. On each side of the archway were pedestals which supported heads of Scipio and Caesar. The game was to put out all the lights, crowd all the dogs into the back passage and for each of us to get behind a curtain and pray at the tops of our voices. At a given signal we would dash out as martyrs and the dogs would dash out as lions and we were cast to each other with screams and supplications and roarings. Our screams and terror had just the right effect upon the lions who pounced madly upon us and tore us limb from limb. Major was a magnificent actor. He was in the Hamlet and Macbeth class. He never failed to convince me that he meant to devour me. When doors opened and light streamed forth it always seemed to me that the flares and the spears of gladiators were being added. Mother's voice, beseeching us not to do these things, became the voice of the Roman centurions. Father only asked if Scipio and Caesar were still on their pedestals. He always called Major off. He always took Major from us on these occasions. Without Major the martyrdom came to an end.

Major was so much a part of us that it was inconceivable that his ratio of living should keep a different measure from ours. It never occurred to us that he was an old man while we were still children. It was hard for us to realise that what had left us apparently untouched had put a deathly finger upon him.

One moonlight spring night the mare from the Thompson manse took it into her flighty head to visit our new horse. The yard gates were bolted and barred. They were high enough to keep her out. But she got in. It was assumed that she had jumped the wall on the shrubbery side. The shrubbery was higher than the courtyard and by a certain hemlock tree, known as the bo tree, the wall was low enough for her purpose. Stones were crumbled there and some of them were loosened — and she was in the courtyard, with the horse all wrought up in sympathy for her presence and kicking his box to pieces. Major, apparently, did his best to get her back over the wall and out of trespass. The night was passed in commotion and in the morning MacDaid was blamed and complaints sent to the manse and the wall was mended. Nobody noticed Major. He was missing. He had gone for his daily swim. The river was miles away but he always went to it for his daily dip. On this day he did not return. He was absent. And then, late in the afternoon, he came back. He seemed exhausted. He was changed. He was struck. I was the one who discovered that he was blind. His eyeballs were literally hanging out of their sockets. The mare must have kicked him in the night when he was doing his duty. That he should have allowed himself to be kicked upon a moonlit night was proof that he was growing old. The state of his eyes shocked each of us to the bone. Our hearts were moved towards him by a passionate sympathy. We could have killed the mare. He lay with his head in my lap and I did my utmost to make his eyeballs stay in their proper position. My heart broke for him. Father sent for the vet. All day I stayed with Major, bathing his eyes and face with a solution of boracic acid. It seemed to us the most tragic unfairness that Major, of all people, should have had his eyes put out like Samson.

The vet gave us no hope. He told us briefly that Major's eyes could not take root again — that he was blind. As blind as Milton and we were all his daughters! We loved him more than ever. He was very brave. He accepted the darkness. To him the world had merely gone over to the night. He still had his nose for guidance. He still insisted upon his daily ablutions. Cleanliness was his approach to godliness — and us. He was obliged to carry on as usual. Every morning he set forth. The only difference was that it took him longer to return. We were anxious for him. It was always a relief when he was back. On one occasion he was away for days. Father tried to persuade him to drive in the trap to the river. But the idea did not work. The procedure cast upon him the indignity of infirmity and there was nothing at all the matter with his legs. He refused to sit on plush cushions and be bumped over roads. He had his own way by fields. He had places to visit. His nose sent him after rats and foxes.

It was purely in order to preserve him that Father had him locked into the courtyard. This was a sentence upon Major. He suffered from it as he had suffered from the control of the first policeman. Even when we stayed with him and tried to engage his interests it achieved nothing. His doom was set. He was a warrior and what we offered him in place of adventure had no more value than fairy tales.

The stretch of these months prepared us for his death. They kept saying to us that he was old, too old, that he was miserable and would be better out of his agony. They infiltrated us with an insidious propaganda which won us to his death in the name of his salvation. In order to save him from suffering it had to be done. It became an infinite charity. It was never made quite clear to us what was to be done. He was to be put away for the sole purpose of taking him out of pain. That was what we believed. Nowadays he would have been given an injection and put to sleep. In those days all they could think of was a dose of arsenic. We were told that it would be quite simple. It would be done by the baker. The baker would give him one of his favourite cakes, a maid of honour with a cherry in her white, iced face. Major would eat the cake and, in a few moments, it would be all over.

The mere thought of it anguished us. But, for Major's sake, we gave in. We accepted it.

The day the baker brought the powder was a doomsday to us. None of us asked for a cake. None of us went out to the baker's cart. All the other animals were locked away. That was a day when Major was the only customer. He was chained to the laburnum tree and the baker gave him his cake. We saw the act from the windows. There would have been mutiny if we had not been allowed to see. Our presence was our farewell. After he had swallowed the cake he began to bark. A new and vigorous tone came into his speech and when we suffered ourselves to look out upon him we saw that, instead of dying, he had become young. We were made suddenly aware of his age by the fact that he had suddenly become young. He was leaping like a hart and the yellow-blossomed tree was trembling with the wonder. That was what we saw. In our innocence a miracle had taken place.

We were told that it was a restoration before death. They begged us to come away from the windows.

They did not touch our love.

Major was thirsty. We wished to give water to him but we were forbidden to. It was explained that water would cause him pain.

So he died — asking for water. And we, his watchers, loving him with the wildness of our full hearts, did not know.

Our sorrow, when it was all over, was comfortless. We

were not allowed to touch him or go anywhere near him until MacDaid had buried him. He was buried in the midst of the daffodils in the garden. The spring flowers bloomed above his resting place. We never passed there without transfusing the atmosphere above his body with our deep and faithful love. We never accepted the fact that he was dead forever, or that we were separated in eternity. He was simply upon one of his absences, being transformed beneath the soil into some new version of himself. He was immortal. He had gone out, leaping under the yellow tree. He would return, bounding freshly from some ledge in Paradise.

Chapter Sixteen

Grandmother was idle. She wore a little Shetland shawl over her shoulders. She was telling James about her brother. When he was a little older than James was he had gone to Spain to fight in a Carlist War. He had a horse he adored, Black Bess. There wasn't a white thread on her. Grandmother's brother leaned down over her from his saddle, as he rode through the Spanish villages, and picked up white geese for his supper with his sword. The geese were as white as doves, he had told her, and their flesh tasted like ptarmigan. When he came back from the war he brought Black Bess with him. He was riding her one day upon the City Walls when a Protestant offered him five pounds for her. It was the maximum legal tender from a Protestant and, as a Catholic, he was legally obliged to accept it. He did not refuse. He simply turned and headed the mare over Waterloo Gate. The jump broke her legs and she had to be shot. He put her out of agony at once. She was his and he loved her. He could not bear for any other man to have her. We understood. The death was cleansed with the love. Grandmother's brother died shortly after that. He followed his Black Bess.

She told us about Catherine. She had adored Catherine who had become crazed for love. Nobody knew whom she loved. Grandmother feared it was some young priest who was entirely innocent, but Catherine had spread her heart and lost her reason. It was Grandmother's assigned duty, as a girl, to follow Catherine. They were so afraid that she would walk out into the river. She was absolutely without sense. Her life was a flight of Time. It had no measurement she could go by as by a clock. At any hour of the day or night she would raise her voice and sing with the sweetness of seraphs. Grandmother had a lovely voice of her own but, she assured us, it was as nothing compared to Catherine's. Catherine's was a gift from the stars. It drenched you with wonder. 'And mind you,' Grandmother said,' I have heard Adelina Patti sing more times than I can count.' Adelina Patti and her sister were her friends in New York.

'But Ahn,' she said, 'Ahn was the wild one. No wonder she never married. There wasn't a man born to match her. All the boys were in love with her and Ahn was in love with none. She never found her peer. She never found a man in the world who could have ruled her.' She became for me a being deprived of loss — just as some are deprived of gain. Catherine had been denied. She had suffered an Ophelian frustration. Ahn had suffered the opposite. When Ahn was still a young woman she had gone on a tour through France at a time when young women were not supposed or permitted to go on tours at all. She had brought back a full edition of Eugène Sue which her bishop had commanded her to burn. Ahn had refused to burn any books for any bishop. All of them, Grandmother explained, were very wilful girls. They had parents who were sweetness itself, but as daughters they were infused with headstrong qualities that had brought them nowhere. Jane was the only one who could be said to have succeeded. 'If you could call it success,' she added and sponged from it, by the inflection she gave it, its full attainment. Jane had all things except passionate love. The single thing she did not have seemed to tear from her the uttermost value of what she possessed. She was formulated upon us as a mendicant, a mendicant of pearls and sables standing upon some everlasting threshold with her hands as empty as though she begged for bread. Jane's 'wilfulness' was wrought by the most awful determinations. It neither went from her as a caprice nor did it land her with any rewards that *mattered*. She emerged from all actions like a rod of iron, compelled to stand up and take the blows from right and left. Nobody felt sorry for Jane. She was a complete victim of circumstances. Society weddings and Civil Wars swirled about her with the ease of grand opportunities. She came out triumphantly from everything — except upon the field of love. Where love was concerned she was derelict and this made all her triumphs flavourless. It made her success as bombastic as a child's balloon. A pin could prick it to nothingness.

On the other hand my grandmother and the bewitched, daft Catherine, who experienced the most romantic loves, were the wrecked ones, the ones who went under. It was such an illogical matter that it split our conception of standards to an nth degree. No laws could be found to govern these ethics. They were as elastic as whims. Whether you did right or did wrong made no difference. It was an affair of persons and allergies. It depended upon whether you were a Jane or a Catherine. It most clearly depended upon whether Love took you in or left you out. But one thing was absolute and that was that you never got away with *everything*.

My grandmother was visible to me. I beheld her in the flesh. I always imagined Catherine as a floating virgin, not upon Ophelian waters but upon air; a form in diaphanous garments with a sash like a scroll. She was brought to a stand when rocks magnetised her by the points of her elbows and when she stood it was not as one stanced from a base but as a flower blown by a wind that was bound to get her. Her lips were always parted for an enchanting utterance and, away up beyond human vision, she was tethered by the ends of her hair held by gods or archangels. I always saw Grandmother's sister Mary as a ponderous young woman in an apron, rooted by activities in a kitchen that was abundantly equipped with cooking utensils. Pots and pans were her Aesculapian signs. About her was an odour of newly baked bread, issuing in warm whiffs from the oven. Somebody was always appearing to ask if they could have a taste.

We were bound by enchantment when Grandmother told us about her family. She took us back into the fairyland of people who were entirely different from their actuality. She gave them to us with an astonishing verity when they were not as we knew them. Her Ahn and Brigid were not our Ahn and Brigid yet they were the same. Grandmother was the youngest in a family of eleven and not one of them, she remarked, ever came out deaf and dumb from anything. She was not entirely *for* the family doctor. She did not condemn him as Father condemned him but she diffused a great and sincere doubt of his efficiency. This was not the doctor who had a daughter named Valetta. He was the doctor with the ten children and a beautiful wife, who, for some reason, which was never gone into, 'was destroying herself'. There were only the two doctors available. Mother would have had the other doctor, she said, 'if it were not for his wife'. I was made conscious of the fact that there *were* doctors' wives, even if they never came with the doctors. They were doctors' problems which were kept at home.

Mother paid her doctor by the year. No matter who was ill in the household it was understood that he could be sent for at any hour of the day or night and in any sort of weather. She had a lawyer on the same system, but the lawyer could only be seen when it suited him.

She took me to the lawyer's. His name was written backwards upon a frosted door. All his books were the same size, and all in mourning. They were bound in black with funeral cards for the titles. He had a very hungry clerk who ate his moustache — and put it out again.

Mother was in great trouble, she told the lawyer. She was demented because Mr Tilly would neither answer letters nor call upon Mr Dawlay. The lawyer said that Mr Tilly was a robber baron and that the only thing for Mother to do was to beard the lion in his den. Mr Tilly, it appeared, was the owner of the factory at the beginning of Carlisle Bridge. When you drove down Carlisle Road, past the doctor's house where his car and coachman were always standing, you saw the square factory. It had very clean windows in which stacks of shirts moved and from which sewing ma-chines whirred like beehives. When you drove over the bridge and got exactly to the middle you saw that there was almost as much of the factory below the bridge, level with the riverside, as there was on top. It always affected me like a dog that you hadn't expected would bite. It was a very bare building, very cold and *closed*. It held itself together like a set of clenched teeth.

Mother said she would take me with her when she went to Mr Tilly's.

We drove there through the town and up towards the new cathedral and out along the high Creggan Road. It was a windy day. Every time we passed a garden all the flowers were nodding. When we got to Mr Tilly's gate Mother said that I was to stay with MacDaid. MacDaid was to drive me up and down the road. I didn't mind at all not having to see Mr Tilly. It was very brave of Mother to see him alone. She said that she would be out again presently.

MacDaid drove me to a place where we could see the river and the railway station where we took the train for the shore. It had the low insignificance of a woodshed from that distance. Beyond it were the quays where I had walked with Father, where the water *plonk-plonked* beneath the boards and I had to catch his hand. On the slope opposite, on the Waterside, we saw the path coming down from the military barracks. We saw the wall of the barracks with the toy soldiers in the sentry boxes. MacDaid spat when he mentioned them. The tiny ferryboat was pulling a silver line through the water across to the Guildhall. We drove up the road and came back again to the same spot. MacDaid made me look down the hill, through the trees below us. There was a set of buildings enfolded by a wall like the picture of Cistercian monasteries. Inside the wall there were bunches of men wearing tam-o'-shanters. They were weeding and digging and watering — a group of gardeners. 'Do you see them?' MacDaid said with a terrible, dire significance in his voice. Yes, I said, I saw them. He told me it was the County Asylum and that all these men were mad. 'Look well,' he said in the dire, ponderous voice, *'you might see somebody you knew there!'* His voice frightened me. I looked very intently down upon the mad gardeners and recognised none of them. They were all wearing tam-o'-shanters. Then MacDaid jerked the reins and we went back to Mr Tilly's gate. MacDaid drove through the gate and right up to Mr Tilly's steps. Mr Tilly's parterres were a hundred times larger than Mother's. He had no pansies. He took his velvet out in dahlias.

It was a long time before Mother came out. Having got as far as the steps MacDaid could not turn and run away again. He had to wait, and Mulligatawny and I had to wait with him. It would have been easier riding up and down upon the road where I could have looked again down into the County Asylum.

Mr Tilly had a door with goddesses pouring pitchers. When it opened to let Mother out a lot of brass things raised their heads in the hall behind, a pair of antlers and an umbrella stand and lines on the wide staircase. There was a very slippery floor with bright rugs which slid beneath the feet of a pair of setters. Mother liked the setters. She patted them. She did not like Mr Tilly and when she held out her hand to say good-bye to him she took great care that it did not touch his stomach. His stomach sloped under her sleeve, almost to the elbow. Mr Tilly, on the contrary, was delighted with Mother. He came down the steps with her as though he were holding up her parasol. But she had no parasol and his hands were empty. When Mother got up into the trap and MacDaid handed her the reins Mr Tilly looked smaller. He was looking up at us and you hardly noticed his stomach. He had a folded, criss-cross cravat with a gold hunting crop on it. The setters swished their tails like silk. We drove off in a dash, with all the dahlias bowing down almost to the earth.

When we got to the place in the road where the County Asylum became visible through the trees Mulligatawny was going so fast that I did not see the men. MacDaid's voice remained in me, fraught with a curious urgency. There was something sinister in his necessity. I was flayed by it as the woods were flayed by the windy weather. We were travelling with such a speed along this high road, and down below us the river was running *with the same speed* in our direction. We resembled two trains in a landscape, racing against each other.

Then we came down Marlborough Street and crossed over to the Strand where I could see the damson tree in its little panel of garden. I felt for it as though it were my own tree.

Grandmother scolded Mother because there were no visitors. Nobody came unless to collect for a bazaar or sodality. Mother said: 'I see the Loughreys at church on Sunday. I never speak to them.'

'That's just it.'

'I write to my friends.'

'Letters, my dear, *if* you are content with *them!*'

Thus is a child thrust cumulatively into life. We are mobilised from the tones of voices, the throw of hands, by what we overhear — for it is never given directly to us. It takes a long time for the pattern to grow.

The Nazareth House nuns came to see Mother. While Margot was opening the door to them, Mother put the match to the drawing-room fire. They were received with fireworks. I was sent for to shake hands with them. I was asked again if I intended to be a nun. 'Neither a nun nor a priest,' I said, as decisively as possible.

The tall thin nun argued against Mother. Grandaunt Brigid was, at times, in her dotage. She had no desire to see Mother.

'And yet,' Mother said, 'she hid this Last Testament in the tea caddy!'

'That is proof,' the thin nun said definitely.

'None of them ever lost their wits before eighty,' Mother argued in return. Her will was speared against the nun's but the phrases melted out against the noise the fire made. When the nuns left Mother stood by the side window, staring out over the rhododendrons for a long time. Beyond the sycamore tree one could see across the hired field to the side road. From the window she could see the nuns upon the road, travelling like beetles.

The dining room was repainted a pale opal green. Two pots of paint were left on the floor in the window embrasure. There was the pot of green paint for the walls, and the ochre-coloured paint for the woodwork. In the morning somebody took out the bottom of the birdcage as usual and the two canaries dropped into the paint. One was drowned in the green paint and one in the yellow. Their little dead bodies dripped like wet wood in the shape of birds upon the carpet. Mother was very unhappy. Margot came and looked at the birds for a long time. 'What possessed them?' she kept asking. Nobody answered her. The delicate gilt cage was empty. There were no birds within to crack the seeds open behind the red and white glass screens. A little linen bag full of hemp remained untied behind the shutter for months and months and then it disappeared.

Grandmother had a visitor — a bishop. She took him into the dining room. It was her favourite room since it had become green. She made him sit in the rocking chair where he found two calves' teeth. She had to explain that one of the dogs had found one of Major's jawbones in the garden. Major had buried calves' jawbones all over the garden. They were always appearing — bleached like flints in the sunlight.

The bishop gave her the teeth after he had examined them. He did not sit in the chair as though it were a rocking chair. He regarded me like Father MacMenamin.

'I hear,' he said solemnly, 'that you are interested in grave questions?'

I did not know what to say to him. Which question did he mean? He asked me if I knew the Commandments and the date of the Council of Nicaea. He laughed uproariously when I gave him the answer. He put his hand upon my shoulder and told Grandmother that I was all right. 'But remember,' he told me, nailing my look to his, 'there are also transgressions against the Holy Ghost.'

Mother came into the room. She was wearing one of her shirtwaists with starched gigot sleeves. She was wearing a black grosgrain belt with a jet buckle and when you saw her at the back you saw the safety pin where she had clipped her skirt and the shirtwaist together. She was like a little girl before Grandmother and the bishop. She said I was to run away now. As I got to the door I turned to take one more look at them and I heard Mother saying: 'Well, your lord-ship, I owe him my four children.'

'I admire your charity,' he said, smiling at her, 'but he is better where he is — *in the asylum*!'

I was frozen on the threshold. I did not go out. I ceased to see or hear. Who was in the asylum? I saw the awful, lost and bereaved *prisoners* and I became a prisoner. My heart was chained down to the floor, groping, groping — and obtaining its own answer.

I hid myself in the china closet until the bishop went away in the carriage. I heard Grandmother cross the hall to her room. I went into the dining room. Mother was holding her hands out to the fire. They were transparent. There were lines of blood between her fingers.

'Mother!'

'Kathie!'

I got myself towards her, dragging myself like lead. She put her arm about me and pulled me close to her. I felt the rounds of her back curls against my cheek. I kept my eyes from her. She knew. She said gently, as low as the fire: 'What is it, darling?'

'Mother, tell me, what is an asylum?'

Her arm squeezed me closer. She thought. I cried out: 'Tell me the truth.'

'An asylum is a refuge.'

'A refuge?'

'A sanctuary.'

'What is a sanctuary?'

'Darling, it is a place where you are safe. In the old days it used to be in the churches. If you were hunted and reached the door of the sanctuary you could knock there, hold on, and nobody had the right to touch you.'

I saw MacDaid's gardeners — the men with the spades and hoes and slow, lazy movements. I did not understand. But I knew that she was not lying.

There was silence, then she said: 'If you are in an asylum nothing can harm you.'

'Is Father in an asylum?' I asked, plainly, as deadly as rain that had to fall.

There was another silence and then she asked me: 'Who told you?'

'Nobody.'

'Kathie!' She thought I lied. It was my turn to hold her close. What did it matter? 'Nobody,' I said.

'Child,' she said, 'dear Child!' the way Grandmother had said it about Grandaunt Ahn. 'Your Father has been ill. Soon he may be well. He may come back to us.'

Neither my heart nor blood beat out any response. The worst had happened. I was taken out by its knowledge in the bitterest reality. I saw him — a man in a tam-o'-shanter with a hoe. Half-truths are more dangerous than whole ones. They consume us both with doubt and with certainty. In that moment I was scourged with whips because I had denied him. Disaster had found him without enough support. I became part of what had failed him. It was as though he had asked me to help him to the road and I had withheld my help and he had fallen by the wayside. In that remote prisoners' field he was abandoned and forsaken.

'You see, Kathie, he has to have certain foods. There are certain things which he must not eat or drink. He is better already.' My muteness urged her on. 'He is getting better. He was a very sick man. Now he is already improved. I have good reports of him.'

'Why didn't you tell me?'

'I was afraid. I did not wish to make you unhappy.'

It was no preservation for what fell now disastrously, illustrated by an accidental image of what had bled me for other men, men I did not know.

The days went on again from then. They went on with an apparent casualness. In me there was nothing casual. I had been awakened to a law that was worse than the Ten Commandments. It was not a code you sinned against. It sinned against you. I was the victim and not the aggressor. Something had been done — upon a remote field and with a

remote power that left me more derelict than those witnessed prisoners.

MacDaid was sowing nasturtiums. His brown worsted
shoulders were within touch of my hand. I could have
stooped over him and put my lips against his ear. But I
stood upright and rigid and asked the question: 'What are
you ill with when they put you into an asylum?' He did not
turn. No quiver of acknowledgement touched his worsted
hairy shoulders. His finger still made the hole in the ground.
The question had cost me too much for me to be able to
repeat it. I had spun and lost. And then his voice came, dark
as the earth he touched:

'Your Da, for instance, a dipsomaniac or just plain crazy
and out of his mind. How should I tell what they put them
in for. But once they get there only the Good Lord can help
them.'

A word that began with *dip* was so inadequate. It gave
me worse than nothing. I worked upon it. I thought that
MacDaid had made a mistake. He had argued with Mother
when she said kail was colewort and ever afterwards he
never mentioned kail without saying, 'Plain kail' with a
sneer. I established for myself that his dipsomaniac must by
gypsomaniac. That was the nearest approach I could get to
Father. They had imprisoned him because he was a wander-
ing minstrel. He had declared himself a troubadour. This
was perfectly clear to me.

But I did believe what MacDaid had said about only the
Lord being able to help. Once again, as I had prayed to the
Virgin for a miracle, I began to pray to God for Father.

Chapter Seventeen

A subtle change came over the household. It was not so much a change as a permeation of what was already there. The furniture seemed to shine differently and fires burned brighter. Mother put the silver out again on the dining-room sideboard. We *used* it. Instead of catching occasional glimpses of Queen Anne pitchers with scalloped edges in a trunk in the attic with sugar basins to match, there they were on the breakfast table. The polo cart was sold by the auctioneer who sold the hired fields. It brought eighteen pounds. Mother said it was really Elizabeth's money but she was obliged to borrow it. Another time she asked Elizabeth to exchange it with her for Frances. Elizabeth agreed. She was very proud of owning Frances.

Mother was always writing letters. She wrote them at the bureau in the drawing room between the windows, sheets and sheets of them at a time. She addressed them to Grandmother or a Mrs Euman in Scotland or a Lady Bellew in England. Mrs Euman sent us postal cards of Abbotsford where Sir Walter Scott wrote all his novels. Her letters said that Jessie and Charlie had visited there.

Mother said to me, putting tea roses into a bowl: 'Those were my friends — Finola Sullivan and Gundred de Trafford and the Mostyns of Talacre. I was at school with them. We were all in Princethorpe together.'

Princethorpe was a Benedictine convent in Warwickshre. I acquired these wisps of information like dates in a history book. Knowing that King Alfred had burnt the cakes was exactly on the same level as knowing that Mother had been to school in Warwickshire where they had beer for supper and bare refectory tables with no cloths.

When we asked Grandmother where she had been to

school, she answered: 'I was educated between the knees of my saintly father and our bishop.'

Grandmother took me to a 'Mission'.

We drove away in an autumn dusk to the Long Tower Church. Grandmother had a deep affection for this edifice because her father had built it. Instead of going the long way round by the Glendermott Road Grandmother insisted upon MacDaid taking us by the side road and down by the steep wall that descended to the Waterside Chapel. From the trap I saw the pink leaves on top of the wall, and the uppermost branches of oaks on the other side. The chapel gate looked very small and slight after the grandeur of the wall. It was spun like a spider's web in the twilight. We had to skid down a short sheer street into the main Waterside street when we passed the chapel. We came out upon the small row of shops — the harness-maker's and grocer's and tailor's — directly to the bridge. The water was surging in a deep flow with edgeless waves. It was almost up to the bridge's understaples. It gave our reverberation a more solid sound as though the water were *solid* when we drove over it. We went up Abercorn Road to the left instead of Carlisle Road to the right. It was neither dark nor light. We moved forward in greyness and the view was telescoped. What was near was larger than usual and what was far was invisible until we reached it. We came to the little narrow streets that flowed like arteries right into the churchyard. They were so tiny that when you walked you always had to step off the pavement when anybody passed you. You were so close to the houses that you could put your hand into the windows and touch the geraniums.

MacDaid stopped and we had to get down and walk. But just at the moment Grandmother caught my arm and terror ran through me to the heart like the little streets running to the Long Tower. A moan was rising out of the greyness. It was as though the twilight air had become articulate. It had become a Voice that was uttering its woe and anguish. And then I saw a most awful wonder: rising towards us from the well of shadows came the gigantic naked figure of a man.

His arms were extended and his form was carved out of the evening with the astonishment of a vision. I was frozen with apprehension. This was Gulliver and a martyr. He was thrust towards us with an inexplicable pity. His head lay slightly to the side. His feet were fastened as though he bore manacles. He was a giant — and he was deprived of freedom. The voice was his voice. It was the thunder of several voices just as his body had the magnitude of many men.

Grandmother put her arm about me. 'It is the Mission Cross,' she whispered, 'carried by the Dominicans.'

It was a crucifixion to me. I was enfolded in it as completely as though I stood upon the Mountain and watched the skies split open and the Day darken on Calvary. And yet it robbed me because it was only a cross. I had beheld the Man of Sorrows. It was not his nakedness that had revealed him. It was his folded feet, closed with such impotence, unable to support his motion. That was the awe and the wonder and terror for me. The form had been spiked through the twilight. A man would have walked.

This was the God to whom I prayed for Father, Christ whom they had crucified. I prayed with faith, with ardour, with all my heart and soul. I was, in the strictest Christian sense, *obedient*. I bowed down and was humble. I submitted myself for the salvation of a man's soul.

That was the period in which I came nearest to earth, as well as nearest to heaven. I was devoted to a cause. It was to restore my father. I suffered the process with the fervour of those who pray for the restoration of kingdoms and monarchies. I became its passion.

And then, in some fashion that I have lost chronologically, the heat became spasmodic. It emerged from night vigils and personal sacrifices into occasional remembrances of Father 'in that place'. This is the effect of peace. It balances us, brings us down from the extremes. Even my longing for him steadied out into acceptance. He was absent. He had been absent before. One day he would come again. Subconsciously I awaited his return.

Two more astonishments occurred to me and I was swept again into an extreme and different sphere. I was given a book at Christmas. Somebody (I think it was Mrs Euman) sent me a Christmas card. How slight are the levers which can rule our fates!

Nobody said to me this is a good or a bad book. Nobody said to me this is, or is not, poetry. The magic plunged with its own swords directly into my being. The name of the book was *Wuthering Heights*. It was a cheap edition. It was so cheaply bound that when you opened the pages wide they came asunder. I began to read it in a corner. Snow was falling. There were *marrons glacés* opened in a box with paper edging upon the horsehair sofa. James was lying full length on the furry rug pretending to be Napoleon with Italian soldiers. Doors would open and shut. Somebody threw date stones into the fire. Elizabeth was wearing a cracker cap with streamers and she had a pair of lattice tongs that went out and touched James' hair and came back when he told her to stop it. When she put her foot with the new slipper down on the rug James lost one of his best battles. Mother was wearing a grey wool dress with bishop sleeves and a black belt. Grandmother was cold. She kept on her mantle which she had worn at church. None of the dogs or cats were eating the fruits or nuts. They were waiting for the turkey. The tree was in the drawing room and the drawing room was in an awful mess because nobody had cleared away the packing papers and paper straws. It was a very real and definite Christmas world.

I belonged to it until I began to read. I dissolved from it as I read and entered Heathcliff's world. The story not only absorbed me. It altered me. It took me away forever from the world I lived in. It awoke me emotionally. It took me into a realm to which I belonged more than I belonged to what happened about me. This was the atmosphere in which all meanings beat. It was where what was *felt* was understood. The loss of the Father was transformed for me into the finding of the Lover. This ghost who called Cathy into the night of *Wuthering Heights* enlisted me not only by name but by spirit. Heathcliff's knocks knocked upon me as the knocking in an immortal tragedy. This was the evocation, the call. It was what I had awaited. It was my baptism, my immersion in Jordan. I was exalted and withheld. I glowed with what had nothing at all to do with Christmas. And nobody knew. Nor was there one to whom I could make it clear. It was entirely my own. I stood up in its essence, autonomous, knowing that I was right.

If I had been asked to write down or express in any form what I was right about, I could not have explained.

I sat up into the night finishing the book. I lay awake with Catherine's broken heart in my arms. I slept with Heathcliff in the winter snows. This was *true*. It was adequate.

It was in the surge and tide of *Wuthering Heights* that the poem in the Christmas booklet caught me. It, too, had magic. It was the full translation of Fitzgerald's *Rubáiyát*. I learned it by heart immediately. It went on and on beating in me from its stone flung into the bowl of night until the steps passed on the grass. I told Mother that I knew every word of it. She refused to believe it. She demanded, there and then, that I should repeat it in vindication. I repeated it. 'What made you *learn* it?' she asked.

What could I tell her? I could not answer myself. I did not know that I had come upon the world of literature. I entered where words were not simple statements of fact, or equivocal with confusion. It was the realm of language fused from conditioned souls. How was I to realise then that I also as a child had established my own fusion? I had been touched by the Paraclete.

That was the Christmas I was twelve years old.

Chapter Eighteen

In the spring the beech leaves came out folded from the womb. They were a tender pure green, precious as gems against the hard trees. The oak leaves were stronger and darker, splayed as though they were meant for a purpose like a beaver's tail. The beech leaves were speared. They pointed themselves into the gathering sunshine. The ash had that black-green quality of sea-grown things. The winds whitened it to silver. No fire burned like an ash fire. The sycamore had fingers. It was a tree of hands and, resembling hands, the blood showed red against the light.

We climbed trees. We laid stones together. We made a wall for defence. We sawed logs. There is a place of balance with the double saw where the teeth saw of themselves. At that point the action is nothing but mercury. It was the place with the mail cart where the driver and the driven were held by the same speed. There is a core where effort is transported upon all fields, physical or mental. It is where the saints come, and poets. It is where the scientist *finds out*. It is where the battle is won or lost. It is where God and the Demon are equal. It is where life and death lose fear.

There were spells when the doctor came and regarded me sternly and I was made to rest. These rests only made the intervening wildnesses more wild. More had to be done in them. All illness or mobilisation was contrary to my nature. Many years later when I had emerged from a grave operation a distinguished surgeon said of me that I had 'a nature which did not express disease'. I had been immunised early. It was a pure matter of reflexes. My mind stayed upstairs, aloof.

The tedium of days in bed had a new relief. There were always books. I discovered the Brownings in the bound copies of the *Cornhill Magazine*. I discovered Thackeray. And, because I discovered him *first*, I preferred him to Dickens. It took me some time to learn that, although Thackeray could stand upon his head in actual life, Dickens could stand upon his in books. Dickens' sense of humour has never, however, appealed to me. I have never been allergic to him. I discovered Tasso and Dante and that madman, Thomas Carlyle, and Sir Richard Burton. I told nobody what I read or what my reading meant to me. It was not that I was secretive but that, quite simply, I was unable to thrust my findings upon others. What I needed, of course, was somebody who would have paid attention to my tastes, but nobody took the slightest notice of the books in my hands. Father would have noticed. It sufficed for Mother that they were not penny dreadfuls. It sufficed for Grandmother that they were not on the Roman Index. Although with an Ahn in the family who had clung to Eugène Sue in spite of a bishop I do not think that any special warfare would have been declared. We had a reading tradition which gave me my liberty. It was only later when I began to express my mind that I was hailed as a danger. I was still young enough for this special indulgence.

It is curious how the mind and the body can walk apart. They can develop unconsciously of each other. I had that sort of mind and that sort of body. I was balanced with innocence.

And, like all who are innocent, I was something of an idiot. When I look back at myself I realise that the young can be given anything, shown anything, exposed to anything. The one exception is pain. I would preserve them from pain. In all the rest they preserve themselves. They have the blindness of youth. They are immune as love is immune, their sight controlled by their own integrity.

Early upon a blowing morning I went for a ride on Mulligatawny. We crossed the fields to the quarry. It was a gentle ride. Mulligatawny's hocks were wetted with dew. His mane smelt of the stable. I saw the early rabbits with their telltale behinds committing their scampers before Mother called them in to breakfast. I saw wrens on the thorns, tiny as catnips. I saw the ploughed fields and the cattle from the farm mottled upon the upper road. I saw the valley as I rode homeward, a bowl into which the morning was flung. A plantation valley, its woods fastened to the solid roots of solid houses. A northern valley with stones on its shoulders and that special bareness that brings the spring with a special delicacy. It is from the bound winters that the grace flows freely, that the flowers emerge pale as Proserpines who have kept their love. No blue is cleaner than the northern blue. Other blues may be deeper and richer but the blue of the north has the sea and the wind woven into its texture. Even the flax fields maintain it. They offer it with the full chemistry. The slightest motion of the stalks reveals it. It is a substance rather than a colour. It has the quality of form, of cranes carved upon a Strasbourg steeple. In Ireland it is needled upon the land with an amazing subtlety. It performs the miracle of restoration. It returns what has been taken, so that no monument is needed.

This morning I was steeped in this mystery and I was drawn through it like threads, dyed with its intangibility. It was as though the Celtic earth had dipped its fingers in the miracle and no ritual that had ever been performed in it was absent. I was its heir.

And yet I was weighted. I was not light in it. In the yard I slid from Mulligatawny. I saw his cream flank streaked with a scarlet stain. I thought he was wounded and searched and found nothing. I went into the house. My skirt dragged at my body. I felt as though hands pressed upon my shoulders, as though a voice commanded me to walk in this way because it was the way. I did not understand, but I was strongly aware of the omen.

We had neither a Mademoiselle nor a Carey. We were in one of those gaps when diminished dividends had deprived us temporarily of formal education. 'In August,' Mother had declared, 'when my dividends come in we will have a new Mr Carey.' When people left us, they left. Or is it that my memory has refused to register their farewells.

I stayed in my room for hours. I refused to appear for

meals. I had discovered a most frightening thing and lay
there, subjecting it to reason and my imagination. My
imagination won. I was convinced that I was suffering from
an *immaculate conception*. Absurd as this may seem to an
adult mind it was extremely real to me. It caused me the
most tormenting anguish. I was absolutely convinced that I
was punished for knowledge as Eve had been punished for
eating the apple. I had found out about Gautama and virgin
births. Children appeared under rosebushes, accidentally,
and at the pure whimsy of God the Father. At the time I had
been strengthened against Mary because of this. It excused
me by a definite logic from Mariolatry. Now the revenge had
come. Even Mr Carey had assured me that one cannot *think*
denials upon the Gods and not pay for it. And there was a
passage in the Old Testament where you were warned not to
think about rich men or 'a bird would carry it'. It was evident that my birds had *carried*.

Mother stood on the threshold and asked me what was
the matter. I was utterly unable to tell her. No words would
break from me. I do not know how she found out. She sat
down beside me, simply paying a visit. Her thin fingers
were knotted so that the rings came out with the wrong
nails. It was the afternoon. I heard MacDaid in the courtyard, bringing in the goat's milk for James. He was remote
to me as a stranger in a foreign land.

'There's MacDaid,' Mother said. I said nothing. I was defeated by the powers of destiny. I was as remote from
Mother as from James. She was inside herself and I was
inside myself.

'Kathie,' she said. She was disturbed. She was frightened.

'Don't stay.' I released her.

She did not go. She said quickly, getting it over. 'I think I
know what it is. You know, it happens, darling. It is nothing.
It only means that you have become a woman.'

I looked at her with wild, unyielding eyes.

'That is why I showed you the pictures of the native men
and women, so that you would know that you were
developing.'

I had understood nothing. I had seen no resemblance between those awful creatures and myself. I saw none now.
But I understood that Mother knew what was the matter
with me. 'I didn't know . . .' I began and could not finish. I
did not know that I was *not* a woman. Father had said ages
ago that it was too bad that I was.

'Don't be afraid,' Mother said gently, comfortingly; 'it
will pass.'

I put my hands over my ears.

That was how I was initiated — with the full flight and
fright of the imagination.

Chapter Nineteen

A man came to see Mother. It was cold but she did not light the fire. She was grave. Her face was as cold as the weather and she stood like a statue. She sent me out of the room to tell MacDaid to yoke Mulligatawny.

Grandmother came to the door. Grandmother cried. She was very sweet to me, warm as though I were chilly. 'Darling,' she said, 'let us dye some eggs. It will pass the time until your mother returns.' She told me that Grandaunt Brigid could always make anything with her hands. She had woven all their bonnets, sewn all their dresses. Jane couldn't even thread a needle. Jane was the boy of the family, always off on a romp somewhere. Ahn was always either writing or reading; Mary was the cook; Catherine was mad; and Elizabeth was the beauty of the family. Each of them had their uses. 'I,' Grandmother sighed, 'was the failure. I failed, not as Catherine failed, but with all my senses. In a sense, my darling, I resemble your father. Only he was wild and I was tame. I was on a quest and he was on a rampage.'

The turkey eggs came out like sparrows' eggs. The emeralds in Grandmother's snake were very green. Margot went in and out. When she pumped up the water she did it with a fearful and angry haste. The water splashed on the flagged kitchen floor.

Mother came back. The fire was lit in the drawing room and we had tea there, with pastries from the baker's which Mother had brought home with her. Father was in Nazareth House, she told us. She had supervised his removal.

'Can any harm reach him there?' I asked logically.

'He is out of harm.'

It seemed to me a complete answer to prayer yet I remained without exaltation. Nothing rang within me in vindication. 'Is he better?'

She did not look at me. She looked at Grandmother. 'He is better.'

The scene was fixed in me stereoscopically, very close and clear and from a duplicated vision — through her and through myself objectively. It was lit artificially and I was unmoved. I could not understand it. The prayers for his recovery had burned from me. This, the result, was nothing but ashes. 'Is he better?' I heard myself asking. I should not have minded if she had not answered, but she did. She said coldly: 'Kathie, I said he was better. Don't you believe me?'

It was a rebuke and I was rebuked by it. I was frozen against judgment. Why, if it were true, did it mean so little?

'Don't you like your cake?'

'Yes,' I answered. Cakes were cakes. This one was delicious.

Mother smiled. But afterwards, when she turned towards the blaze, her profile was sad.

'He knows he's in Nazareth House?' Grandmother asked, and set me off again — listening as though I pulled a wire so tightly that he hummed.

'Of course.'

'That is quite extraordinary! He and Brigid!'

'It was Aunt Brigid's choice. I wish she had never gone there. They refuse to give up the china. Aunt Ahn always said I was to have it. It is in the convent cellar. It will be broken. I offered them anything in *exchange* — a dinner set, *anything*. . . .' She broke off upon the anguished word. Her hands fluttered despairingly. We had such a lot of china but she wished for this that had belonged to the little house that had been made by her grandfather. Somebody always said of it: 'You don't get gold such as that nowadays.'

Grandmother was not so sad about it. She had no sense of possession at all because she had never been able to possess the one thing she had desired, the love of the young man in Lincoln's army.

It was Palm Sunday. Grandmother had taken us with her to church. The statues wore purple cloaks. The Gospel was extraordinarily long. Then the people filed up to the altar for the blessing of the palms. They moved like Birnam wood in *Macbeth*. Their arms became branches that ended in the shape of a cross made of the aromatic palm.

We drove home in a great hurry. Mother had not come with us. She was absent. But she was there when we got back. She looked at me and from me to James in a peculiar fashion, as though she had to choose between us. She took James. I followed. 'James, my brave son, I have something of great sadness to tell you. You know, darling, it is a long time since you have seen your father. Now . . . he has died. . . .'

I stood there. I heard. And it struck no chord from me. I was numb and dumb. Mother tried to comfort me. I did not *need* the lovely words of love she was saying. Something had happened. It was far away, either out of reach or I had yet to come to it. I was struck. That was all. I knew that I had been struck. There was no pain. I do not know what James felt. His mind and heart were his. We could not transmit the feeling. Presently I realised that James was going to see Father. I do not remember if I was asked about it, but I, also, was going to see Father.

The world was exactly the same as we drove through it. The descent from the hills and woods to the place in the land-scape where we could see the Walled City, as Mrs Patch had seen the sunset. It was a city built upon a wide river, the Northern Rhineland, they always said. It had the Rhine beauty. It bore the same wooded demesnes upon its breast. The city rose in a stony heart above the freshness and every stone in it was sacred, marked by spear or prayer. It was a saint's city, a foundation where men had established their faiths from the Celtic beginning. They had been passionate Druids and passionate Christians from always. Nothing that passed through this place remained untouched. It took on the cloak of the past. The *touch* went forwards as the laying on of hands.

The convent was the same. The bell clattered and the steps took ages to come. All the signs and passwords were said and, finally, James and I were led down into the cave to the chapel morgue. Everything was bare and cold and clean, swept with an ungovernable newness. Time had grown nothing upon these walls. When she walked, the nun's dress smelt of serge. Her rosary made tiny wooden notes against her stride. Her wide sleeves moved like wings.

'There, children, there!' She pointed. She knelt. We knelt too. A statue lay draped upon a narrow board. The sister rose and went from us, behind us. James moved closer to me. I did not move at all. I did not pray. I felt *nothing*. I was neither afraid nor unafraid. I simply wished that it was over.

And then! I raised my face and looked at *him*.

He was lying in the white shroud with the immobility of Death, the beauty of Death. At first I did not recognise him, because his black hair had turned to silver. It was swept back from his profile like metal. His eyes were closed. They did not open. They would never open again, never again dance with his old wildness into mine. His voice would never again utter his living mockery. He was chilled into everlastingness. It was then that the ice broke in me and grief gathered and flooded and overcame my heart. 'Father!' I cried to him. It was the last cry to the Father, the desperate cry. And he gave no sign. He would never again be able to say what had to be said — and *neither would I.*

All that I had withheld from him deliberately, returned deliberately upon me. I suffered the remorse that confronts us before the Dead when the charity that we have lost remains lost forever. Mutely but passionately I cried out my full love to him, the love that had never perished. I had only taken it away from him to punish him as you punish a child. Now the punishment was mine, not his. 'My darling,' I screamed in secret anguish. 'What did they do to you?' I saw him with the prisoners and there came in upon my consciousness the full meaning of his confinement in *that* place. They had broken him. They had destroyed him. The last time he had come, when he seemed nailed to the threshold, they had already got him. I knew now — when it was too late to save him.

I returned to him. I came back from that first scene when I had threatened him with withdrawal. Nothing in me had ever been withdrawn. It had been withheld. Like a fool I had declared to him that he should have nothing, when I had power to give it. Now I was giving him everything and he had no power to take it.

It did not reach me when they told me that he was *not* truly dead, that the dead went to heaven. My reason only accepted that he was blind and mute and unanswering, out of my reach. I sobbed. I did not mean to cry but the sobs broke from me and when they tried to tear me away from him I clung as I had clung when the constabulary men had tried to take him from me years ago in the house by the shore where the linnets danced upon the sandy paths.

Chapter Twenty

We grow up. We are shot through incidents into the morality of the world. The process is active and retroactive. We go back and forth. But the constant that steadies us out is the beauty and mystery of life. In our first freshness we miss nothing of it.

An actual moment always comes when we find ourselves without shelter, *outside*. The Dream cracks and we are impelled to join the pilgrimage, to become one of others. No matter how strongly our will rises against it we find the yoke upon our spirits and we become subject to an obedience that strives to escape senselessness. Logic is our one shield. We raise it in all confusions. We reason when we seek God and wish the ways of man explained. What troubles us in our beginnings is the hazardous quality of our initiations. Death and wonder and delight drop upon us from the blue. We are staggered or struck or enraptured by them. But no matter how they are expressed, the act of their eventuality remains steady and what pierces us is irrevocable.

These are the points, perhaps, where we leave the animals. We depart from singleness. We awake into the higher and stricter discipline of our kind. The religions have evoked rituals for the acknowledgement of these stages in our evolution. It is agreed that the baptismal vicar no longer serves for us; we must stand upon our own feet and become responsible for our own acts. Since the beginning of human organisation it has always been the priest who took over the ceremony of initiation. There has always been a ritualistic recognition of the bestowal of another mechanism into the bloodstream of the earth's mastery. When that registration has hardened and weakened in its significance a new and stronger system has always thrust itself up to supplant it.

The law has held fast and still holds fast to the principle that none of us is forgotten. Each of us has to enter the battle. Why shouldn't it be done with drums? It is but fitting that there should be a visible seal upon the invisible transformation. Buddhists crown the child when manhood touches him. They admit him to the pity of kings. Christianity *confirms* him. It is a magnificent word for it — confirmation.

Whatever the term may be it covers the same thing, the agelong process of induction that covered the sacrifice of innocence. It is the hour when the conscience strikes, when the will begins to know its balance and guilt becomes operative because it can mark a mistaken choice. We are foredoomed and chastened by our individuality in the universal contribution. We are not alone, yet each one of us has to make the choice alone, and there is no escape except by death, as by the chrysalis.

My small private statement against the religious ceremony is that it has become so rigid and fixed in time that its stress sometimes misses association. It can hang in space, meaningless. The sacrament and the understanding do not necessarily coincide. The stress is laid too strongly upon the ritual instead of upon the fact where it touches the child's awareness. In my instance there was no logical combination. The two things did not go together. I was one of those who suffered nothing but disillusion, an awful and drab negativeness. Nobody took the trouble to explain to me that the sacrament I was made to undergo was actually a very beautiful signature of my personal growth, that it was a benediction. I remained abstract and unapplied. The result of this inability on my part, or negligence in religious education, left me practically for all my life with God and humanity on separate sides of the picture. It is when the child is shocked into separateness that he takes his own flight into the Unconscious. Until that flight occurs he is withheld, folded fast into the pristine dream. When he enters reality he has need of God and if God is to be laid upon him with the hands of man then it is essential that there should be no misconception in his understanding.

There should be a definite and logical link between the ritual-istic gesture and the hunger and thirst in the child's spirit.

This induction of the young is nearly always dated with sex because sex is what most often creates the curiosity which necessitates the crisis. Sex might, perhaps, be the complete answer if the earth were governed entirely by the strict division of male and female. It *is* the complete answer in a physical universe. But, if it is to be allowed that we are, after all, making the entire earth journey towards a state where sex is not dominant, then we must allow equally for those aspects of our being which draw us by similitudes towards a fuller world.

Psychologically speaking sex is not the Law. It is opera-tive under the Law. It is the Law which binds us. It is the obedience commanded in the Garden of Eden. It is knowl-edge and the use of knowledge, the widening out towards the magnificence and unity in which we occur. Halfway through life most of us find this out, and change directions. We turn from egotism into the full scheme. Saints and sin-ners discover this reality sooner than others. They travel faster; saints because they are born to wisdom, sinners because they find out early through a surfeit of indulgence. But, saint or sinner or average human being, it is always the child upon whom the choice first strikes. It is the child in his innocence who is cast into the hazard. All the tendencies take shape from the first drift.

Nobody is able to say to the child: this or that will take place and it will occur upon a Tuesday. The moment cannot be foretold. It has to be waited and watched for and the guidance has to be administered with a discretion that makes it almost impersonal. The child must not know that he is being aided for he is obliged to stand up, victim or hero, in the singleness of his own endeavour. Nobody else can do his measuring or choose his weapons. His own mechanism has to set up his own defences.

I was shocked by the immobility of death in the person of my father. This was my blow in Time which put me out of shelter. Other blows had been struck at me, but all that had ever cheated or defeated me rushed back again in the instant of his death to destroy me utterly. This time I was not able to go back to the Dream. His death brought no return. He did not come again as he had come after the policemen had taken him from my arms by force. His silence endured. His absence endured. And I was shattered into the dreadful *knowing*, into knowledge. I ate of the fruit. I was made conscious of mortality, of his inevitable withdrawal. His speechlessness drenched me with its argument. It was my third experience of Death. Major had been compelled by the same absence. But I had not *seen* Major dead. I had seen him die and his dying had been falsified by the appearance of a return to joyousness. He had been given an overdose of arsenic which had whipped him into a *dance macabre* of exuberance. Fortunately for us at the time the awful truth was kept from us. It would have torn our hearts. We did not know that Major was suffering.

I had seen Major's son lying with the stillness of death within the oblong space of scraped earth that he had sanctified by preparation. His foreknowledge of death had given me a profound lesson — one that I was to learn cumulatively. It did not reach me fully at its particular moment because my strongest emotions were pitched into the outrage of his treatment. I was too maddened against Margaret. And also my love for the little creature was not ultimate. I loved Major more and was thankful that it was not Major that Margaret had abused. When Major died I escaped the frigidity of death. With my Father there was no escape. There was absolutely no amelioration or mercy because *my conscience was guilty*. I had made a mistake.

The love, the presence and absence, and the contrition were all there together, transformed by anguish into an aspect that nothing could obliterate. This was a stark going out of the house, a departure from the realms of preservation into a vast and frightening landscape where every tree was naked and all roots hidden. It was the pure and devastating reach of winter spread prematurely upon a child's consciousness.

Facts and rulings caught me and sequences took form. This followed that. My father was my father. My mother was my mother. Behind them were others, all relative and disposed in my personal world.

This was the *shape* of life, the form in which it was going to be played.

Chapter Twenty-One

I remember going into the house of my paternal grandmother. It was a Sunday and either the house was dark or
the weather gloomy. I was aware of a deep shady strangeness in which all objects appeared as though beheld through
water. They were transfused with the quality of things seen
in a marine world, visible but irresponsive to human notions of utility. The furniture had a boxed air. It was confined
in cubes. My grandmother was a pale, dark-eyed woman
with dank hair clapped like shutters against her cheekbones.
There were two younger women: Aunt Ellen and Aunt
Annie. Their faces had the same thick pallor and opaque
eyes as their mother's and they were moved by an abstruse
and passionate emotion that acted between them and me as
a separator. We were declared to each other as enemies.
Everything they said or did was controlled by an unseemly
and critical standard. What they gave was not given as the
purest hospitality but as a declaration of policy. There was
no grandaunt atmosphere, no bestowal from the core. When
Ellen insisted that we should be given hot scones the
proposition moved forth from her with the gesture and
gravity of a proclamation. Everything they did *for* us was
done *against* somebody through us. It took away all sweetness, and even the scones became Kantian in the
determination by which we had to eat them. It was entirely
without humour. Although we did not understand it at the
time we were the means through which they unloaded their
antagonism to my mother. They were the opposite side of
the medal which, in the grandaunts' house, was all against
Father — and always with a touch of mockery. This was grim.

Only in the grandmother was there any lesion. Beneath
what she kept guarded, harshly and aridly without words to

dress it, there was a curious tenderness. Her smile exposed a sort of grandeur in that mean and bizarre room. Nobody explained to me that it was a tea-room. Her smile was so significant that even now, looking back to it after all these years, I am freshly conscious of her love for my father. I know, as I knew then in the silence, that she loved him with completeness, beyond the stretch of argument. She loved him with the integrity of that mother love which enfolds infancy and is indestructible. No matter how he failed her later, or how she failed him, the love came from her in these pure terms. I remember her presence, lit by this testifying smile. I was touched by it. In a state deprived of fineness she was what replaced it and made it unnecessary.

The younger women, her daughters, were closed from her. She was lost to them, struck entirely from another mint-age of the same metals. They were too sharpened by their bitternesses to know what they lost in her.

None of them ever came to our house except Hugh. He was Father's brother. He stood either beside Mother or behind her, a brown man in brown clothes, marked by a permanent reticence. No word ever seemed to come from him, nor any gesture or embrace. Unlike the others he was not black and white. He had an autumn quality, a brown ruddiness that was marked by quiet. He did not *disturb* the atmosphere. He merely appeared in it. In one of those fleeting interchanges that passed between my mother and grandmother, Mother remarked of him that he was a 'reasonable man'. He was marked for me by his rationality and the softly drooping texture of his moustache and eyebrows.

It was Mother also who made a statement about Annie. She said: 'She swings her arms. She has always been detestable.' So there I had her: a short dark young woman who was detestable and swung her arms. I saw her and Ellen always in that strange Sunday gloom, utterly without flowers.

On another occasion, giving something genealogical to a rare visitor for a reason which was never clear to me, Mother said: 'My husband's second name was Montagu. It should really have been Montaçuete. His grandmother was a Spaniard.'

It is by such straws that distinctions are fastened upon us for life. The pride, the awful family pride, seeps through from these trivial indications back into its native place in our blood. The germ catches us and we are stamped by stray characteristics, classified by these intimate differences and differentials. All families suffer from the malady. No social level is immune. It is the law of inheritance.

I remember Mother kneeling before a trunk in the attic that was full of bundles of letters. She was searching for a letter with an American address. Packages were opened and tied up again after incidental readings of letters that had nothing at all to do with her quest. 'I shouldn't be wasting my time, but there is nothing more tempting than a letter,' she would say and then hurry to another package. There were letters franked before the invention of envelopes; letters from Spain, from France and — most of them — from America. There was a letter written by Ahn to Catherine from Bundoran. There was a pressed poppy in it, a wild poppy browned by age. 'My dear and lovely girl,' it began. 'She was almost old enough to be Catherine's mother,' my mother explained. There were letters from somebody named Natalie to Aunt Waters — Mother's Aunt Waters. There were photographs: daguerreotypes taken before I was born of Grandaunts Ahn and Brigid exactly as I had known them.

Mother showed me a photograph from America. It was a cabinet-sized photograph with a piece of tissue paper glued from the top to keep it from being scratched. It represented a man and a woman sitting on two chairs like islands, entirely surrounded by children. There were eight or nine of them, ranging from infancy to various stages of adolescence. 'This,' Mother informed me directly, 'is your father's brother Edward. He ran away from home when he was twelve, to Moville, where he stowed himself away on a steamer leaving for America. When he was discovered and brought up before the captain, the captain took a fancy to him and taught him how to use the compass. And when the ship landed in the States he took him into his home and adopted him and sent him to school. He is a printer. This is his wife and children. They are your first cousins.'

It was so astounding to possess anything so alive and tangible as first cousins that I was absorbingly interested in the photograph.

'His wife's name is Obadiah!'

The inflection with which my mother stroked the word fastened it securely into my consciousness. At that time it was simply a name with a foreign distinction. It was neither male nor female.

That was my first and virtually my final contact with this large family of cousins. Somewhere in the United States today some of them or their descendants may exist. I have no clue to them and no proof that would ever make them positive to me as relatives beyond this peculiar first name of their mother or grandmother. If any man or woman were to reveal to me suddenly in a railway carriage that their grandmother's name was Obadiah, I feel certain that my blood would tingle with recognition. So far this has not happened. The chances are mathematically against it. The name Obadiah remains confined to that scene in an attic of a house in Northern Ireland where the dried poppy lay as brown as a mummy in Ahn's letter to Catherine.

Once when driving through Williamsburg from Vermont I saw the surname on a string of removal vans and became excited, with that one-never-knows urge which can make us yield to extraordinary impulses. If I had been alone I might have tracked those vans. I was not alone. I contented myself with the knowledge that somewhere in the region of Williamsburg people who might be my lost generation existed. I was once daring enough to write to the author of a book on economics who bore the name — but he had no Obadiah. I have seen the surname in the telephone book where nobody but a fool would dare to tackle it. My last surge was a radio announcement that Rome was about to enter a priest bearing the surname for canonisation — an early American saint from Florida, I think. But how, in a human world so numerically involved in a common descent from Adam, is one to particularise and become confirmed in the closeness of anybody dependent upon such a shred as Obadiah?

I do not know what happened to those three women, set in that distant Sunday gloom of a house with furniture arranged in store settings. Not once, in any shape or form, was my paternal grandmother's death spoken of within my hearing. She might, for all I have proof of to the contrary, have been an Immortal. I have a very intangible notion that the younger of the sisters came to America. When another Annie with her surname committed suicide in an apartment house in the West Nineties shortly after I began to live in New York I had positive qualms. It was too late by then to communicate with her.

It cannot be claimed that I ever knew these people. They were my father's people and I loved my father. He never indicated them to me on any occasion. All that I have of them is limited to a Sunday visit and a few inadequate remarks — extracted simply by my own vigilance from what my mother or grandmother said about them. It was only because the will towards them was in me, noted by my own acuteness, that these remarks carried. Otherwise, they might have been made about anybody, and lost.

Their deprival stripped me of contemporaries. Edward and Father were the only members of their family who begot children. Mother was the unique contribution to her generation on her side. James and Elizabeth and Brigid and I were as shelved off from our kind as the animals who went into the ark two by two. Any fresh start had to go on from us.

All this cast me with undue stress upon my grand-mother's generation. The youngest of a large family she was the one who had somebody to talk about. In families some-body has to be talked about. Grandmother was the one to do the telling. Anything that slipped through my mother went back to Grandmother's family.

As a person Mother's own aspects were sealed with an unostentatious reserve. My approaches to her came very slowly. Too slowly. I think they stopped and were arrested on the night I fell down the staircase in the terrifying darkness and Father picked me up. She waited then to finish the song she was singing: *Kathleen Mavourneen*, her voice rising like a fountain and sprinkling my terror with crystals. It was years before we went on again. Years that were, perhaps, too late for her. I have lived to assess them. There should never be these frozen interruptions in the flow of any love. Yet, in spite of this reserve, this irremediable reserve, it was she who was the constant in our daily living. Others came and went without responsibility. She remained. She never forsook us. The fact that we were fed at all and had blankets on the beds has to be credited to her. She was the one who had roots. She had them in us. Grandmother and Father could disappear at any moment. They indulged in escape. . . .

Father escaped finally and absolutely. It was very curious that in a place so accustomed to his absences his last absence should be felt like a presence. It removed certain sentinels. He, who could not be said to have watched over us in life, made us feel by his death that guardianship had been killed. Mother was the one on whom the blow fell. The mere fact that she was a widow seemed to involve her in situations that never dared to approach her when Father was alive. His presence and absence had nothing truly to do with it. It was as a figure under the Law, as her *husband*, that he had bestowed upon her the strong shield of a protection he was utterly incapable of giving. No sooner was he gone than she was obliged to drive in several times a week to consult her lawyer and agent. She had positive sieges with them. No details were ever given out before us. We were simply conscious of the fact that Mother, like a country, was at war. She always seemed to be reading and signing papers. She seemed to have a habit of reading them after she had signed them. Her writing bureau had drawers stacked with long documents tied in a peculiar fashion with bright green shoelaces. We discovered later that she sought solutions to immediate necessities that she would not have sought if Father had been there to check them later with his stormy criticism.

All the time he was alive she, for the sake of peace, avoided argument. When the threat of argument was lifted she arrived at the signature of treaties. By the time any of us was told enough to understand, she was as involved as Europe in financial problems that were extraneous to our private life. It took years for the obligations to gather.

Father's death marked the beginning of a road. Once we were set out upon it, it had to be travelled. It took us into a change of climate. It was not only that we were growing up. We were moving forward as steadily as the planets towards that position of the earth where the ground hardens.

The squeezing came gradually.

Grandmother began to stay with us permanently. At those hours of the winter days when fires burn their brightest; on summer evenings when the sun sets over fields and gardens; in long afternoons winding like country lanes through walks or storms or rains; or through an indoors marked with work held in quickened hands, kneeling against chairs with silken frayed edges and taking pins out of long pink packages, the hearthrug covered with tatters — I can hear her voice and feel the warmth of her presence as she unpacked the facts.

'I am not your godmother, Kathleen.'

She was James' and Elizabeth's and Brigid's. Each of them had been held in her vicarious arms at the baptismal font and dedicated to the Virgin. Each of them, even James, had a Mary in their names. I was the one who had no Mary. I was excluded from the fraternity. My godmother was an Eliza Gill. She was Mother's friend, and she lived in New York and wrote letters about Ellen Terry's son. By way of compensation for the loss of my grandmother's sponsorship I had two godfathers. Each of them was a James Hassan and they were totally unrelated by blood. They were joined simply by their heavenly parentage to me. I felt myself to be a Hassan just as James and my sisters were Marys. Later on, when I began to read Mozarabic history and came upon the recurrent mention of Hassans I always glowed as though I had come among my own people.

Although excluded from spiritual ties with my grand-mother I was linked to her by another that resembled that between a drowning man and his rescuer. She had saved my life. I was bound to her exactly as Major had been bound to the fireman.

'Yes, child, I am as responsible for your being alive as though I had given you birth.'

As usual the story began at the end. It went backwards in segments — a piece when you were nine and a piece when you were ten and so on. It started without sequence and when the sequence came it was not what followed but what went before:

'I landed that morning from America and drove directly from the boat at Moville. I was strangely perturbed and impatient. At the time I put it down to my urge to see you. The moment I received the photograph of you, in your embroidered robes on your mother's lap, I had to come. All had to be forgiven. I had to hold you in my arms. I couldn't wait.' She paused here and her expression became loaded and distant, taken off into meanings which she did not intend to express. When words came again you always felt the slice that had been cut out of them.

'Well, as soon as I got to the house a laundress was there, on the doorstep. She knew me apparently. The first thing she said was: 'Oh, Ma'am, I'm grieved to the core about the little baby.' I asked her quite sharply what she meant. She told me that she had seen Kerrigan, your mother's maid, go off in a cab with a lot of baggage and Kerrigan had told her that 'the baby had had a fit' and that she had not the courage to tell the mother or face me. She had confessed to the laundress that she was running away before I came. The poor laun-dress did not know what to do. She waited for me. She had made a futile effort to get into the house. At that time your mother was an invalid and not allowed to leave her couch. When I heard this tale I got into the house. I found you lying limp and lifeless and as blue as though you had been struck by lightning in your cradle. I gathered you into my arms and took you right out to the carriage without a minute's hesitation and told the coachman to drive as fast as possible to the nearest doctor's. The doctor told me that you had been poisoned. That vile woman, Kerrigan, had given you something and left you. I think she was convinced that if anything happened to you your mother would die from shock. I don't know. I arrived in the nick of time. I saved your life.'

This recital suspended me upon a high Kerrigan note. Who was she and what was she? She had gone away with 'seven trunks'. She was as full of magic as the Seven Dwarfs. Why should she wish to kill me — a perfectly innocent person? 'Why,' I began, 'why did she do it?'

'She was a vile creature.'

The answer explained nothing. As the victim of a potential murderess I was done out of the evidence. I was driven inward and it is no wonder at all that I exulted secretly in being as good a character as any in the *Family Herald Supplement*. I was in the line with those you leaned out to listen about when Mother told Mademoiselle about *Dene's Hollow*, or *Robert Elsmere* or *The Woman in White*. Life became exciting and factual and, in these moods, poetry vanished. I came down from heaven to earth where things did not sing but happen. Poison was a weapon used by the Borgias and witches and had been applied to me. I joined the innocents: the Princess in the Tower and Marie Antoinette and Mary, Queen of Scots. All that was missing was the historical significance. I had to wait for that. What could be my heritage if it could move anybody to do away with me while I was still in the cradle? I could not put the pieces together. All that I knew was that somewhere and in some fashion they were impelled to unite.

At the time it became stabilised as one of those stories which either should not have been told to me at all or should have been told fully. The subtlety tormented me. It turned into a gross exercise in imagination. A direct 'Why?' had brought forth nothing. Instinct warned me not to probe. Silence and vigilance together were the only means by which the door could be kept open a crack. I had to guard and trim my curiosity, to wait with the amazing patience of youth which drags heavy weights in Time towards the understanding of forbears. We follow them. It is unfair to blindfold us. Their caution is simply that they are unable to confess failure before us, to expose themselves to us who are still undefeated. They are afraid to admit mistakes before those who do not appear compelled to make them. They traffic with our blankness and confuse us with their scruples. So our wills are forced into war. It is an old story, a continually repeated chapter in mankind's study of man. The young begin with forfeits. We pay — with poison in the cradle and all sorts of *mis*understandings. It would be better to begin clear. It would be stronger to separate us completely from the sequence and bring us up outside the pale of family life, on a Rousseau plan.

I was born just too early for the solutions. I was the child of a darkness that was only beginning to break in large enough masses. Psychology was only beginning as a science. It was only beginning to move out from ecclesiastical domination and politics into the kingdom of the little child.

The atmosphere of our household thinned out into a chilly economy. MacDaid ceased to come daily. He came when he was sent for. When Mother had to go into town it was Margot who did the harnessing. Margot was still there but something seemed to happen to our washdays. They seemed distended in volume and demanded more and more attention from Margot. The attention she gave to them was taken from the attention she gave to what was being cooked on the stove. Stews began to be permanent, varied only by the amount of barley or lentils that supplemented their ingredients.

Grandmother appeared in the kitchen one day with Mrs Beeton's cookery book. It was propped open against the coffee-pot, blown open at the coloured plates in the middle where blancmanges glittered like yellow citadels and crimson jellies shone like gigantic rubies in diamond dishes. Vast quantities of blackberries had been gathered by us for the occasion. Grandmother said that we had to economise. She

borrowed one of Margot's enormous white pleated aprons
that went all around her and declared that, on this occasion,
she would make the jam. Jam cost nothing but sugar and
time. Her time might just as well be wasted upon jam as
upon memories of tragedy. Margot protested that she could
still make jam. She insisted upon saying it and she fixed
Grandmother with both her eyes so hard that the gaze
seemed projected from her like blows. Grandmother almost
cried. Half tears appeared in the corners of her eyes and
were pressed back by her fingertips. She was urged to take
Margot into her confidence. 'I confess to you, Margot, that
what troubles me is the maggots. Do blackberries without
maggots exist?'

'Boiling takes the danger out of them,' Margot grunted.

Grandmother shuddered. She said despairingly: 'I must
make myself go through with it.' She said the berries looked
perfect. She regarded them very critically and then, catching
my eyes upon her, she declared: 'The fact is, Kathie, I have
never paid any attention to food. I have just enjoyed eating
it. I should not begin to discriminate at my time of life.'

Her first lot of jam refused to thicken. She blamed the
fruit. Blackberries were three parts rain water, she asserted.
She sat in the Windsor chair with a wooden spoon dripping
claret spots upon Margot's apron and she asked what
should be done to make the jam into jam. Margot said: 'You
should have let me make it.' She grumbled about her apron.
Grandmother begged her not to worry about the apron. It
could be replaced. What was disconcerting was the unwill-
ing jam. A bunch of carrots was lying upon the kitchen table.
She decided to put them into the jam. She asked Margot to
scrape them and chop them and she would try them. Margot was shocked. She had never heard of such a thing. Jam
was made with fruits. She had never in her mortal life heard
of carrots being anything but a vegetable. Grandmother had
made up her mind. Experiment was working in her. She had
the mood that made her cut out dresses two and three times
until they had the right shape. Now it was the jam that had
to have the right shape. She swept the dish of carrots into

the jam. 'I prefer carrot jam to blackberry soup, for that's what it is at present. all that it needs is a touch of salt and pepper.'

She was delighted when the carrots took on the blackberry dye. She held them out in purple dice upon the spoon to Margot. 'I've invented a new fruit.'

Margot ceased to protest. She was stirred to interest when the jam became a success. The carrots really did the trick. Grandmother burst into the most extravagant optimism. 'I must try mushrooms and turnips.' When she pronounced this exaggeration Margot said feebly and pathetically that she wished the jam could be made in the dining room or bedroom the way toffee was made. Grandmother was delighted that she had invented a jam. 'If I made enough of it,' she told Mother, 'I could supply the grocery stores. We could exchange jams for other things.' Mother had no ardour about the matter. Grandmother fell back upon her original intention. She had stocked us with jam so, unless the baker's van ceased to come, we would always have bread and jam to eat. Starvation was held off.

In one of those gusts of affluence that always had an air of beginning and ending upon the same day: with Mother bringing packages home and having a 'party'; one of those extensions that were connected with the signature of documents, it was decided that James should be sent to college. Governesses had always depended upon Mother's dividends. When the dividends failed, education was postponed. Now the consideration fell singly upon James. Mother explained that James was now the man of the family. His education was absolutely imperative. He had to have a profession. She discussed the problem with James, who seemed, judging by his expression, not to have the faintest conception of what it was all about. It was decided that he should become a barrister. Mother had wished Father to read for the Bar, and he hadn't. He had got out of it. James was too young to escape. First of all James was to be sent to a preparatory college.

James and I read Whately's *Logic and Rhetoric*. Logic was

necessary to barristers. Logic became a game. You could, we discovered, argue about anything — provided you set up a formula. You could prove that nothing was something and that black was white. All that was needed was a triangle. Any triangular arrangement contained proof from any aspect. Black was a colour, white was a colour: things which were equal to the same thing were equal to one another. James and I had an argument that lasted over a period of years: Could a *fact* be physical? We could prove that 1066 was a historical fact but it was another matter to show where it was physical. When we had it all set up in perfect physical condition it could, in places, slip as a pure fact. Whately, by some strange means, led me to Berkeley and Hume and we were then involved in proving that we existed as human beings. The whole world was apparently a figment of the imagination, if you believed Berkeley. You could go to the edge of the precipice and cast yourself forth if you did it in the right spirit.

We came out with the facts pretty well in their places and believing in our separate identities. The battle led nowhere but it was, while it lasted, a very real exercise in discovering the other fellow's weaknesses. That, we were told, was what logic was for.

When James went to college it was to a boys' college in Dumfries, conducted by the Marist brothers. Mother's sole recommendation for it was that Conan Doyle had sent his son there. She had obtained this information from the college prospectus. She learned afterwards that this same son had had a mental breakdown — so the recommendation was not a recommendation at all. But the *Strand Magazine*, which was then publishing the Sherlock Holmes series, was one of her favourite readings and the fact of James being in Conan Doyle's son's college linked her (logically) to Sherlock Holmes.

Shortly after James went to Dumfries I received a letter from the college censor, a Brother Tatiana. I always thought of him as a girl. In the process of reading the boys' letters which, he assured me, was necessary in order to prevent defamatory doctrine from entering their institution, he had come upon my correspondence with my brother. By the time I had read this much I was hot and cold with apprehension. What could I have written that could be regarded as defamatory? But it wasn't that. I had done no wrong. Brother Tatiana was simply, in his own words, 'enchanted' with my letters and he wished me to communicate with him. He made it impossible for me not to do so for he challenged a verdict on Saint Augustine which I had expressed in a letter to James. Saint Augustine was nagged by his mother out of Manichaeism. I had written that it was Augustine who had done the final stiffening of Christianity. I admitted that it was a beautiful relationship between him and his mother. They had leaned out of that window at Ostia on their return journey and suffered the exquisite tenderness that preceded eternal separation. His mother was about to die. But I maintained that he had gone against his own will in the renunciation of the dual power of God and the Demon. I do not know why I unloaded these letters upon James. I think he was simply the target for the burden of thought that preyed upon my idle mind. Certainly James never answered me. His notes in return simply asked for pocket money or footballs for the college. James never approved of anything I thought or wrote. We had a desperate battle about the Brontës, especially Emily. James had read a detrimental criticism written by a conservative gentleman about Emily and he had accepted it as doctrine. James said she was wild and that I was wild too. It was a period when I was experimenting with hand-writing. I wielded a pen like a paintbrush and some of my capitals were, according to James, three feet high. James judged me by my capitals. It was only an adolescent phase, an outward sign of an inward necessity. I was reading everything I could lay my hands upon. I had to have some channel for the digestion of philosophy and history and romance and poetry.

Brother Tatiana replaced James. My letters to James became incidental to his. We wrote about the rose gardens of Paestum and Browning and Kirke White and the Border wars and Parnell and the thirst of the dying. Anything that sprang from where my mind was exercising. It was I, not he, who set the subject. This correspondence was a flower that ripened and died rapidly. It was a fragile, wind-blown affair.

Mother took me to visit James' college at Easter. We were invited to witness the college sports. We stayed in a hotel in Dumfries where we arrived late in the evening of a very cold day. I was tired and excited to a degree that can be measured by the fact that when Mother came to say good night to me after I had got into bed she stood on the threshold and greeted me: 'Kathie, are you going to sleep in your hat?' I had forgotten to take off my hat.

We drove over to the college the next morning. The weather was raw and cold. The earth had a bleak, lost quality. There was a great crowd of people. The event was open to the public and it was impossible to distinguish who belonged to the town and who to the college. James only appeared at intervals. He had an unhappy air and most evidently did not wish to be seen with us. He bestowed his misery upon me. It was certainly not my element. It was all so indefinite and scattered. Something was about to happen, and then when it did happen it bore stillborn marks. It had not enough motion. We wandered about greeting strangers who greeted us. The game was very muddy and had not enough coordination to interest me. My football education had been so neglected that I did not know what was happening and I hated the ball when the masses of struggling forms fell upon it. I was relieved when it took the air. The sports field was slimy. The grass upon which we walked at the edges was grey and tough under our feet. A middle-aged man with gingery hair who was wearing a soutane stood and talked to Mother. She said presently: 'This is Brother Tatiana!' He smiled at me. There was no enthusiasm or warmth in our meeting. I lost him when I met him. What flowed form his pen upon paper was far more intimate. His presence gave me no touch at all. There was nothing you could put a finger on and say: 'This is where it stopped.' The whole interest between us melted away as snow melts out of its own temperature. There was no disappointment. It just came to an end. In Dumfries I was much more interested in the ghostly presence of Burns. I stood on a threshold and was aware of Burns turning his glowing face upon me, smiling, cracking a joke and rising and going out singing into the bitter weather. Brother Tatiana vanished as a real person and Burns entered my life, a poet who kept as closely as Jesus to his origins.

It was while James was at college that I was sent to a Young Ladies' Academy in Derry. I was entered three weeks before the end of term, two weeks before the term's examinations, which were a test for the Intermediate Examinations to be held later. This was a Protestant school under the direction of three very distinguished and brilliant sisters, the Misses MacKillip. They were not very interested in me, a little girl who had arrived at the wrong end of the term. They were absorbed in the progress of their examinations. I was classified according to my age which put me into the grade of a girl from Sligo who was the pride of the school. Her name was Charlotte Warner and she moved in an aura of scholarships. She had a magnetic effect upon me. She dispensed an electric atmosphere that excited me. I was drawn towards her by a quickening process that scattered my own darknesses. We sat in desks at right angles so that I was able to squint at her when I wished, which was often. She was quite unaware of me, taken up with urgent matters which entailed her complete attention. I, alone, was conscious of the miracle that *together* we attained some fusion. I did not know what it was. I only knew that it glowed like light, and that we both stood in it and generated it. I have always been conscious of people's brains. I was aware of Charlotte's because of its bright functioning at that time. She was magical to me. I was supported by her presence.

The mathematical Miss MacKillip discovered that I was deficient in Euclid. The only thing I knew about it was that Euclid himself had sat in the sand, mystifying scholars with his symbols. I was given the first two sections of Euclid to work upon as a preparation for my work during the following term. It was only as a pure matter of routine and as a sort of courtesy that I was allowed to participate in the examinations. It was easier to have me in than have me out. I stepped into classes that were in a test state and where all questions were sharpened. I had the advantage of freshness. It was all a wonder and of the deepest interest from the brightness of the girls' faces to the tones of their voices and the quality of their answers. I was astonished by an accuracy that could mean nothing; it was quite tasteless. It was the sober truth, a statement of facts, and it was absolutely dead and left me then and for always puzzled by its worth. The author in the literature class was Washington Irving. It seemed the purest waste of time to deal with him or give him thought. I read the textbook through from beginning to end in a fever to discover one gleam that would alleviate his tedium and I did not find it. I did not understand. Who and what was he that he could be chosen to exercise the mind? Two sisters in the long desk behind me answered all the questions correctly. Their truth was not my truth. Their names were Gladys and Kathleen Scott and they wrote magnificent essays. I made every effort to appreciate what drew out their values but I failed to find it. I was more interested in them than in Washington Irving. Gladys had strong raven-wing hair that rippled from her like a mane. Kathleen's hair was curly. They had dark, wide-spaced eyes and the sort of skin that made you think of damsons. I used to wonder if they liked Washington Irving. They were such fine specialists in his meaning. I never dared to ask. I never became intimate with them. I remained an outsider — with them when recess came but not of them, as was Laura Gailey. Laura, who knew nothing about Petrarch or *his* Laura who, also, wore a green dress. Laura Gailey's dress was not embroidered with violets nor did she walk in the valley of Avignon. She hardly ever walked at all. She skipped and danced and there was about her a brown velvet liveliness that made me think of goats and pansies somehow combined. The only discipline that was in her blood was that which went to music.

There was an older girl whose name I never remembered. She had a desk by an open window in a classroom through which I had to pass. Her face was always in profile against branches of trees laden with spring blossoms. Her auburn hair flowed in waves against a breeze. She had a complexion of cream and roses and there was about her an air of such delicacy that she seemed poised as an angel upon the pink-white light of the flowers. I never seemed able to think of her feet in shoes. They were always bare and white as alabaster with pearls for her toenails. Girls said in hushed voices: 'Isn't she lovely?' She was the school beauty. It was true, but she was only an aspect to me. I was not aroused by her as I was aroused by Charlotte Warner with her strong features and her eyes as clear and hazel as mountain water. Nobody ever said Charlotte was a beauty. She was too grave.

These girls became everlasting. They are with me to this day as in a dream, as visions upon a field one was obliged by some hazard to cross. They have the haze of eternal youth and have remained unspoilt by any circumstance. Everything about them and surrounding them is preserved and perfect. They were companions in an hour that had its own splendour. They came in like the sea on that shore by the Bay of Shadows and went out again. It is what they did not leave that has stayed. It is their intention, their unfulfilled promise that has remained.

During the Easter holidays the senior Miss MacKillip came to call upon my mother. They were closeted in the drawing room and I was not brought in to share their testimony. I was shut out, troubled vaguely in spirit — as one who had sinned in ignorance. Miss MacKillip departed without seeing me and I was told that, for some reason or other, I was not going back to that school. It appeared that Miss MacKillip had wished for me to return. The examinations in some strange fashion had brought me out level with Charlotte Warner and Miss MacKillip had implored Mother to give me to her as a pupil. The terms were evidently not within Mother's means or outside her pride. Whatever the excuse was, it shut the door. I was touched for the briefest instant by a scholastic yearning, by the flags of recognition, then it all vanished and became nothing. It was Charlotte I missed. It was Charlotte I longed for. I was convinced that her companionship was a necessary requisite for my best attainment. She was an urgency in my personal integrity. We had some cathodic power in common that would have enabled us to perform miracles in darkness. I never saw nor heard of her again. I was born under stars that made schools as fleet as comets. They trailed across my sky in sudden and unlasting glory.

Chapter Twenty-Two

When it was decided that Elizabeth and Brigid should be sent to a convent in Warwickshire the entire household was disoriented by the preparation of their trousseau. They had apparently to be provided with as many sheets and pillow slips and towels and personal garments as though they were getting married. They had to have dozens of chemises and petticoats and nightgowns and knickers and handkerchiefs. All the cottons and cambrics and embroidered edgings and insertions in the attic were brought down for their benefit. Tables and chairs were stacked with heaps of white materials and fittings-on were continuous. One could hardly enter a room without finding Elizabeth or Brigid in the process of pulling a dress up over their heads or letting some disintegrated-looking garment fall in a pool at their feet. As innocent little girls who were being drafted to boarding school, they were completely beguiled by the immensity of their provision.

This particular convent had been chosen by Mother for the reason that it was a sort of stepchild of Princethorpe. While she had been at Princethorpe an order of German nuns had been chased out of their homeland by the Catholic persecutions. Princethorpe had given them a house and some land. It was to these German nuns that Elizabeth and Brigid were being confided. Mother was certain that special care and attention would be bestowed upon them as the daughters of a Princethorpe pupil. They would certainly learn German and music. At home they were learning nothing for there was no governess. Any form of Mademoiselle in the house at that period would have had our internal economy gratuitously revealed to her. Governesses could not be expected to accept an erratic diet. Bread and jam on the days when the butcher forgot to come could not be distributed to a governess with large spoonfuls of Parrish's syrup to make up for a lack of phosphates.

Mother tried to inure Elizabeth and Brigid to their life in a convent by telling them about her own school days. She had loved Princethorpe. She told them about her friends Finola O'Sullivan and Gundred de Trafford and about the suppers in the refectory — a bare table with beer in tankards and everything tasting good. She told them how, when she was a pupil there, she was not allowed to take a bath unless she wore her nightgown. This fact disturbed Elizabeth considerably. It almost shattered the excitement of a journey across the sea to another land 'like going to France'. She declared firmly that she did not wish to go to a place where you had 'to get wet with your clothes on. Where did you put the soap?'

This preparatory period was also marked by visits from an Englishwoman. She was one of Mother's mysteries. Her husband was connected with insurance policies and the policies were the cause of the visits. Her name was Mrs Clayton. She resembled Mrs Corkery, the minister's wife. Mrs Clayton always drove out to see us in a low phaeton with a dappled pony. She always brought us a small soup dish filled with what she referred to as 'buttered steak'. It was a Glossop speciality and she was an adept at making it. The steak was grilled lightly and buttered and then scraped with a sharp knife into a paste that was excellent for sand-wiches. She adored our countryside and was always comparing it to her native Shropshire. She never got out of the phaeton. She had had some sort of nervous collapse that made walking precarious. In her own house she always seemed able to get about — from chair to chair and room to room. Her husband was a little pig-like man, very fat and pink, with a blond curly beard like Jason's. He never arrived with her in the phaeton but he always appeared in time to take her away. He would come scrunching up the avenue and hop into the phaeton and she would lean across and tuck the goatskin rug in about his knees; then they would sit there and make conversation until the dappled pony could wait no longer for any foolishness. As soon as Mr Clayton appeared policies were discussed but one went on thinking of primroses in Shropshire and woods that had sheets of wild hyacinths. Mr and Mrs Clayton seemed to live in separate worlds. They did not seem to belong to each other even beneath the goatskin. The pony always made them depart suddenly. He would swirl upon the gravel and Mother would turn her eyes upon her pansies when he edged the lawn. Then the next thing was that he had his back to you and Mrs Clayton's gauntleted hand was raised like a benediction above her bonnet.

The Claytons lived in a furnished house in Carlisle Road. They had no children of their own but Mrs Clayton was very fond of young people. She invited us to a Christmas party. It was during the holidays when James was at home. He drove us in and we put the trap up at the hotel. Elizabeth, who had a special flair for parties, was too impatient to wait. She went on in advance and was the first guest to arrive. She said her greetings very prettily, Mrs Clayton recounted later to Mother, and then she added casually: 'The juveniles will be along presently.' Mrs Clayton was enchanted with the phrase. She mistook it for a pure Irishism. She never knew that Elizabeth must have derived her juveniles from a Latin grammar. It was a word nobody used and it must have fallen upon her in pure inspiration — a word in a party dress to match its occasion.

Father always said that Elizabeth was a very self-contained lady. He said it was her early political training that had rationalised her. She was always casual and had that gift of meeting unusual events with adequate ease. She was full of laconic surprises. Somebody read out of the morning paper at breakfast that a soldier had fallen out of the public ferry when crossing to the Barracks and that he had been rescued by a dog which belonged to a little girl. Elizabeth said: 'I was the girl.' The dog was Major.

The Carlisle Bridge, which had been in public use for years, was officially opened by the Duke and Duchess of

York. The Royal visit was a very social occasion. During the actual ceremony the Bridge was closed and nobody was supposed to cross it until after the Duke and Duchess's carriage had gone over it. But there, meeting them in the middle of it, was Elizabeth, all dressed up for the occasion. The Duke made her a deep bow, holding out his hat towards her as though he expected a sweet and Elizabeth made him a deep bow in return. She did not bow to the Duchess because the Duchess was bowing to the other side and did not, as Elizabeth explained, 'catch her eye'. The Duke was driving with the Mayor and the Duchess was driving with the Mayoress who, it was maliciously rumoured, kept the sleeve of her dress that had touched the Royal sleeve in a glass case in her drawing room ever afterwards. Elizabeth kept the grace of the occasion in her heart.

I was miserable after Elizabeth and Brigid went to the convent in Warwickshire. Brothers and sisters are never meant to agree. It is a natural law that they should disagree and tumble over each other in conflict. Examples can be picked to prove it from eagles in the nest to puppies in the stable. As children we fight out our growth upon each other. It is not until we are grown men and women that the sympathy arises. We do not understand when we are very young. We do not know that we are neither for nor against each other but merely sharpening out our individualities. I was to find out years later that James and my sisters had their own particular tribulations, their own particular inductions.

What I was conscious of after their departure was the grinding desolation that spilled itself through the house without them. It recovered for me the dereliction of earlier miseries, the ennui of an enforced idleness when I was obliged to listen as they played in the cornfields by the sea. The void they left accentuated the quality of the rooms I passed through so that they resembled a Christmas tree that has been stripped of gifts but remains garnished with artificial fruits. The rooms remained bright enough but they became hollow and stripped of expectation. They became exaggeratedly empty so that sunbeams took on voices, and shadows seemed to have power to explain themselves, and memory took on the terrible equity of an equally terrible tranquillity. I was pointed like a pencil in a peace to which I did not subscribe.

I was enfolded there with those who were older. I was closed with my own dream upon others who had awakened. It was all significantly strange to me, marked by a comprehensibility that allowed me to take them in without understanding them. I was aware of my grandmother's unrest. A curious urgency possessed her and she seemed impotent to deal with it. I did not know what the check was. In the old days she had never been held down. You had never known, as my father said so often, whether she 'would be there for breakfast'. Now she wished to go and she did not go. She remained. She was subject to some unexplained obligation that wrought and worked her as spasmodically as a fever. It made her erratic in her behaviour. It made her declare herself with strange and sudden moods. She would appear before me brusquely, catching me, baiting me: 'Kathleen, will you come into town with me to visit Nazareth House?' We never went there now. It hurt me. It brought back my father. Yet I could not refuse her for she had demanded as though she demanded pity. Then, when we were actually in town, safely in the hotel sitting room, she said: 'I have no intention of visiting Nazareth House. It was only an excuse. I have never been able to go there since your father and mother brought that awful lawsuit against them for the family china. They were bound to lose. Your father should never have done it. Your mother should have known better. They might as well have attacked a Conclave of Cardinals. The china should have been got by guile.'

What disturbed me was her habit of subterfuge. It was unusual for her. She need not have invited me to visit Nazareth House. In the hotel sitting room she had an air of not knowing what to do with herself. Then we went out and we turned upwards through Bishop's Gate and out in the direction of the convent until I believed that she had changed her mind again. But she hadn't. She said: 'I had to go to the hotel but it was only a blind for MacDaid's benefit.' We walked without haste, as though we were going nowhere. It was the same Bishop Street on the other side of the Gate but it suffered a change. It seemed to widen and become rural. The houses became smaller. There were glimpses of trees and fields. Grandmother took me to one of the little houses. It was owned by a Miss Elliot. Grandmother was sorry Miss Elliot's sister had died.

Miss Elliot reminded me of Grandaunts Ahn and Brigid. She was tall like Brigid and she had Ahn's eyes, dark and deeply set. She told us simply about her sister while she prepared tea for us: 'She had a pain in her heel when she got up in the morning. She thought it was a cramp and would go away but it lasted. "My dear," I urged her, towards noon, "it is such a lovely day, don't you think you could walk as far as Pump street and let the doctor look at it? You may have sprained it or something. I once rammed my hand down upon a piece of needle and was unable to probe it out. I had that piece of needle in me for two years. It went in by my finger and came out by my heel."'

'It might have gone to your heart,' Grandmother said.

'I thought it might be a needle she had. You never know. I watched her go. It never occurred to me to go with her. In about an hour's time, when I thought she should be getting back, I went to the door again and there she was, coming through the gate towards me. I came right back and began to dish out the food I had prepared. When all was ready to go upon the table there was still no sign of her so I went to the door again and she had vanished. I wondered if she had slipped down to the Long Tower to say a prayer or two, or gone into somebody's house. I stood there, wondering. I was standing there when the messenger came from the doctor to tell me that she had just passed away. She died of a thrombus in the consulting room at the moment I saw her coming towards me.'

I felt the ghost of Miss Elliot's sister in the room. This was the same behaviour as Canon Newland's. It had the persistence of those who have departed with too great haste. Miss

Elliot's speech had that quiet exactitude that made it all seem normal and not to be wondered about. She and Grandmother shed tears together, then they drank tiny glasses of amber brandy and Grandmother turned the grief inward upon herself: 'I am unable to bear the monotony of my life. I feel that I must run away from it. It has nothing at all to do with Katie. It is simply that it has become unsupportable.'

Miss Elliot laid down her glass. She was shocked. Travel had not the substance of death to her. 'I do not understand it,' she said soberly; 'I quite simply do not understand it. I, myself, have never been a day away from home. I have not even seen the Giant's Causeway which I am told is one of the Seven Wonders of the World.'

'Well, not quite,' Grandmother remarked slowly, gathering up her defeat; 'they have the same formation in Dalmatia.' She sighed and turned her profile so that her sadness was visible. Her lips were still wet with the brandy. She listened while Miss Elliot gave her full details of her sister's funeral. She said nothing beyond syllables of sympathy. But her own urgency remained with her. There was another time in her bedroom. I went in upon her and she had the contents of her bureau drawers spread out upon her bed. She was not packing. She was folding garments as though preparatory to packing. There was a little heap of while silk stockings with navy-blue clocks embroidered on them. Every time she doubled a pair of stockings inside each other she drew them across her cheek caressingly. She said: 'I should never have settled down. I should never have come back. I should have marked my dream. I dreamt once before I left America that I had sent my trunks on to Ahn and Brigid and that they refused to take them in. Every time a trunk was put down upon their doorstep they shut the door and the trunk went sliding down the hill, shooting down. Ahn and Brigid never approved of me. They accepted Jane. She had more money and I was extravagant. Money never meant anything to me except to spend it. Jane never spent it. She invested it in various projects — like turning out priests at Maynooth. She was a perfect mill-wheel for motives. Jane succeeded and I failed and that is all there is to it. She bought them over with gifts. She always gave them what they wanted. Her last gift was the carriage and horses which enabled them to make that tour of the Lakes. It would have altered your mother's life if they had not been away when Jane died. She took ill and died in their absence. She died of cancer within six weeks. If she had not died, or if they had not been away your mother would never have married your father.'

I did not dare to ask for reasons. Questions, I had discovered, only blocked answers. It was safer to wait, not to check the flow. Anything might come up in the current. She had an air of asserting that Aunt Waters would not have died *if* they had stayed at home. All was thrust dependently upon their flight to the Lakes. The meaning came out clearly that it was Mother who had needed to be rescued and none had been there to do it. I held my breath, offering an intense muteness as the only encouragement.

Grandmother sat down upon the edge of the bed. She began to settle the things she had arranged back into the drawers. 'Yes, dear child, everything hangs by a thread. As soon as the news reached me, as soon as I heard, I left New York.' She moaned and pressed her fingertips to her temples, pressing down her sorrow. She regarded me with a wide, distant bereavement, as one completely outside the pale of her testimony: 'How was I to *know* that Jane could go so quickly! She was injured at the opening of the cathedral. She was pressed in the crush against the top of her own pew. She was so stout . . . and then she always laced herself too tightly, no leeway at all. And, imagine it, she was wearing her diamonds! She thought it was a fitting occasion for diamonds. She never wore them. She was saving them for Katie. She had planned to have Katie presented at the Viceregal Lodge and she was hoping to marry her to the Attorney General. He was much older than poor Katie. She had him to dinner, and Katie, in all her innocence, was charming to him. So there it is: the plans of mice and men, and women such as Jane,

gang aft agley as Burns so truly said. It was cancer. The
agony she went through was frightful I have been told.' She
shuddered it from her. Her voice was awed with the fright-
fulness. She fixed me with an analogy. 'They say Queen
Elizabeth had a frightful deathbed. Strong women give
battle. But Elizabeth earned it. She was a bad woman. Jane
was not bad, only mistaken. She had no blood on her hands.
Poor thing, she went through her martyrdom. And, when it
was over, there was your mother, shut up in Edenbank with
a pack of servants under the dominion of that vile woman
Kerrigan. I always say that Jane spoiled Kerrigan. She took
her everywhere. She was her personal maid and every time
Jane crossed to America with Katie they took Kerrigan with
them. She was a very impudent, ambitious woman.'

Kerrigan became a clue. She drew me into a sphere of
melodrama where knives flew and villains sprang from the
shade. Reasons fluttered in that electrified atmosphere, but
nothing came out upon which they could be pinned. Mother
was the victim and Kerrigan was the villain. Kerrigan had the
knight's move. If I could trace her jump all the rest would
follow and I would be able to tell *why* my mother had married my father. Edenbank was a solid, comfortable house built
in the same style as the house in which Canon Newland's
ghost still walked. Aunt Waters had built it on her return from
America. She had a passion for building houses. She had built
several in New York. Whenever any American fact had to be
attached to her in time it was noted before the house was built
in Spring Street or before she built the house in 9th Street or
East 51st Street — between this and that house — always a
house. Edenbank stood high upon the Creggan Road with a
full view of the Rhine-like river. It was where my mother had
lived as a girl. It was where she had had Orr for a groom. It
was where, she had told me with her own lips, she had *never
had enough to eat*'. Aunt Waters suffered a Victorian panic if
her waistline swelled beyond sixteen or seventeen inches.
'So,' she told me, 'I never had an egg for breakfast.' The
standards of my own life seemed so superior to what hers
had been that it aroused my pity.

The details of these expended lives filled me with constant astonishment. They were so irrational, so incredibly illogical. Things happened without reason. Books could be read to the last page where some sort of solution was invariably to be found. Something stopped at the right place and time in books. In real life nothing ever stopped and there was hardly ever a solution. If a solution happened it always seemed to be by hazard. It never occurred to me that I, in my turn, would take on any sequence. It never occurred to me that anything that had happened to them could affect me. Their lives were entirely their own, bound by their own problems. I can still feel the unbearable confinement of having to be present when they revealed themselves to each other. I was trapped in their company, condemned to their virtues and tendencies. I would come in upon them sitting by a window or fire, filled with my own private exultations, and the very manner of their looks, of how they turned upon me with some incredible expectation, made me their prisoner. At that time I was reading everything I could lay my hands upon. My mind bristled with labels from Averroes to Zoroaster; with theories from Thales to Hagel. I actually dwelt in a world which had no cognisance of my mother or grandmother. My intimates were others. I knew Spinoza, the poverty of his little room, how his mind worked and his heart beat and the day they changed his sheets. I saw him as closely as Dante by the balustrade, a man with black hair which the thin Dutch winds freshened when he walked upon the brick streets. I knew all about him down to his day of doom, when they put over upon him the awful curse of the Synagogue — the black candles dripping their flames into the vats of blood while the words of excommunication mounted like a river in spate. I knew what his depth was, and how he descended to it and *rose* again. He was the Jew, the Job, the Hamlet element in the fortification of Truth. He was Wordsworth's Toussaint L'Ouverture, the Man swept by delectable agonies in the human process. I knew Machiavelli in Florence, writing his creed for kings, always washing his hands before he went into his sacred

library to balance out good against evil and evil against
good in a sandwich that has been the basis of politics down
to this day. He has lasted because he took account of what
was wrong as well as what was right. He was neither for
Christ nor for the Devil but for the weaknesses between. I
knew Teresa de Ahumada and walked with her in Ávila, in
Veas when she met Gratian; when love touched her or when
death came out first, more ardent than life. Poetry swung
through me as a bell in a belfry, vibrant from every cause. I
was consumed by these secrecies, and to the two women
who looked upon me so innocently I could confess nothing.

It had nothing at all to do with my love for them. It was
only that I was young and that they were older. I was
growing. I was alone and there was so much to take in. I
could not explain it to them. I could not explain it to myself.
I could only suffer the absorption, silent to the point of
mutiny. It was hard to bear. It hurt — in that queer removed
fashion by which you suffer when a form in black breaks up
the sunshine in a country road. It is wrong and you don't
know why it is wrong. I used to wonder what I had to do
with them. I was going in a different direction. It takes such
a long time to discover that we carry their histories in our
veins and that, at the given signal, we are coordinated to the
same bloodstream. What has shaped them is bound to shape
us. There is no escape.

I would listen to them, obedient in circumstance if not in
spirit. What was spent in them was unspent in me. They had
already scattered what I had not yet attained. They went
backwards into the past. I had to go forward with effort still
unbroken in my arms. As women they were done. And yet
every tap they touched me with became indelible, fraught
with the gift of registration and of memory. What had been
spun into their pattern with the threads of a final exhaustion
they had the power to weave out upon me. They had the
power to quicken it from loss. I was the focus of a final
rendering which had to reach me cumulatively. It only came
out by fragments.

'If John had not been what he was, we could still have

been Parnellites,' Grandmother asserted.

Mother only partly agreed with her: 'Also, she said with a grave implication, 'it is our religion.'

'Yes, but chiefly John.' Grandmother did not weaken.

It was rags and tatters to me. In spite of politics and creeds, if Father had been different we might have belonged to our neighbours. Father became a clue like Kerrigan. I was afflicted all over again by the shame and doubt that had assailed me before the Thompsons, because he had slept in haystacks and paid strange shoemakers with cheques instead of cash. I was stung and then washed by a spasm of passionate tenderness. No blame could touch him now. His immortal stillness was his shield.

'Jane would have made a fine bishop,' Grandmother said; 'she was brought up at the knees of bishops.'

It lapped over upon me from scraps of conversations that it was always what men *were*, and what women were *not*, upon which verdicts depended. Women were negative. Judgments were cast upon them in darkness, never in the light. It was what was said in a whisper. Women were controlled by marriage in a way by which men were not controlled.

'Our marriages!' Grandmother bewailed often, and always wrung her hands. All of them seemed to have married without approval or against their wills. Grandmother told my mother about her own mother's marriage. It was a happy marriage. She had married for love and never regretted it. But she had married against her parents' wishes. She had eloped with a young man whom they considered 'beneath her'. His financial status did not enter into it. He was condemned by another standard, as one of a lower order. 'They thought he wasn't worth her.' Grandmother explained. 'He was a McNulty and she was a Kinel-Owen in spite of the name Smith which had been thrust upon them during the Denomenclature. As a girl she remembered it. She remembered the transplantation when they were told that their lands no longer belonged to them legally. It was a terrible period, a disastrous time. People have forgotten it now, but when I was a child the stories were still told. The anguish was still remembered. People still knew it. Now they are beginning to forget. My sister Ahn had a wonderful memory. She never forgot anything. She never had a dotage. She kept thoughts crystal clear to the last. I hope you will do the same.' She fixed me with a look that was a sort of seal. It fixed me with Ahn's testimony. It stamped me into her tradition although, at the time, I remained external. I remained separate.

She always had this power to declare meaning upon me. 'We are reduced to women,' she said to me on one occasion so strongly that I took on the reduction and became its ebb at the lowest. Our race ran, she asserted, to strongwilled women and short-lived men. Either foolishness or the sword struck down our men. It made me tremble for James. He was not yet a man but he was going forward in that direction, and he was all the family now had.

Grandmother unloaded distant details upon my mother. Mother would go on with her sewing or reading. She listened and was polite about it but what Grandmother told her never seemed to interest her. She had heard it too often, perhaps. Or she was engaged in balancing it out in her mind in secret. She had no comments. 'My parents,' Grandmother said, 'could never have married if the Earl of Bristol, the *Protestant* Bishop, hadn't started a fund for the restoration of the Long Tower . . . Saint Columba's Church . . . it was built upon the site of his abbey. They eloped.' She always bit off a thread, or snipped something with scissors or fingered her shell earrings at this point. Then, when it had had time to sink in, she added the touches: 'She rode pillion behind him, on a white horse with a scarlet saddlecloth. They came riding down through the woods upon a morning in spring and were married.' I always saw my great-grandmother as an Angevin princess, her veil floating against the neatness of leaves in a Froissart landscape.

'It was a happy marriage. Her parents found out that their opposition was mistaken. They thought he wasn't worth her. She was their beloved daughter and they were

still Kinel-Owens although their name had been changed.'
She looked at me with the phrase still upon her lips. She
sighed. 'Names and lands and *everything* were taken from
them. They were forced to transplant themselves and you
know how it is in *any* moving — so much is left behind.' I
saw rubbish bins filled with the residue of emptied closets.
But it was worse than an ordinary removal. They were
turned out as beggars. It was only their spirits that had
escaped. Their souls had kept their clothes. My great-
grandmother had kept a few Irish silver spoons in her
breast. She had guarded them with a secrecy that had the
quality of miracle. They were as imbedded in this secrecy as
the heart of Jesus which shone through the shirt for the
Blessed Mary Margaret Alocoque. They were part of her
flesh in the image of my imagination. 'Yes,' Grandmother
went on, 'he was worth her. He was a very fine character. He
was the first Catholic allowed to reside within the city ra-
dius after Dowcra's Law.'

I asked what Dowcra's Law was. A law could be asked
about, certainly. She did not answer me. She looked hard at
Mother and said, 'It was ironical.' Her voice was bitter.

I did not know what it was that was ironical. I was only
aware that the irony rested, as shadowy as a menace in the
quiet room. There was the peppery scent of winter chrysan-
themums in the air. The brown blooms were snipped with
yellow. I became strictly aware of the room and its contents
and the two women who sat in it. Ever since Elizabeth and
Brigid had left us we had taken to the drawing room. It was
the brightest and coldest room in the house. It always
needed a *red* fire to warm it. Its grey and gold walls were
fadeless. Its white gilt-edged panels were spotless. The
acanthus leaves in the carpet kept the freshness of a forest.
On the pale marble mantelshelf a pair of Dresden china
donkeys travelled perpetually towards the centre, carrying
their children in panniers. The little girl's dress was the
exact shade of pink roses. The boy's fat thighs were crinkled
into a blue as blue as heaven. Each guided a donkey with
golden twisted cords which were threaded through holes in

their palms and holes in the donkey's nostrils. It always seemed to me that these reins were more real than either the children or the donkeys because they were not made of china. Mother's special favourite was the tall French clock. It stood on high thin pillars which gave it the air of a stork. She never allowed anybody else to wind it up. It chimed out the quarters like bells in a wilderness of meaning, saying that this and that were irremediably so in the midst of any tumult. It had the fragility of glass. It was kept, sheltered, beneath a dome. It was the most potent of all the inanimate objects in that familiar room. It had a voice which gave it an argument. The everlasting laughter upon the faces of the Dresden china children became real when the clock struck. And when Mother played upon the piano, when the ivory keys went in and out like musical echoes, one felt that they were waiting for the clock to call out to them when it had had enough, for a sign which would set them silent, gone quiet as players withdrawn behind the green silken flutes held in place by the fretwood screen. The furniture was walnut; the chairs and sofa upholstered in a horrible amber velvet that clung to your clothes as stickily as honey. On an octagonal table in the centre of the room de luxe editions of the poets were displayed, piled with deliberate carelessness in little heaps: Browning and Tennyson in Morocco bindings; Shelly and Byron and Keats embossed with gilt foliage; Kirke White looking like a missal, with broad tabs of watered silk ribbon to mark the right place to open; Mrs Hemans in bright blue cloth with tiny, parsley-like flowers. The books were as beautiful within as without. Father had always picked the Byron. Tennyson was Mother's choice. Grandmother never read poetry, she sang it. I read them all. There was also a Family Album, fastened with a silver clasp as large as a buckle. Its contents never ceased to be interesting. Grandmother was there as a girl, a fleet long-waisted figure in crinoline with her dark hair looped. She seemed poised for flight, her lovely Greek face caught in a tense, dark dream. There was something about her that always made you wish to hold her and keep her. On the opposite page was a photograph of her dear and beautiful Mary Anderson, Madame Navarro, beside a photograph of Adelina Patti's sister. Father was in the very centre of the album, framed with life-sized Gloire-de-Dijon roses. It was his beardless period when you saw that he was Hugh's brother and James' father. He resembled them both. The photograph which I preferred was the group which had been taken after my return from Glasgow and Dr MacEwan's care. It showed me with crutches and the awful steel patten, but the crutches were laid aside and the patten was buried in the deep bearskin rug upon which Major lay with his head up and his ears and eyes bright with vigilance. He was watching out for the rooster. All of us had the same rooster expression, except Mother who was holding a beribboned Elizabeth upon her lap with a delightful dignity. It was quite evident from her manner that she was not in the habit of holding Elizabeth upon her lap but, at the same time, that Elizabeth was her own child and both beloved and intimate. There was such a bright, delicious harmony about the business, posed there for the man with the rooster. Father's beard was pointed and his eyes as wild as usual. James had his whistle in his pocket. I had a corded basket threaded with a piece of the tartan ribbon which I wore for a sash. There we were, fixed for the future, fastened into the patterns we were bound to follow.

Chapter Twenty-Three

The saga of Jane was unfolded.

Mother said: 'Shy was a tyrannous woman.'

Grandmother said: 'She and my brother John were the wild men of the family. He went to Spain. She went to America. She should have been a boy. She had a man's will.'

'Oh, you all had wills,' Mother ventured quietly.

'Yes perhaps. But Jane was ugly. My mother wished for a son and Jane came. She came before either of the boys was born. She was always plain, plain Jane.' It was a time when Mother and grandmother were wearing black *passementerie* capes, embroidered with thousands of tiny jet beads. They wore beads on their boots and shoes. The capes had taffeta foundations and the necks were ruched with prinked-out frills of black silk. They wore bonnets with ospreys or posies, tied beneath their chins with meticulous bows. They smelt of black silk and orris root. Grandmother liked it when she was dressed up. She would sit for as long as possible before going into her bedroom to take off these outdoor garments. She went on about Jane, smoothing out her gloves and making her handbag creak. It gave a little leather squeak when she opened it. 'When she was growing she was good for nothing, a hobbledehoy. She came in the middle of the family, neither belonging to those who were above her nor to those who where below her. She was a changeling, decidedly in the wrong family. Brigid never could bear her. They were opposites in every respect; then she was neither an intellectual like Ahn nor domesticated like Mary. The two boys who followed her stuck together, and Catherine had me. I was always with Catherine. Jane always walked alone. She was not drawn to books and she was not practical and her fingers were all thumbs. I have heard Brigid say hundreds of times that Jane's stitches were like nothing so much as a horse's gallops, leagues between. She couldn't sew on a button.'

Jane was revealed to me as a particularly forlorn duckling in a strongly individualised family. If it had not been that she had deprived my mother of eggs for breakfast, she would have aroused my sympathy. As it was I saw her objectively and was merely curious about her. She was both the failure and the success, the one who had touched both the bottom and the top according to my grandmother's own standards. She was actually a person of destiny, as bound as any Napoleon to her events and doom. She was a subject of prophecy. It was a prophecy that had sent her to America. She had suffered a visitation as directly as Abraham who had an angel upon his threshold. In her instance the angel was a deaf and dumb beggar who came to the house selling needles and tapes. Jane, the idle and the lost, was the one who opened the door to him. She was then a girl in her teens. She was filled with a great pity of the poor beggar. She responded to his inarticulateness as a Samaritan. She brought him water in a basin and a towel and, when he was clean enough to eat, she brought him bread and milk. She ministered to him, smiling her wide ugly smile. Suddenly he began to make urgent gestures to her. She was frightened until she realised that he was violently endeavouring to convey some important truth to her. He waved his fingers up and down in an undulating motion to show her that she was going to cross the sea. He began to scrape imaginary coins into his palm to indicate that she would acquire riches. Jane believed implicitly in his forecast. Her pattern was set from that moment. She did not care when they laughed at her credulity. The beggar had shown her a way of escape from a family to which she did not very particularly feel that she belonged. He had cast her outward, forward into a place in a larger world. It was the period of the emigrations to America which had begun after the Famine. Jane spoke impulsively of going to New York and was crushed into silence by her father's opposition. He would not hear of such a project. He put his foot down. He reasoned with her. He did his utmost to dissuade her from the idea that obsessed her. He committed her to the Catholic bishop, Dr MacDevitt, who was both his neighbour and his intimate friend. Dr MacDevitt did his best with the rebellious girl. He had been educated in Paris. He tried to convince her that the outside world was evil in its essence and did his utmost to guide her from the wildness of trusting it. Jane believed him. She never doubted that he knew what he was talking about. But America was not Paris. Thousands had already gone there and nothing apparently but good had happened to them. She quoted her father who quoted the old Earl of Bristol who had maintained before his death that it was the Irish who had helped to lose America to the British. That, in Jane's estimation, was anything but evil. But she was unable to break down the opposition against her desire. Her mother sided against her. She had allowed Ahn to go to Paris. She had accepted her eldest son's service in a Spanish army. She had accepted her youngest and favourite son's departure to England, but he had died there and that was too much. She could not bear to let Jane go. She could not bear to risk another loss. She recalled to Jane the circumstances of her brother's death. She had been awakened in the middle of the night by the noise of the furniture in her son's room being dragged across the floor. She had risen from her bed and gone upstairs to the room from which the tumult came. Every piece of furniture was quietly and peacefully in its accustomed place. At breakfast, the next morning, she announced that something had happened to her beloved boy. And when news came, weeks later, it transpired that he had died upon the night of her warning.

Jane saw that she would never be able to persuade her parents to accept her ambition. Suddenly she became a reformed character. She gave up all efforts about the American plan. She ceased to speak of it. She allowed the subject to wilt and die upon the lips of others. She became simply a dependable and reliable girl. She began to guard her secret, keeping it folded within herself. She changed. She began to

oblige everybody. Nothing that was asked of her was refused. She copied French memoirs for Ahn. She took out
basting threads and carried hot irons for Brigid. She washed
dishes for Mary — but all at a price. They had to pay her, a
penny here and a penny there. For some things her rates
went as high as sixpence. She also began to act like a lady of
charity to others outside her home. She was seen carrying
baskets of damsons or apples to houses into which none of
the others ever went. It was assumed that somebody was
sick there. Jane never explained herself. She was closed up
into a rigid, adolescent pride, apparently at the stage where
girls become slightly queer and individualistic. It was only
years later that the family discovered with horror that Jane
had a price for her apples and damsons just as she had a
price for her services. Moreover, she took them only to the
households of men connected with the sea, to the families of
sea captains and sailors and ships' officers. Jane was a girl
with an idea that dominated her. She worked towards its
fulfilment as men in prison strive towards their liberation —
with all her will and the advantage of any and every opportunity. She *had* to go to America as definitely as migratory
birds had to go to Africa or return again to northern climates.

Time brought Jane to the day when she actually had her
ticket to America bought and paid for. At that time you
could go to America for the sum of five pounds. She also
had a surplus, a sum sufficient to tide her over a period of
initiation. She had a distinct plan and scheme. She had
evidently weighed what she could do against what she
could not do. She had made a collection of her sisters'
dresses, made by Brigid's exquisite workmanship. Nobody
ever wondered why Jane kept dresses which she did not
wear. The others had discarded them, but that was not why
Jane preserved them. She had her plan.

She intended to depart without a word, to go forth from
her home like a thief in the night. She was compelled to act
clandestinely because proof had been given her that none
would willingly ever allow her to go. Nobody believed in
her. If her brother had not died in England things might

have been different. But he had caught pneumonia from sleeping in a damp bed in Dickens' Dotheboys Hall, then an Inn, and his death had become the label of her defeat.

She did not, when the time came, go like a thief in the night. She was preserved from that larceny by her mother's vigilance. Just as she was about to creep out of the house her mother came into her room. Jane froze in an agony of suspense. 'I heard you moving,' her mother said quietly. She saw her daughter in the morning twilight, all dressed up in bonnet and gloves. There was no time for argument. Neither of them argued. They faced each other in shadow, in a sort of limbo where life for the girl waited. Quickly she cast herself upon her mother's faith. She told her everything — that she had her ticket, that the boat was due to sail, that her trunk was outside in a handcart with a boy, ready. She pleaded with the strict eloquence of those who have been subjected to prophecy and been made obedient to an *idée fixe*. There must have emanated from her some extreme discipline, some determination so pure that it won her mother, for her mother accepted the situation. She consented. She not only gave in but she assisted her. Very quickly she brought her own savings and thrust them into Jane's hand. Who knows what private ruling in the older woman's soul gave her the strength and clairvoyance to believe in this mutinous girl in her extremity? She trusted her. They clasped each other with a passionate brevity; they wept a little — and that was all. Jane went forth with a blessing instead of a curse. She was able to go freely and not sneakingly. The only fly in the amber of her relief was an enormous featherbed. It was the one clause her mother maintained — that Jane should take her own bed with her. She insisted upon it as a charter for her peace of mind. If she could be sure that Jane would always have an aired bed to sleep upon it would diminish her anxiety. Jane had to give in about it. A featherbed was a trifle in the midst of such decisions. But it must have been as much of a problem as the last-minute thrust of a fat woman's companionship. It must have been hard to *place*. She couldn't squeeze it into her handbag or run out with it in her arms, and the ship was waiting.

Jane's mother watched that dawn come by a window. She watched the river. She must have heard the strange moaning music of the emigrants come up upon the wind. When the family was gathered around the breakfast table she told them that Jane had gone. She defended her. Then she ceased to talk about her. She kept her for her prayers. None of them ever knew what magic she used with her husband but he never, at any time, was heard to say a solitary word against Jane. Gradually Jane's letters began to bring them her news from America.

It was my mother who told me what Jane did when she got to New York. She found a room and installed herself and the featherbed in it. She went out and bought writing materials and spent her first night writing elaborate letters, each addressed to a 'Dear Madame', and assuring the recipient that she had arrived from the European Continent with the latest styles and fashions and intended forthwith to open an establishment which would specialise in ball dresses and riding habits for ladies. She intended also only to use the finest materials and the most exquisite workmanship. Perfection in fit, taste and design was to be her motto. The letters were written in a fine, pointed hand-writing which she had practised out upon Ahn's French memoirs. She sealed her letters and the first thing the next morning she took them with her, out into the foreign, alien streets. She did not mail them. She inquired where the fashionable residences of New York were and, with her own hand, thrust her letters into the mailboxes of these establishments when she found them. She went back into her bare room, where the featherbed was bundled into a closet, and waited.

Her first client was an Astor, Laura Astor Delano. Her first task was an Astor wedding. No more fortunate opportunity could have fallen upon her.

Jane did not know what an Astor was. All she knew was that she had a client. She received her with a regal air in her poor room, excusing the lack of furniture with a grand gesture of exasperation. She was all upside down, she declared, in an afflicting state of *déménagement*. Her furniture had not yet come. She did not know whether she was standing upon her head or upon her heels. She then launched forth into comparisons with Catherine the Great. Women were always tortured in their ambitions. She had her life set upon a plan that needed the magnificence of queens to support it. Somewhere out of her subconsciousness she raked up scandals about the great in Europe and displayed these intimacies before her visitor as though she were displaying silks and satins. She came out with incidents about eminent persons which could only have reached her ears in childhood when she had overheard her sisters repeating tall tales which had been recounted by the scandalous Earl of Bristol who, it was well known, lived like a petty prince when he went abroad. If Jane had any uncertainties about the truth of what she was saying she was quite certain as to why she was saying it. Her extremity had to have a rationality that would both magnify her to her visitor and enchant her. What was significant was that this lady, whose carriage waited at her doorstep, was a potential customer. Her life depended upon her. She took her measurements with the discretion of a Court Physician feeling the pulse of a Dauphin.

What was significant in the eyes of her visitor was the beautiful workmanship of the dress Jane was wearing. It was one of Brigid's. It had been made by Brigid, and Brigid had the hands and fingers of an artist. So it was Brigid, who had never approved of her, who sold Jane to her first customer.

Jane's next move was to engage a sempstress, the best sempstress she could find. She discovered an excellent one. That, again was her luck. Providence — and her mother's prayers — was with her. Her strong faith in the deaf and dumb man's prophecy was with her. She could not sew. She had never made a dress in her life. But having obtained an order she could afford to hire somebody who could sew. The rest would follow. She had learned one thing from watching

Brigid: she knew when a dress fitted and when it didn't. She knew how a dress should express its wearer. She had heard Brigid say often enough that what Ahn could wear was not what Mary could wear, and that what she herself could wear would never do for Jane. So Jane was aware of differences. She also knew the value and quality of materials and she had a good taste for colours. She knew what was not vulgar.

But Laura Astor Delano liked Jane for herself. Her wit and character charmed her. Jane had not served her apprenticeship to Ahn for nothing. Escaped from the judgments of her family she suddenly took on their quality. She and Laura became friends and remained friends until Mrs Delano died.

And Jane succeeded *as a dressmaker*. In a very short while she had a real workroom with several women working for her. Her clientèle increased steadily. In a few years the riches the beggar had prophesied for her were pouring in upon her. It was through her connection with the Astors that she began to acquire land and build houses. She grew in dignity and splendour and the letters she wrote home assured her mother of her safety to such an extent that permission was given for Elizabeth to go to her after Catherine died. Elizabeth went out under the chaperonage of Mrs Gavan Duffy.

It was this Laura Delano who offered Jane a curious gift. She offered her an island in the East River. She didn't know what to do with it. She had a feeling that Jane, who was able to work miracles, might have found some marvellous use for it. But Jane fell down on the island. She refused it. She was a busy woman; she had her hands full. What, she demanded of her friend, could she do with an island? She would have had to buy a boat to reach it and hire a man to row the boat — and she had no time to waste. Ahn would never have refused an island. Ahn had imagination. She would have kept it purely because it was an island. Jane had not that particular sort of imagination, and her experience was against it. It would only have been a trap for added responsibilities which must have been, even then, quite onerous for her single shoulders. She was actually so prosperous and flourishing that she had no time to enjoy her success.

Another curious thing happened to her, one which had a very direct bearing upon her success. At the very beginning of it she was approached by a young Frenchwoman who had heard that she required fine needleship. She told Jane an extraordinary story. She was the daughter of a French nobleman who had escaped with her from France when she was barely sixteen, at the time of the Revolution. They had escaped with their lives and not a vestige of belongings. On the ship which brought them to the States her father became gravely ill and died. Upon his deathbed he insisted upon her marriage to a young man who was one of the passengers. This young man had paid her some attentions but she knew nothing about him and was utterly astonished to discover that he wished to marry her. Her father was tormented on her account. He felt he had to confide her to somebody and there was nobody but this young man, who wished to become her husband. The moment they arrived in New York this girl of sixteen was taken off in a carriage by her bridegroom to a strange house where he confined her to an attic. For years he kept her confined in this attic under lock and key. He never allowed her to go out. All that she saw of New York, she said, were the birds flying across the skies. Her husband did not beat her or maltreat her in person. He simply made her his prisoner. He was a very strange individual. He never went out in the daytime, only at night, and night after night in succession. He habitually brought home sacks of jewels which he melted out of their settings He sold the gold and the gems. He never explained anything to her, neither where the jewels came from nor why he had to melt them down. She was convinced that they were Royal jewels but where or how he obtained them was a mystery to her. She assured Jane that she had had moments when she was convinced that she had lost her reason during the Revolution and that everything else that had followed was a nightmarish dream. Her confinement endured for years. And then, finally, when she had utterly abandoned any hope of release from her husband's vigilance he went out one day and did not lock the door. He was only going out for a few minute to buy food but she profited by his carelessness. She fled. She might have met him upon the stairs. She flew like the wind down the stairs and out into the streets and onward without looking either to right or left. She did not stop until she was so out of breath that she could not go on and then she took refuge in a doorway. Every second she expected to see his shadow. When she realised that she had truly escaped and that he was not following her she went out into the street again and walked until she came to a church. A clergyman was kind to her. He gave her money. He sent her to the house of some French people. It was there that she had been given Jane's address. She walked into Jane's house on Ninth Street and Jane believed every word she told her. She would not reveal either the name of her father or her husband. All she gave was her first name, Natalie. She became Madame Natalie. She was a godsend to Jane who made her her forewoman. She became Jane's right-hand man. Together they maintained a high standard of taste and efficiency. She worked for Jane until her marriage. It was Jane who advised her to marry. It was Jane who advised her to forget that she had ever been married or that anybody existed who might ever make a claim to her. 'Put him out of your mind completely,' she advised, and Natalie took her advice. She married a very rich man with an estate in the country. She was happy. She began to feel safe and protected. But every now and then, my mother said, a queer haunted look would fill her dark eyes with a fearful sadness.

Mother had stayed with this Natalie when she was visiting New York with her Aunt Waters. She was then a very young girl. They had stayed with her in a lovely house in the country, surrounded by a park. Everything was beautiful and serene and both Natalie and her husband seemed very happy. It was with a most terrible shock that when her Aunt Waters opened an American newspaper, shortly after her return to her home in Derry, the first thing she saw upon the first page was that Natalie had been murdered. She had been shot in her own park a few days after they had last seen her. 'The last thing I remember of her,' Mother said, 'was her standing upon the terrace, waving her good-bye to us. Her husband was not there. He had gone out with a gun to shoot larks.'

Her death remained as great a mystery as her marriage. It was never discovered who had shot her. All sorts of conjectures arose in me: perhaps she had confessed her past to her husband after seeing Aunt Waters. Perhaps it was her husband who had shot her. A man who could shoot larks, I imagined, would be capable of shooting his wife. But Mother always thought that it was her first husband who had found her.

Grandmother revealed to me that Jane had no luck in her love affairs. She fell in love with the wrong men. Her grand passion was awakened by a clerical student. He was an Episcopalian and she was utterly unable to reveal this to her parents. It was also utterly impossible for her to deceive them. She had tried deceit once and it was one of the most gratifying things in her life that her mother had found it out in *time*. She waited until this young man was ordained. She had built a new house in E. 51st Street and she was determined to live in it as a married woman. When everything was ready for the wedding she wrote a long letter to her mother in which she asked for her blessing and, at the same time, proved to her that she intended to marry the man of her choice whether her mother approved or not. It was a strong, reasonable letter in which she uttered her sincerest thoughts. She believed firmly that the consent would come. What actually came was a letter that announced her mother's death. She died before Jane's letter was delivered. The letters had crossed. Jane was stricken with a deep and lasting grief. She was filled with an unbearable remorse in which the death of her mother took on the force of a judgment. It became a verdict. She felt that she had failed her mother and the failure plunged her into regret for her rebelliousness. She regretted that she had left home. She did not, perhaps, regret the justification of her success, but it became void to her. It became tasteless and valueless. In this mood she broke off her engagement. She wrote to her fiancé that she was now prevented from marrying him. She explained that she could have fought the living to get him. She could not fight the dead. The cause and the argument both died on her. She refused to see him. For her the whole matter of her love came to a definite end. She entered into possession of her house in a state of mourning.

A curious thing happened to her. There was a night in which she was unable to sleep. She rose from her bed and turned on the light and there was a large black dog upon her threshold. When she looked at him he vanished. She went into the corridor and there was no sign of him. There was no sign of him at the head of the stairs. There was nowhere he could have gone. He had simply disappeared. The next morning news was brought to her that her fiancé had committed suicide. She always associated this with the black dog. The image added to her woe. She was convinced that she had helped to damn this young man's soul.

From this period onwards a change took place in her character. Her spontaneousness and courage vanished. She became a grave, stern woman. She became overreligious. She began to subscribe to public charities and good causes. The private, happy charity of her large heart and spirit disappeared. She planned to return to her native place.

Grandmother said: 'She *had* to come back. It was stronger than her will against it. Her roots were here. Why, Katie, we have the earth and stones of this place in our blood.'

They became silent before me. I did not possess their understanding of some full truth. Their meaning was suspended. I was swung out with them upon its fringes, touched by their wind from the past.

'It would have been better for us all if she had stayed in America.'

Grandmother shook her head. She denied it. Jane, she said, had nobody to hold her there.

'She had me,' Mother said bitterly and desperately.

'Yes. I tried to get you back. I should never have given her to you. You were mine, Katie.' She stared at Katie. Their faces were contracted with a secret opposition. The silence struck, iron-hard between them. It not only stopped speech. It froze it at its origins. I was touched as by ice. Pain and injustice and some hopeless and irrevocable fate held us all in a vice. We were obliged to turn our faces from each other as from what could not be witnessed.

'I was the payment,' Mother said at last, her voice lapping like a wave that had struggled to reach the shore.

'No, Katie. You were apart. You didn't know. I was the one who paid. You see, you see I couldn't bear that you were a McKenna . . . that was at first, before your father died. If only I had known that he was not going to *live*, I could have borne it better. It was all so obnoxious to me. None but myself can know. I made a mistake, a very terrible mistake. Then, when he was dying, I regretted what I had done.' She sighed. 'It was then too late . . . and I had not the courage for the opposite reason.' As though afraid that Mother would argue, she went on, quickened: 'I promised your father on his deathbed that I would go to see his people if ever I should be in Dublin, particularly his two sisters. To tell you the truth I was afraid to go. They would only have blamed me for leaving him . . . so I never went to Dublin.' She shuddered as the subtlety slipped from her, the means by which she had evaded the keeping of her word. The unvisited women in Dublin seemed to hang over us in the room, waiting, waiting, waiting. 'forgive us our trespasses as we forgive those who trespass against us.' The prayer moaned itself upon the train of the excuse. It was a plea from the depths of her spirit. She avoided my mother's steady full eyes. She said: 'There were a lot of nephews, I believe, his brother's boys, McKennas. . . .'

'I should have enjoyed cousins.' Mother's resoluteness sprang from her, ripened long ago in some dire necessity.

'Yes. I sometimes thought of that. But they were all boys, Katie, and when we first came back to Derry, when we were staying that first time with Ahn and Brigid you were not

alone. You had the Sigerson little girls next door, Annie and
Dora. You were always with them. They were like sisters
to you.'

'I know. I loved them. I adored Annie. But all the same. . . .'

The unfulfilment swelled out and became oppressive.
Grandmother put a stop to it. 'Well, there it is. But they are
still there, Katie, unless some of them have died. You can
still find out about them.'

I remember the gleam that assailed my mother's eyes, the
sort of hope that lightened the blame in them. I never knew
what effort she made to reach these cousins. All I know is
that a very long time later when I mentioned Stephen
McKenna's translation of Plotinus to her she said: 'I had a
cousin Stephen. We had the same aunts in Dublin.'

The futility of these two women struck at me in a sort of
wonder. It was mitigated in its display by the wisps of facts
attached to it. My horizon was enlarged by something actual
and, at the same time, withdrawn from the actuality. I remained as external to their affairs as to the affairs of Mrs
Thomas Carlisle and the house in Ecclefechan where nothing ever came clear and happy, and where a husband who
could only be reached through *Frederick the Great* or the
French Revolution or upon the terms of *Sartor Resartus* was
equivalent to no husband at all. My people had the same
negativeness. Their truths swelled and fled like clouds in the
sky. What was real was not derived from those who were
alive but from those who were dead. Aunt Waters and her
private chapel and Marat and his bathtub and Necker who
had both a daughter and a diamond necklace were intensi-
fied in their reality. As far as the living were concerned I was
cast out like Emily Brontë's Catherine into a world where no
voice *answered*. Things were uttered but questions were
denied.

I went for long walks with dogs and goats and cats in my
train and sat, desolate as anybody in agony, upon rocks
above the valley and tormented myself with life. It was the
first decade of the twentieth century and this deep unrest
and urging was in the air. I was responsive to it simply

because I was of its generation. I did not know what it was. I remember watching a man ploughing in the fields below me. He was thrusting his iron spear into the rich, dark loam, a multitude of crows swarming upon his heels. I envied him his action. He and I were matched in the solitude, doer and witness. I envied him the force and fertility of his labour. I did not know that I was suffering growth and that the black stir within me was only a good proof of change and progress. The lovely planted valley was a wound to me with its secret firesides, with the closed lives of human beings which never opened to me. I was curious about them, thirsty for their *meaning*. Saint Thomas Aquinas understood this mood. It is the desolation of the unfound, the blind groping towards the unknown. The spirit of man is subject to this seeking. It is as thermal as brotherhood, its heats are in our blood. I was young and it worked in me as a dark and sullen rage, a furious sadness that made everything my eyes or senses fell upon become nostalgic. I would come home with my eyes blazing and not a word upon my lips.

I remember my grandmother turning upon me with astonishment when I committed some trifling rudeness. She had asked me to shut a door and I had banged it. 'Kathleen, what is it?' she cried out, and I was harnessed by the mere tones of her voice to a lasting rebuke. At the time we only stared at each other, out of sympathy, separated into a hard crystallised defiance that gave out upon my abrupt denial: 'Nothing,' I said.

Her own unrest was exposed to me because she was no longer able to contain it. It came out upon the slightest contact or provocation. A stranger was a signpost to it: I went with her to the dressmaker's. She was not having a dress made. She was bestowing upon Miss McLoughlin one of her *passementerie* capes. It was held out in the firelight, a black garment twinkling with clusters of jet and warmed where the material was cut out in stencils by the blaze from the fire. Miss McLoughlin said that it was beautiful. She kept feeling it caressingly, too shy to put it on.

Grandmother said: 'I am thinking of going to America.'

'Beautiful,' Miss McLoughlin repeated. She put the cape on timidly, hugging it to her thin frame. It acquired a gentleness upon her thin body which it never showed when Grandmother wore it. It became *tender*. She gazed at herself in the tiny mirror nailed to the corner of her dresser. I saw my own face, tilted with excitement. I saw myself objectively as I saw the girl Gwendolen who was the niece of the lady who owned the hotel. Gwendolen was fair and I was dark, but we were young in common. These others were old.

Grandmother said, not belonging to anybody but herself: 'I was a fool to sell my New York property. I did it for Katie. I should never have come back to stay. It was Jane's fault. She had such a strong will. We all had to obey her.'

Miss McLoughlin took off the cape. She laid it upon a chair and moved in slippered feet across the tiny, spotless, glowing kitchen. She took cups and saucers off the dresser and laid them upon the strip of cleared table beside her sewing machine. 'I'll make you a cup of tea,' she said shyly, beguiling my grandmother to stay.

Grandmother heard but she paid no attention to the invitation. 'Jane should have been a man. She would have made a fine cardinal.'

'Oh, not a cardinal.' Miss McLoughlin let out a little giggle.

'Why not? She had an excellent mind. She'd have been a marvel in a conclave. Haven't you heard it said that one of the popes was a woman? For that matter they say that Queen Elizabeth was a man?' She shivered. 'That is the bottom of the scale. A woman who becomes a man becomes a devil.'

Miss McLoughlin looked shocked and frightened. Grandmother went on, sublimating it: 'When Jane set her mind upon a plan nothing could stop her. When she wanted Mass said in her chapel the bishop denied her. He said, what was perfectly true, that she was only a few minutes away from the cathedral. All she had to do was to step into her carriage. But no, Jane wanted Mass said in her own chapel. It was right next to her bedroom, only a door between. So she wrote to the Pope and she got her permission from the Vatican. She always got what she wanted, except with love.' She sat down upon the chair with the cape. Miss McLoughlin whisked it off in time. 'Her death was a martyrdom. But every morning she got up and heard Mass in her little chapel. They say her moans were frightful to listen to. In the end she did not know what she was doing. The house was full of priests. I've been told that there was always one going up or coming down the staircase. Jane believed that she was suffering her Purgatory upon this earth and that when she died she would enter directly into Paradise. Imagine,' Grandmother said, as she turned upon Miss McLoughlin in a sort of fury, 'they charged twenty-five pounds a Mass for the peace of her soul. Did you ever hear anything like it?'

'I never heard the likes of it.' Miss McLoughlin stood in the centre of the floor, clasping her hands. Her expression was exuberant, overflowing, urgent with the quality of children who wished for more. As soon as Grandmother looked at her, the exuberance faded. Hastily she thrust her arm forward and changed the kettle from one hob to the other, from the black side to the red side of the fire. 'Would you like some buttered toast, Ma'am?'

'Nothing, thank you, nothing at all.'

The kettle began to spit and bluster. Grandmother stood up. Miss McLoughlin seized the kettle and poured the boiling water into her brown teapot. 'Don't go, Ma'am. It won't take any time to draw. It's a good blend of tea I have, I get it from O'Doherty's.' When she saw that Grandmother did not sit down again she went over to the window and wiped the steam off with the cushion of her palm. Her thin face and straggly-haired head were cut against her scarlet geraniums. She took up a pot of musk and offered it to my grandmother: 'Would you like this?'

'Oh, thank you, I would but I have one already and then my room is on the damp side of the house. Keep it, it is better here. You have the sun.'

Miss McLoughlin put the pot back upon the window sill. 'Nobody ever goes by these days except the people from the farm. That woman has just had her fifteenth child.'

Grandmother stood very upright, joined imperiously to what condemned a fifteenth child. 'She's very prolific,' she remarked coldly but she regarded Miss McLoughlin as though she had committed an indiscretion.

'Please let me give you one cup of tea?' Miss McLoughlin pleaded. But Grandmother would not stay.

Outside upon the road homeward, when we were out of sight and out of hearing of Miss McLoughlin's, she said: 'I talk too much. I never used to.' She was complaining. 'It chokes me.'

There was another version of Aunt Waters' death: 'The unkindest thing Jane ever did,' Grandmother revealed to Mother, 'was to die so quickly and at that particular moment. She died before I got here. As soon as I heard about her illness, I came. I was too late. Before I could land Kerrigan's letter was put into my hand, telling me that she had died and that you were in Dublin — *on your honeymoon.* Ahn and Brigid were still away touring the Lakes. I was struck down — as I was struck down upon the day of my own marriage. If Jane were there, conscious in her spirit of what was happening, she must have suffered my suffering. My will died inside me. I was unable to get off the boat. I stayed in my cabin. I wept and raged like a fool. I stayed on the boat until it sailed again. Neither Ahn nor Brigid ever forgave me for that. What did they know about it! They were old maids. They had not the heart of a mother. When I thought of you, Katie, shut up after Jane's death, in Edenbank with a pack of servants under the domination of that vile Kerrigan . . . well, I couldn't bear to imagine it. . . .'

Mother explained nothing. The tragedy unfolded itself in their silence.

Grandmother gave me a sequence at another time, in another place: 'Your mother has never told me why she married your father. He was engaged to marry Kerrigan and how he came to marry your mother has never been explained to me. He wasn't in love with her, nor with

Kerrigan. He was in love with a girl he knew in America, a cousin. I think he met Kerrigan in America. I don't know. I have never been told.'

'Perhaps Mother wanted to marry him,' I said, with evocative innocence.

Grandmother stared my innocence into its place. 'They were married in the cathedral, at six o'clock in the morning, and by a priest who ought to have known better.'

Chapter Twenty-Four

I was not conscious of any unrest in my mother until it became articulate with a suddenness that involved everybody. She began to write letters continually and quantitatively. Stacks of her smoke-grey envelopes, addressed in violet ink, piled up upon her bureau. She wrote to friends and universities and house agents and foreign mayors. Then one day, for no reason at all, she declared in my presence: 'I see that I must give up this house. I do not know how I shall be able to live without a garden.'

A curious secret thrill was communicated between me and my grandmother. Each of us was thankful. A new horizon was coming. We were beginning to move, like satellites, towards a more valid world. In those brief words of hers our stability was shaken. I, the deprived one, was threatened deliciously with some land of promise. Globes of experience that were labelled for my mother with the names of places — Terregles and Talacre and Traquair and the people who lived in them — began to float out towards me with my own labels. If Elizabeth's and Brigid's letters could contain references to girls with German names like Bluetta, or German nuns who rang bells before daylight and *aspersed* you with Holy Water before you could get your eyes open; and if James had Brother Tatiana and best friends who were called Bliss, and confectioners' accounts in a street in a town on the Scottish Borderland, then soon I, upon my individualised part, would be moving into personal contacts. I, too, would know strange people and perform my own strangenesses. I hadn't the faintest notion what they would be but I was confident that they would be remarkable.

We had an omen to mark the dissolution. A dove was closed into the drawing room. Nobody knew how it had come there. Margot swore that it was not there when she lit the fire. It was only after the fire was lit that she saw it, sailing across the ceiling. She was scared to death and began to shoo it out. During the winter weeks our windows were nailed down on the outside to prevent them from rattling. Only a small margin was left for them to open at the top and at the bottom. It was not a large enough opening for the bird to escape by flight. It could have squeezed its way through if it had approached the opening quietly. When Margot tried to chase it out it became frightened.

Mother and I heard the commotion and reached the drawing room at the same time, by different doors.

Margot cried out: 'God, Ma'am, I don't like it. It's a bad sign. It means something is going to happen to us.'

Mother sent her to find MacDaid and have one of the windows opened. The poor bird did not seem to know that it could escape by the door. Mother was afraid that it would fly into the flames. She was afraid that it would, in its panic, alight upon her beloved clock and send its delicate mechanism crashing to the fender. The poor bird was dashing itself blindly against the deceptive windows and against the walls. Its impotence was uncanny. Its greyness beat against the grey walls and was grey with them. It almost seemed to me that it took on the pattern, that tiny leaves of gold were stamped upon its plumage. Its distraught eyes were small black plates that reddened wildly against the light. Its grey claws had pink edges. Its terror became a pure undiluted terror in the tranquillity of that room. Its frustration became the substance of our own. All checks and limits met in us and combined and became cathartic. Fear became present. We all waited for the opening. We were all caught in the will of this wild caprice and whirled with this bird's wings out of the serenity that was there, battling against the freedom that had not been taken away. How was this bird to know that it was not a prisoner! It forecast upon us its own terror so that we, also, reached this driven and hunted climate where no liberty could be acknowledged.

I often remember that bird and its symbolism. When

Margot declared it upon us as an omen she struck the truth. Mother's fear that her clock, her striker of bells in Time, was in danger, had a real significance. Her fear that the innocent bird would fall into the flames projected itself into the future. And I, the young and untried, was caught in the terror without knowing what it was about. The process of the human consciousness is built up and sublimated in this fashion. Each of us is let out by our own doors. Religion seeks to standardise the signs, to sacrifice the *Fear*, to liberate us. The eternal argument is between God and this darkness.

We were so rooted in that house in Glendermott. It contained our growth and our first conscious flexibilities. We belonged there. It was our *Cherry Orchard*. When Mother decided against it she sold us from our orchard. She did not do it to deceive us. On the contrary she weighed the matter out entirely upon our needs and values. She did it for us, not against us. All over the world roots were loosening. A new and surging generation was crying out for breaks with the past. It was the beginning of a stronger century.

Mother certainly did not make the change lightly. She took months to consider it. She went about the house looking like Saint Brigid — with a balance instead of a church in her hands. She began to make lists and to examine objects. She was more conservative than my grandmother and more stable than my father. It could never have been easy for her to break the shape of her life. The impermanent quality of places in her own childhood had set her a standard of durability that was a secret passion to her. She did not wish to leave Glendermott. She was forced in our interests to leave it. She was the one most conscious of those interests in their full meaning.

She said, standing in a beam of sunshine, with a breeze blowing in the scents from the garden: 'If only I could *see* into the future!' It was the cry of those who are uncertain and do not know what they are doing.

'You see, Kathleen, there is no *future* here.' I did not understand. She saw that I did not understand. She tried to convey her meaning and only confused it for me. She said: 'The July after your father died, do you remember that lump that appeared in Rory's ear?'

I remembered. I stared at her, wondering what the sequence was.

'He was shot, Kathleen. I did not tell you at the time, any of you. I did not wish you to know that people were going about with guns.'

'Why should Rory be shot?' I demanded, indignant.

She made an impotent gesture, a shrug with her shoulders. 'That's just it. It seems such a stupid thing to do, to shoot a dog. I know you don't understand it, neither do I. Either they do that sort of thing or they plant orange lilies in your flower beds — just to remind you that they are *there*.' When I asked who was there she said she couldn't tell me. She didn't know. Nobody ever knew. She brought back to me the finding of the bright vulgar orange flower in her roses and I was shocked all over again with the same feeling, the sense of iniquitous taste. It was distinctly something that would have been better left undone. Its effect was negative. But the knowledge that dogs could be shot and outrageous colours planted in the garden stayed with me. Mother could quite easily have used the occasion to imbue me with political intolerance but she did not do this for the simple reason that she was not politically intolerant. The incident had escaped from her confidence because it was part of what was urging her to leave this place for us, not for herself. She had lived with these mild dangers for years. It was something that was a wider and greater menace that was chasing her away now.

Change crept in upon us like a climate. The idea grew gradually. It strengthened from indecision into determination. Grandmother accepted it from the beginning. She knew that its cause was strong. Its effect upon her was one of relaxation. She began to take her breakfast in bed. She began to say to Mother and Margot and me and anybody she came across that she was 'getting lazy'. Some long tension was released in her. She was the only one who took coffee for breakfast. Her 'American habit', she called it. Margot would prepare her tray and I would take it in to her and sit up upon her high bed while she indulged in her laziness. First of all, before she touched a thing, she always asked for her hand mirror. She examined her face and arranged her hair and put on her cap. She had to make sure that her beauty was still there. 'I am always afraid to become unrecognisable,' she would remark. It was not said for me but for the young man in Lincoln's army whom she hoped to meet in Paradise.

She was lazy in the morning and lazy again in the evening. She never accepted when Mother invited her to a drive in the late afternoons. Mother and I would set out in daylight and return in twilight. It was on these drives that I began to know my mother. She is set within their frame as clearly as the photographs in the family album.

There was a drive at the edge of winter, in one of those evenings when lights hang like stars. The earth was hard with frost. In the Waterside marshes, beyond the Military Barracks, skaters were ringed with lanterns. The river bordered them in a long ribbon of reflected light and suspended animation. It was a scroll without motion. Against it their distant waltzing forms were spun like magic, like figures upon a music box, rhythmic and intensely unreal. I was bewitched by this sudden spectacle caught between the near branches of trees. Mother stopped the horse. His breathing heaved like gigantic bellows. The harness creaked. And far off, borne upon the mystery, came the tinkling laughter and delight of beings who did not appear to be human. They were imposed upon us as a sort of fairyland. They destroyed the earth on us and lifted us up on a plane where everything came with the lightness and softness of feathers.

Out along that road I remember how often we saw into the lighted rooms of houses and gardens or came upon lifted iron gates, dark and fine as lace, their pattern cut upon a bas-relief of shadow. Mother would say: 'That's where the Glendinnings live, or the Loughreys, or somebody else.' The labels came out upon fair-headed girls leaning forwards upon firelit hearths, or a boy blowing a trumpet, or a man standing, muffled, and shaking the weather from him in sneezes, or a woman in a red-cloth coat with yellow furs. These intimate strangers were a foretaste of the cinema to me, pieces of their private lives were exposed deliciously.

In the long summer days the revelations became different. They were less stolen and not so sweet and the gardens were lovelier and more vivid. When Mrs Loughrey looked at me, coming down the aisle in church, I met her eyes with a sort of challenge, wondering if she could guess that I knew that her drawing room was a green drawing room and that her lampshades were pink. When I saw the Harvey boy in the watchmaker's and he stared at me, I stared just as hard back at him, supported in secret by having seen him blown out in an effort to blow a trumpet.

These were certainly my years of abeyance, the years in which reality was held off, years without aggression. I was whirled within moons and dreams, as enclosed as planets in the fullness of space. I had no more purpose than a balloon that sailed with the wind's caprice. I was contained in an extraordinary innocence, preserved in an extraordinary magic.

It was on our drives that Mother broke her reserves, and when she broke her silences it was to cast me upon another magic — the wonder of her heart. 'I could have done anything with your father if I could have got him away from his family. They were his destruction. He never had a real chance.' She defended him. She was on his side. I had misjudged her as I had misjudged him. I could not confess it to her. I could only listen.

Once, when we were driving past Edenbank out towards flaxgreen fields, she said: 'When your father first came to see me he brought me a bouquet of red roses, the reddest roses I have ever seen. I was sitting by the window.'

That was all, but I knew from the tone of her voice that there was more to it than evil. She, as well as the wicked Kerrigan, had had her will in it. She had loved my father.

The young girl who had 'never had enough to eat', whose contact with life had been restricted to the absent — her school companions and a mother who had deserted her and a tyrannous aunt — had welcomed the dark mercurial man I had known as Father into her loneliness. It was not her fault that the marriage had not succeeded. Was it his? How was I to judge?

She said another time: 'That first year, before you were born, his mother and sisters were never out of the house. They took everything and anything they wanted. I did not know how to deal with them. . . .'

I saw again the three dark-eyed women in that doomed gloomy house that I had entered. I was aware all over again of the love of his mother. There were the ones on both sides. All of us had loved him. How then could we have failed him? Here, in the person of my mother, was a woman who had married her first love, as in the person of my grandmother was one who had *not*. What then was the formula? Any answer I attempted only served to close them all away from me, as people who had not known how to deal with their own problems.

We drove to Daisy Hill, Carn-daisy, and Mother said: 'Aunt Ahn told me they made pilgrimages here in the eighth century.'

Everywhere, up hill and down into the valleys, across roads or streets, Mother had something to say and it was always something that was true, something that had fixed itself into her own experience. She would smile at me out of her great dark eyes and pass on the facts. She showed me the stone crottles. 'Ahn always called them croutils. The Latin name is *lichen omphalodes*. It sounds Greek. Turnsole blue, Kathleen, turnsole blue. They use it for the linen dyeing. Do you know how they get it? They make a paste of the plant and treat it with human urine to make it change colour. First it becomes a bright red, then it turns blue. The Dutch thought that they had invented it and they made a great secret of it. They pretended they got it by the juice of sunflowers. That was in the eighteenth century. But the Irish knew the secret in the thirteenth century. It has always been theirs; that is why it is called Irish moss.'

And all that year the process of our own change was moving up on us. Slowly and gradually Mother adopted the certainty that we were going. I remember her standing by an open window with her hands clasped in a buckle at her waist and a sort of passion rising from her stillness: 'I resent leaving this house.'

Grandmother never encouraged her *not* to go. Grandmother had a universal spirit. She belonged to the outside world. Her silence was a tacit acceptance. It filled the entire house and even the landscape with the futility of staying. She cast an ambience that let in upon us the subtle propaganda of a life filled with other people. She obliged me to move towards these people. I could not live in imaginary Pitti Palaces for always. I had to reach a place where Clives and Wolf Tones and Disraelis and medieval saints dropped into their places. I was being lured into the obligation to separate the dead from the living, the past from the present. Little things touched me as by a baptism. We had a very ardent washerwoman. The sweet windy smell of sheets was sacred to her. 'Smell,' she commanded Mother, and Mother had to put her nose obediently into the basket. And the life, the *outlook* of this little laborious woman became significant to me. She became an *other* person — and the world was full of them.

Mother took the final step. She sent for the auctioneer. She went through the rooms with him. He was a fat man, packed solidly into a pale grey suit with a gold chain strained tightly across his stomach. The chain dropped a little when his breathing fell. He disapproved of everything. He reminded me of the salvage men who had walked upon ashes with Father. Nothing, in the auctioneer's estimation, was anything like the worth Mother put upon it. The objects which Mother wished not to be sold were the only ones he wished to sell, to have 'under the hammer'. Mother was worn out by his opposition. When they entered the dining room, where Grandmother was rocking and knitting, she went on rocking and knitting as though they were not there. It was only when the auctioneer had his back to her that she took a good look at him. Her eyebrows shot up like antennae and dropped the instant he turned. Then she looked at me slyly and with a question in her eyes. As soon as he left the room she got out of the chair. She squeezed the knitting into a ball. She made a gesture that condemned the auctioneer and the whole proceeding and brought such a swift misery upon me that I wished to stab him and put an end to it.

Mother said after his departure: 'He didn't like it, but I refused to let him sell the things I wish kept.'

'If you give that man an inch he will take an ell,' Grandmother declared.

The date of the sale was never settled. It was held off on account of other vague actions which depended upon Mother's judgment and discretion. But the sale was inevitable. It was bound to come. Mother said: 'This is a monastic life. It will never do. I have to think of James.' Why our domestic disintegration had to be caused by James was never fully explained. Nothing was explained to me directly. When Mother ever explained a fact to me it was either historical or scientific. It was always in the past, never in the present. Her acts, even when they reached me directly, were always oblique in their intention. They always struck at me with appalling suddenness as when she said, without any warning: 'We are going to Belfast, Kathleen. I have the tickets. MacDaid will drive us down to the station the first thing in the morning.'

I gathered by clues here and there that we were going to 'look' at the university and houses in which we might live. Grandmother refused to go so Mother had to turn to me. She was unable to go alone. The entire event was an adventure to me, tamed by Mother's gloom about it. She cheered up a little after we got into the train.

MacDaid drove us down to the Waterside Station just after breakfast. When he dashed us to a dead stop in the Station Square the station master's house door was open and his wife was sending her little girls to school. Mother was introduced to them. One was dark and one was blonde and their names were Adelaide and Madeleine. Great funnels of smoke were blowing out of the open side of the station. MacDaid whistled and a porter came and took out bags and ran off with them so fast that Mother and I had to run after him. Mother said: 'Where ever did she get their names? She must be English.' And when we were safely up in the first-class carriage that smelt of stale cigars, she said: 'Thank heavens I never married a station master. It must be a nightmare to keep the windows clean.'

The engine kept shunting as though it were practising. But at last we moved off. The train slid along the lovely Foyle River, past familiar wooded demesnes. Mother made me look at the white patch of Boom Hall, showing like a postage stamp among its trees: 'That is where they put the boom that blocked King William when he came up the river. William of Orange . . . in the William and James Wars. Of all places they had to fight it out *here!*' She resented it as a personal encroachment, as something that had interfered with her mode of living. She made it intimate to me so that I saw the little church-crowned city that I knew waiting for the kings, whom I never knew, to clash. They were as clear to me as Mother sitting against the blue buttoned-down railway cushions. She was wearing a brown straw hat trimmed with ribbon bows and bunches of red flowers that had an Alpine name, or she gave them an Alpine name. They looked as though they were about to become berries. They were half berries. She was wearing a new pair of gloves. The fingers were bulged with her rings and the tips were drawn out and pressed flat according to the law which, my grandmother said, showed how 'a lady should wear her gloves'.

The scenery became foreign. The train travelled into strangeness. The deep dark mould of the ore-laden soil lost its warmth and became yellow. The green went out of the grass. The earth dried and hardened and became granite. We were thrust through tall virgin gravestones in which exquisite bright flowers were rooted as though rooted by the wind. Blossoms as deep as sapphires and pink as coral. The rocks shone like marcasite and the flowers shone like gems.

We slowed into a station. 'Coleraine,' Mother sighed deeply. She stared out with a curious, sad dignity upon the buildings. Her eyes took on a faraway, laden and drugged expression. She became the focus of thoughts that hypnotised her. She was emptied from me. It was as though everything within her had been drawn out and she was only a husk. It was useless to speak to her. When words came from her they came soaked from the terrible climate to which she had been taken. 'It cannot be denied that tragedies have happened to us. The dice were loaded against us. It is curious — you can take good people and reduce them to evil, the opposite of their natures.'

The train was moving again but her words remained static, as fixed upon me as though she had compelled me to stand where a murder had been committed. Then she recovered, she became normal again: 'We should have got out there,' she said, distressed; 'I meant to get some sandwiches and a cup of tea. Now we must wait for Belfast.' She shuddered: 'I don't know why I am going there. They tell me it is awful.'

All I saw upon our arrival was the railway station which looked like nothing but a railway station, furnished with the same smoke and dirt as any other railway station. We got into a cab and drove to a hotel for the night, where we had supper in bed, brought up upon an enormous silver tray that weighted our knees under the bedclothes. There was far too much to eat upon it and forks had been forgotten. Rather than call the maid from 'the bowels of the earth', Mother and I ate with our fingers. The next morning we had breakfast in bed. This time nothing was missing and the jam was delicious. It had everything in it and more than you expected.

I do not remember going to the university. It may be that Mother went alone for there were intervals when I was left in the hotel bedroom; and the university, for all I knew to

the contrary, may have been just around the corner. But I
believe that Mother never went to it at all. I think Belfast
discouraged her. We looked at one house. It had a spadeful
of garden with an unhealthy rhododendron bush in front of
a bay window. We went through empty, awful rooms, one of
which seemed piled with old newspapers. Mother thanked
the man who showed it to us. She said she would write to
him later. As soon as we were alone she asked me if I had
noticed his celluloid collar. She said nothing at all about the
house.

I remember standing with her before Robinson and
Cleaver's shop windows where festoons of Irish lace were
draped upon portraits of the King and Queen. Queen Alexandra reminded me of Mother. She had the same poise,
struck upright with gentle dignity upon a bustle. Nobody
was wearing bustles. They were seen only in portraits. 'She
was always beautiful,' Mother said, 'but not as beautiful as
the lace.'

It was directly after that that we left. We went back to the
hotel. The bill was paid and the baggage collected and we
got into another cab and arrived at the station and got into a
train. Nothing was said. I could not tell whether the visit
had been a success or not. It seemed to me that nothing had
happened except the hotel trays and the lace in the shop
window.

This time we got out of the train at Coleraine and had a
snack at the buffet where two men were flirting with the
lady behind the counter. She took no notice of them and
concentrated all her attention upon Mother. She gave us dry
sandwiches from under a glass dome and thick cups of tea.
As soon as we had finished eating the sandwiches and
biting our way into the tea, Mother paid and we went back
to the train. The lady behind the counter went back to the
two men. It did not seem to me to be the same train for it
was going in the opposite direction. I was afraid that Mother
had not noticed this and I did not dare to tell her. Then she
said: 'We are going to Portrush and the Giant's Causeway. I
think I will take a place there for this summer.'

The inconsequence of the adventure increased in excitement. I was enchanted. Mother lowered the window and the salt wild smell of the sea caught us. It was the strong Atlantic coming in with waves that were curled like iron, inky black with wrack. This sea belonged to the granite landscape. The first station we came to was Castlerock. Mother stood up when the train stopped. 'I think,' she said, looking at me as though she expected argument, 'we could get out here instead of going on to Portrush. What do you think?' What could I think? The sea was there. I was exalted by it, entranced by its strength and splendour. Its music filled me like an orchestra. It drew me like a magnet and I was unable to say let us wait until we come to Portrush. Castlerock was just as good to me. Miss Elliot had said that the Giant's Causeway was one of the Seven Wonders of the World. Aunt Ahn had told my mother who had told me that the Giant's Causeway was the Earl of Bristol's hobby. He went all over the world examining basaltic formations that rivalled it. What were the Seven Wonders or a bishop's hobby when compared with the salty flowing sea which was only a hand's throw from our train? I said yes. So we got out of the train again and another porter took the bags.

We walked through the deserted seaside streets full of wind and sunshine. Mother found what she was looking for immediately: a little cottage perched high on the cliffs with white railings and a green porch and the red twines of fuchsias and snow-white pebbles bordering the paths. She settled for it there and then with a woman in a white apron that blew like a banner. The woman gave us tea in a kitchen with a flagged, sanded floor. We had boiled eggs and a plate stacked with buttered fadge. We walked by the sea with our hats in our hands. We found shells that had piled up through the winter, and lay crusted as flowers against the spiny, grey sea grasses. Mother found an orchid, an oyster plant. 'It tasted like an oyster,' she said, but did not advise me to eat it.

Neither of us had any desire to return home from that place. Our will rested there in the grey enchantment, with the sea's music. But we had to go, Mother said. She had an air of waiting for my negation. It was useless for me to give it for if I had pleaded to stay it would have only spurred her to the duty of going. It is only when we are young in spirit that we hover upon these borders. We have these instants when we tremble upon the edges, when we hesitate deliciously before reality clutches us.

So we took the train again. The train became the punctuation mark in a voyage that dealt with states rather than places. Mother was yielding to moods that broke a seal, piece by piece, upon the unrest in her soul.

Grandmother was unduly upset when she heard what we had done. She focused a fiery look upon my mother. 'Katie, that isn't like you!'

And Mother, safe in what she had gained from her indulgence, only laughed at her. She was able to laugh. She was able to enjoy the knowledge that she had anchored us for another summer — and in a place of splendour. 'You should see it,' she said gaily to my grandmother. 'It's white without and white within, the chairs covered in white calicoes with tiny oak leaves and acorns. It made me want to eat cherries.'

The auctioneer came again and was more disagreeable than the first time. 'If you will permit me,' he remarked stingily to Mother, 'to know what I am doing.' Mother was obliged to permit him. She had to listen to his advice. 'Omit no details,' he said sternly; 'be sure to put it down if bed valances are to be sold with the beds or separately. I wish to avoid trouble.'

It was a relief when he left. Strain went out of the atmosphere and things became normal again. Quietly and methodically Mother made her lists every morning. She took possession of the rooms, one by one, and nobody was allowed to stir a chair or take out a book while she was 'counting'. In the afternoon we went for our drives. We drove all over the countryside, discovering it with the season. We felt the earth grow that year with a special intimacy. It was as though we were never going to see spring or summer again. Our farewell was to the place. It was the place that was being withdrawn.

We drove to Omagh. Mother showed me the convent in a stretch of pasturing fields to which she had gone for one year before Aunt Waters had sent her to Princethorpe. She told me about it. 'It was after the Sigerson girls went back to Dublin. I was lonely. But I hated this convent. Every day we had mutton. The nuns raised their own sheep. You can't imagine how tired you can get of mutton. In the winters it used to freeze upon our plates. All of us hated it . . . and we were so regimented there, sent out for walks no matter what the weather was. There was always a strange air about everything that happened there. The Reverend Mother was far too young. She was far too gay in spirit to be a reverend Mother. We would come in from our walks and pass through a room where she was sitting with a group of sisters around a table, embroidering altar cloths. They were gossiping and eating chocolates. We were always hurried past them but you could *see*. You could *hear*. Somebody always made a hush, but not before you took in what was happening. There was some sort of scandal. The bishop disbanded them.' She made it sound as though chocolates were a crime and laughter a mortal sin. But she swept upon me the full image, as bright as a page out of Froissart, of those sisters in their full-skirted habits and white coifs and mischief in their eyes; and the table stacked with sheaths of fine whiteness in which the embroidery silks lay as rich as gold and silver and precious stones.

Grandmother and I were alone one evening. It was early summer. There were wild ox-eyed daisies wilting in a sheaf without water. A blackbird was hammering at the air with his strong mating notes. She asked me abruptly: 'Tell me, has your mother ever told you about Kerrigan?' Before I had time to answer she half answered herself: 'She has never told me.'

It stayed, where she had put it — a question. It was tamed by some vague inadequacy. Neither a yes nor a no would have answered it. It trapped me in the insufficiency of human understandings. It defeated me because it was impossible for me to explain either of these women to each other. I was shut fast into my own individuality. I was looking at an analytical chart of the human brain, which was displayed as foliage, as acanthus leaves parted on either side of the medulla. She provoked me into a terrible surge of darkness. I was obsessed by an awful fear that nothing ever came clear and that life would pass in fields that would be far from Elysian but stacked and cluttered and *reduced* as blades of glass. Something would always trample upon us. In spite of Spinoza's logic or Hegelian principle the *waste* would be there. I remember staring at her, wondering how I should deal with it. She mistook my expression. She thought that the denial was for her. 'Don't answer me. I shouldn't have asked you.' The door opened and closed.

Mother and I went into the new cathedral. The day was beaten by a strong wind. It had rained. Stones were cleansed and blown dry again. As we came round a corner the edge of sandy wall made me think of a man in a pink tunic with a white-fleeced lamb upon his shoulder. There were wide shallow stone steps. Our steps scrunched into the gravel, seaside gravel, all white and grey stones from the shore. Nobody but ourselves was there. The edifice waited as a gigantic shell for Sundays and services, for May twilights with the vespers for Mary. Away down below us the Foyle flowed as it had flowed for centuries. It was a witness upon time and human impotence. Behind us were the dark-aired cells of the confessionals with their baize panels. Mother was in a strange mood. She was both young and old, both sad and strong. I could feel the darkness in her, running fast as an error. I was lit to match her, responsive.

'I know why Aunt Waters had to come back here,' she said. She declared it upon me passionately. 'I know why she was religious. It was in them all — and it's in us. It will take as long to get it out of us as it took to grow. Do you realise, Kathleen, that we are associated with, with this. . . .' She made a sweep towards the cathedral that took in the whole landscape. '. . . We cannot escape from it. I did not understand her at the time. I was too young, too against her. I begin to understand.'

We scrunched towards the gate. We saw the sweep of Clarendon Street going down towards the river. The older, upper streets had smaller houses. We walked along the Creggan Road and Mother showed me the Bishop's Demesne. She pointed into dense trees. It was the Protestant Bishop's demesne. 'All this land belonged to us, belonged to the Kinel-Owens. That was our name,' she laughed bitterly, 'not Smith. Why, there were so many of us, they hardly knew what to do with us. Ahn used to tell me. She was a wonder, Ahn. She remembered so much. She had a marvellous memory. She could remember the Earl of Bristol telling my father that there would be no Spanish War because the "English had sold their honour in order that they might sell their cotton." Imagine it, Aunt Ahn was a girl in her twenties when my mother was born! That makes her a generation older. She never forgot anything that was told to her. She used to speak of Gargarelli who expelled the Jesuits from Italy as though she had known him. She used to say it to me, as I am saying it to you now; our people have always been on the side of the Dominicans.'

And as it was said to me it was as though she put the old feud into my hands. It was as though she gave me the Guelphs and Ghibellines to feel. These people became mine. She gave me Ahn as a girl with her darkness unwithered, learning French from Dr O'Donnel who had learned it in the Collège des Lombardes in Paris. I saw the blur of the low streets near the river where the little house was with its damson tree. I wondered who lived in it now and could not convince myself of any living people supplanting the presence of the two black silken figures — Ahn, whisking her satchel like a kitten upon her knee, the china with its shining gold rims. They would be there, for me, for all time. So do our ghosts endure.

'That is how we preserve the truth,' Mother said; 'we give it from person to person.'

Her truths have certainly lasted. They were as seeds

sown in my inexperience, coming up as I ripened for them and they for me.

It was from Ahn that my mother had received the five Irish silver spoons. Brigid was furious about it but Mother refused to give them back. Ahn maintained that her mother had given them to her and that she had a right to give them to whom she pleased. Her mother had been given them by her mother who 'had carried them in her bosom', against fearful odds. 'They are more precious to me than gold,' Mother declared to me. I believed her. I never had any reason to doubt the truth of what she told me.

That summer hung as golden as a promise or a harvest upon our lives. It had about it the satisfaction of some ripeness. The time for some change had come and we were woven with it. Grandmother receded upon her own private wisdom. She became quiet, the unrest no longer broken upon her lips. She was resigned — as one who sees the end in view.

Mother was both determined and disturbed. She was the one who was forced into action. If the preparations she was impelled to make were made against her inner will, they were performed outwardly in the name of James, her son. It was for James that she was doing it. She had no satisfaction except that which is derived purely from a sense of duty. No feeling is colder or more exacting in its performance.

I, being young and innocent of the behaviour of the world to which I was travelling, was stirred and filled with an exciting optimism. I was filled with the wildest courage and hope of the untried — and undefeated. I did not know the change for what it was — the emergence from a state of dream into reality. I did not know while it was happening that I was stepping out into my own generation. I was approaching what was to separate me from these older women.

Later, I realised that my pattern was made from these people. They were my family. I had been born into their lives. I had had to acquire theirs. I have endeavoured to explain how they became mine, gradually and by a slow growth. I was imbued with their meaning. Whenever I have sought as an intelligent human being to comprehend the values of life, as we are obliged to live it as individuals, I have been driven back by necessity upon them, upon what made me through them, and them through others. I have had to deal with that heritage. I have had, as have others of my generation, to ask what is this that is handed down to us. Has the mould any significance? Must we accept it, or must we break from it?

Apart from my father, I was confined to these two women. They were my shell. I had their blood in my veins. Without seeming to impose themselves upon me, they actually did impose upon me a very certain quality. Question it as I might — and of course I questioned it — their influence had to be dealt with.

What puzzled me always about them was their extreme pride. They were supported by a censor, in Freudian terms, which made them immune to insult. They were held up by a very definite integrity, by what kept them whole in the centre of ostracism. I have never come across a reference to Irish pride without associating it with them. I was too much their victim, or subject, not to be conscious of them as victims, or subjects of this pride. I was bound to ask what it was that made them so 'untouchable'. What right have any people to pride of this quality, to any pride at all unless they have something to be proud of? Pride without a legitimate cause is the purest arrogance. Neither of these women was arrogant. What they possessed went deeper. It supported them in secret.

In the present-day world which is seething with differences, it is a common argument that racial distinctions are to blame for wars. There is a very real cry against race. The Count de Gobineau is to blame. His theory was gobbled up by the Germans who digested it into a creed for a dominant race. It is as though one should come out entirely upon the side of the lions in the forest, that no other animals should be permitted to survive. This is entirely against God who has promised us that a day is to come when the lion and the lamb will browse in the same pastures. The simple truth is that there is room for all of us. There is a working principle for all races and the success of the world depends upon our admission of it. Wars are not caused by our differences but by our monopolies. When the differences are adjusted and properly distributed it will be found that we each have a gift to bestow upon humanity, even if it is nothing greater than a lesson in climate. We serve for some purpose. We represent, in our turn, some mastery of the earth.

What has to be sifted out, in a world with rising democratic standards which increasingly demands our consideration of others, is our true racial values. Not our values to ourselves but our values to others. We have come into the democracy of our days by various ways and means. We have come into it with various backgrounds. The strength of America, the foremost democracy, is that she has amalgamated her people with these backgrounds upon their values as individuals. The time may come when she may have to amalgamate them racially. She has all the machinery. What she has attained in the evolution of the newest science, psychology, gives her the material for such a measurement. As a measurer of these values she may become the clearing house of the world.

It is purely as a contribution to these scales that I offer this statement upon a veritable background, in answer to: What is it that does not die in us? What do we carry? Where is our place in a general and universal adaptation?

It has become stale to scoff at the Irish. Destructive criticism is the easiest thing in the world and people who have been reduced to beggary are exposed to it. Anybody can be mocked at but what does the mockery serve? Napoleon remarked that when the Bourbons appeared at the Imperial Court they 'behaved like parvenus'. Tradition can be betrayed by appearances. What really matters is not the pomp and circumstances but the human values, the universal contribution of any groups or races to the world in general. If they have nothing to give, nothing can be taken from them. If they have something to give, then the time and place for that giving is bound to occur inevitably. Purposes are very persistent. They have a timeless patience. When their hour strikes it may be that it endures but for a moment. It may be that their endurance only declares the course of some evil, but if it serves to eradicate some malady in an unhealthy world science will certainly not deny it a place.

Pride may be another term for registration. We have to find out what is registered. I remember understanding the pride of those in Provence who claimed direct contact with Christ because one of the Marys who had stood by the cross had come to their land. The Saintes Maries were there to prove it, a little place by the sea, below the smooth Alpille hills. There is a pride in Arles to this day that sweeps at you through the eyes of people in its streets and cries to you from its stones. You cannot enter Saint Trophime without *feeling* it. It is the touch, the 'and did you once see Shelley plain?' that fills us, in spite of ourselves, with reverence. It is not snobbery. It is deeper.

Appendix[*]

The Kinel-Owens were an *erenach* family in Derry. They were closely associated with the history of Derry for many centuries and I think the fairest way to get them into their proper place is to give a brief history of Derry.

Niall of the Nine Hostages plays the same role in Irish genealogy that William the Conqueror plays in English genealogy. Most of us seem to have sprung from either of these men, unless, of course, we wish to go back beyond Angevin and provincial kings to Adam who was our first father. What does it matter? Either it does matter or it does not matter at all.

Niall had twelve sons to whom his territories were apportioned at his death. The share that fell to his son, Eoghan, or Owen, was named Tir-Eoghan, or Tir-Owen, or Innishowen or Tyrone. This was in the fifth century.

In 546 Columba, a young man in his twenties, founded the Abbey of Derry. He was related by blood and sept to the ruling Eoghan clan. He built the Abbey in a series of cells or *cille* and it is for this reason that he is referred to as Columcille or Columba of the cells. He began with twelve associates. Among them were two grandsons of Eoghan, the son of Niall of the Nine Hostages. The names of these grandsons were Lugain and Baither. Among the twelve was Columba's maternal uncle, Ernan; and a boy, Bran, son of Columba's sister. There was also a young man, Russen, whose father, Rodan, became Abbot of Innisfail. There was a young man with a name that waited for Shakespeare — Scandal, the son of Bressen. And there was Eochod — to whom we owe the record of Columba's life.

There is no record of the type of the architecture of the Abbey. But McFirbis, a historian who collected all the Gaelic material available in the seventeenth century, protests against the assertion that there were no stone buildings in Ireland

---

[*] In earlier editions of *The Magical Realm* this Appendix appeared as Chapter Twenty-Five.

before the Danish invaders. He quotes an ancient poem, written by a certain Flannagan who was a *caiselór*, or architect. He also gives a list of *caiselórs*, or *cashellors*, builders.

1. Cabar, architect — *caiselór* of Tarah.
2. Goll, surnamed the *clochair* — mason, *cashellor*, to Nadfrech, King of Cashel in the time of Saint Patrick. This was contemporary with Niall of the Nine Hostages. Goll, it is recorded, erected the 'Palace of Cashel'.
3. Righrim and Garban — the two *cashellors* of Aileach.
4. Troigh — *leathan*, builder, of the strong tower of Tarah.
5. Boic, the son of Blair — builder of Rath Crogan.
6. Bainche, surnamed the 'Barrow River' — architect of Emania.
7. Cricel — builder of Rath-Aillone.

Aileach is that place by the sea where, as a child, I looked down from a road full of roses and fuchsias upon the place where there was always either an inch of water or an inch of land. It was from there that the Flight of the Earls took place in the seventeenth century. I delight in that king's name, Nadfrech. It always smells to me of the pyramids.

There is a Johnsonian translation of a Scandinavian manuscript which contains an illustration of Tara, or Tarah. It is described as 'consisting of circular walls enclosing the Daedalian Castle of the King'.

When, centuries later, Aileach was demolished, it is recorded that 'O'Brien carried home a trophy stone to Limerick.' This was the stone that was afterwards known as the Treaty Stone of Limerick.

Another fact put on record about Aileach is that it had a *grianán*, a stone house or temple dedicated to the sun. This brief statement is another clear sweep to Egypt. And it gives us stones. It would be curious if a Druidic people who could move *menhirs* and *dolmens* should not use stones for their dwellings. Gaul is full of *megaliths* and Druidic remains, but it also has contemporary castles and humbler stone dwellings, which proves that there was no Druidical law against the use of stones for dwellings. France is a country in which archaeological traces have remained in a fine sequence. From her Chellean days downwards her mode of life has left remains. She was never subjected to the same measure of destruction as Ireland. It is justifiable to assume that the Irish did use stones for their dwellings and that these were destroyed whenever they were centres of warfare. It is justifiable to assume that the Abbey Columba built was not made of laths or wattles. But, whatever it was made of, it was a Christian centre where Christian principles were taught. It was also the nucleus of the city of Derry.

In 565, twenty years later, Columba did a very strange and significant thing. He abandoned the Abbey and settled in the island of Iona, where he established a seminary on land given to him by Picts. This seminary, it was bargained, was to contain a burial ground for *Kings and Queens who were in exile from Ireland*. It is significant that a man so grave and earnest as Columba, a man who cannot be accused of capriciousness, should give up the work and interest of years. The secret of his departure lies in those 'exiled Kings and Queens' for whom he had to consecrate a burial place. What exiled them, exiled him. The situation was not unlike that of today when kings and queens are again in exile. Saint Columba was as much involved in the politics of his times as the Archbishop of Paris is today. This is not the place to go into this matter. Let us accept that a change in *form* was taking place. When Ireland became Roman Catholic she became intensely so. When the Roman Church was founded it rose to power upon the ruins of Rome. It took over the temporal power as it fell from the administrators of the Roman Empire. It took over the existing machinery of this administration. The early Church laid its grip as well as its blessing upon all the Christian states. The Irish Court at Tara, the Court of the High King who was head over the provincial kings, was torn between the old system and the new. It was torn between the conservatism of those who stayed at home and the liberalism of those who went abroad and came under the influence of Rome and France. It was torn by the weaknesses of what was dying and the rising craft and graft of the new advantages. Saint Columba was a purist. He was a saint and on the side of the idealists. He was neither for the pomp and splendour of the ecclesiastics nor for the ambitions of the politicians. His business was with God and not with the world. So he took his own special way of teaching with him and consecrated the burial ground for the royal exiles. These high-minded and noble Picts who settled in Scotland in the sixth century were the first Protestants. They generated a criticism of Irish Catholicism that was to endure. Their protest was to become one of those great oaks which grow from little acorns. Much later, when the controversies had become silent, the remains of Saint Columba were brought to Ireland and laid beside those of Saint Patrick and Saint Brigid.

His Abbey lasted in Derry until 783, when it was destroyed by fire. Only the belfry was left standing and around this belfry a new Abbey was built. It must have contained treasures for, when the Danes came to Derry twenty-one years later, they looted it and massacred the students. It was again restored.

In Dr Coyle's *Collectanea* it is recorded that its treasures were again stolen in 985 by a 'Maol Leachline'. *Leachline*, or *Loughlin*, was the Gaelic for Dane, and *maol* was a word which signified a religious servant. Dr Coyle gives its derivations. It was a Christian designation found in the Coptic Church as *mal* or *mahal*, in Arabian as *malik* or *memelik*, and in Persian as *mahamsavi*, a shaved or tonsured person.

Derry drew the Danes. She was available from the sea by her broad navigable river. A little city, perched upon a hill, fortified by her Abbey walls. Every time they fired her she rebuilt the walls. She emerged from these onslaughts with the title of Termon-Derry, Derry of the Sanctuary. The prefix *termon* was used to define the *erenach* land, or lands enclosed within the Abbey walls. Usher interprets the term as a Latin definition. Latin was the common language of the early Christian epoch. He explains the word as: 'A terminus in a Holy Place. Three estates constituted such a terminus: the King, the Clergy and the People.' The *termon* lands were described as of two sorts: *mensales* and *casuales*. The *mensales* were the church lands proper — those used by the monks. The *casuales* were the lands within the *erenach* walls which were let to lay tenants or holders.

These brief facts are to be found later in English documents. They are indisputable. They mark Derry as a monastical city from the fifth century. It was because of her Abbey and its treasures that she was constantly attacked and plundered. The process became her special form of growth. She was not diminished but enlarged by her *afflictions*. The same sort of thing was happening among the Franks and Gauls. Out of it was to come feudalism. The power was not yet in the hands of the 'barons'. It was held by the Church.

The particular conflict in Ireland was between the temporal power of Rome and the native, Brehon code. The Irish kings were tribal, they were subject to a head king, an *Ard-Rí* who ruled at Tara. The Irish for king — Rí — is another word that hints of Egypt where the king was known as *Ra*. These kings were not chosen by direct inheritance but by their ability to rule. It was only if the reigning king's son proved to be the fittest, that he was chosen. The system was as democratic as the election of a republic's president. On occasion the heir was chosen because he was a 'sister's son', the matrilineal process. It was not until feudalism that royalty became agnatic.

Next to the king in the community the foremost men were the *tanist* or lawgiver, the *ollain* or poet, and the *shanachy* or historian. After them came the craftsmen, silversmiths and forgers and weavers, and the tillers of the soil and the soldiery or *kerns*. The classification, allowing for its primitive conditions, had much the same pattern as is to be found today. The only difference was in the economy. All contributions were made in kind and repaid in kind. The weak were protected by the strong for whom they fought and laboured. The people were bound by families and groups, *septs* and clans, forged into an entity against all external dangers.

Derry had two rulers. One was the ecclesiastical ruler of the Abbey. The lay ruler was known as the *Erenach*. The Abbot governed all things connected with religion. The *Erenach* governed all things connected with the laity who dwelt within the walls. The *Erenach* collected the dues for those who enjoyed the protection of those walls. There was a curse, known as the 'Erlar Curse'. It was applied to those who 'went over the wall'. Those who ran away from their obligations. The name Eric means simply a man subject to tax.

The *Erenach* of Derry was always a member of the Kinel-Owen branch of the ruling clan. If you go back to the beginnings you will discover that as long as there was an abbey and a lay *erenach* the *erenach* was a Kinel-Owen. The Kinel-Owens were associated with the Abbey of Derry in the same fashion that the Abbeys of Saint Germain-des-Près and Saint Denis and Saint Riquier were associated with the Capets in the early Duchy de France.

These abbeys were all cores of an extending faith. France and Ireland were Rome's eldest daughters. In the first centuries of Christianity the Irish saints and bishops were in the first line of doctors. These new priests were exegetical. They were establishing a doctrine. They were impelled to discover a *sensus* behind all existing systems and social groups. They were rational in the

highest and most constructive degree. They had the noble and
large behaviour of men in a universal process. As Saint Anselm
said, their chief objective was to establish 'an intelligent order'.
The Irish priests bore their due share of the adjustment. Derry
made her contribution. She produced a line of abbots and
bishops who sought to deal intelligently, and honestly, with the
problems of their day.

Cachuile is mentioned in 724. In 937 Finnachtach is referred
to as a *coarb* or abbot who 'was skilled in the old language.' The
reference to the 'old language' marks the period of stabilisation.
The reform of language is a signal of all new systems. It was the
problem everywhere just then. When the empire of Charle-
magne disintegrated it can be noted that Charles the Bald of
France and Louis the German 'pledged themselves in each
other's language' in 843. This marked the definite trends of the
lingua teutonica and the *lingua romana*.

To return to the list of Derry bishops or *coarbs*, there was
Malfinnen in 948. In 967 there were Dengus and Kinaeth — both
of the Kinel-Owen family. In 1066 (the date of the Battle of
Hastings) there was Dunchadh O'daimhin, another of the Kinel-
Owen *sept*. In 1122 the Abbot was Congalach, who was the son
of the *'erenach* or Keeper of the Walls'. Literally, the Waller. He
died when he was ninety-four years old, covering almost a century with his own life. He was followed by Giolla, better known
by his Latin name of Gelasius. Gelasius became Bishop of Armagh where he filled the episcopal chair for thirty-eight years.

These were Christian abbots and bishops. Their rank declares them. They must have been supported by congregations.
They were not ignorant men nor could the people to whom they
ministered have been ignorant. There must have been at least
one class or group to whom they could have appealed intellec-
tually. They were the guiders in a hierarchical management.
Under them very fine labours were performed. We have the
illuminated books as testimony. We have the silver patterns; and
we have the passionate poetry that was to surge from its native
background into the medieval classics. It is no myth at all that
Ireland had her era of scholarship.

The amalgamating factor was the Norman Conquest. Unlike
England, Ireland had had no Roman conquest, no military
conquest. The Roman dominion that reached her was Christian.
The difference between the Roman conquest and the Norman

conquest was that the Normans fused themselves with the Celts wherever they found them. Culture and *courtoisie* happened to be their fashion, and manners and fine modes of thought were the period's urgency. In Ireland the Normans became 'more Irish than the Irish'. There must have been some very clear appeal in the Irish atmosphere for the Normans were by no means the sort of people to delight in wild men of the woods.

The Normans did not settle in Ulster. They settled in Leinster. I would not mention them in connection with Derry if it were not for a very oblique detail that has always caught my eye in medieval French literature, the William of Orange element. There were two Williams of Orange; the one connected with the Battle of the Boyne and Derry and an earlier one who fought the Saracens and was precipitated like a challenge, or a menace, into the *chansons de geste*. I am unable to think of them as real persons. They come up for me always as *symbols* in two phases of Celtic effort.

The first peace of the Catholic era was used to gather up the crumbs of what had perished culturally in the transition. The songs of the roadways were cherished and edited. Legends were taken up. Anything of any worth that had been harboured in any group consciousness was restored. It was in this warm, charitable atmosphere that the Irish basic themes of Tristram and the Grail and Joseph of Arimathea flourished. Either they had originated in Ireland, *or* the Irish version of them was the most popular. Afterwards, they received a Welsh and Breton restatement — in Mallory's *Morte d'Arthur* and Marie de France's *Lais*. Marie de France used the Irish form of *loid* for her lays. The small things point the clues. This influence came to France from the North. Another stream went southwards where the Pepin Cycle, the *Song of Roland*, swept through the Pyrenées under the name of *Garin de Monglane* or *Guillaume d'Orange*. I find it most odd that a William of Orange should be associated in time and essence with a Celtic wave. It is prophetic, like the germ of a malady. I can prove nothing from it beyond this wonder as a sign upon the Celtic path.

Another French writer of this particular period was Crestien de Troyes who treated the Tristram theme in parts, one of which he entitled *Erec*, which shows his origin.

I cannot tear myself away from this period without mentioning the *bestiaires*. I find it psychologically curious that the human consciousness should illustrate its periods of transition with a recourse to animals. New civilising processes seem to stabilise themselves out of the woes and throes of disintegration by a charity that includes all living creatures. Saint Anthony (who incidentally was an Egyptian) in the fourth century was an example. In times of ideological uncertainty humanity exercises a special humility. The saints and poets seem able to commune with animals. They come down to a common consciousness in which nothing that lives or breathes is left out. The beginning of Christian literature was stamped with *bestiaires*. The beginning of Christian sculpture was stamped with gargoyles. Today we have surrealism and Kafka. In the *bestiaires* and gargoyles the pity and misery and confusion of dumb creatures is exposed with a sort of anguish. It is as though the human consciousness were sharpened to the full limit of the defenceless states, as though mankind can be chastised back to the first reaches of life when it comes to a reamplification of its purpose. A state of charity arises in which no sparrows fall or lilies grow without acknowledgement. The courage of the lesser beings is something normally inexpressible. It is without redemption, the purest and most continuous hazard, unless we admit them into the unconscious. Once we do that they become our 'brothers and sisters', as they were for Saint Francis.

In 1095 Derry, Termon-Derry, was burned again and again restored.

In 1100 a new thing happened. Derry was besieged again but not by foreigners alone. This time and for the first time the foreigners were aided by Irish armies under the 'leadership of Murchertach of Munster', and it was an attack upon the Church and the government of the Church. The Roman Church had acquired a power that was further reaching than the empire it had supplanted because it was a power that functioned upon two planes, the spiritual and the temporal. It controlled men by their ambitions as well as by their souls. Such power is always dangerous, a terrible test of strength and weakness. Politics were in the hands of Kings and Cardinals. The 'barons' were subjected to an intolerable pressure. As a class they were responsible for everything — the furnishing of men to fight or men to labour for those above them. They were responsible to the people below them and the rulers above them. They were ground between the upper and the nether millstones. It was only natural that they should rebel and assert themselves. In England, King John had to make promises. In France, Hugh Capet was obliged to listen to appeals. The tide was rising through Christendom. The laity were demanding separation from the dominance of the Church. This manifestation of social growth had two effects upon the clergy. Those who were consecrated solely to the service of God began to seek or found establishments where the politics of men could not enter. Mendicant orders began to form. Those who were ambitious and mundane strove to increase the pomp and glory of the churches.

Derry had her two sorts like the rest of Europe.

When the pure elements began to break away from her the Abbey produced a man of the world. The Abbot O'Brolchain took it upon himself to establish Derry as a bishopric. He decided to glorify the Church. He decided upon ecclesiastical magnificence. He decided upon a cathedral. He set out to turn the Abbey, which had been a centre of holiness and learning, into a sacred edifice where pomp would impose the full sway of Rome. He went up and down the land crusading for his mission. Princes and rulers supported him. He was given oxen and horses and golden rings. Derry gave him four hundred and twenty ounces of pure silver. Golden ring-money is mentioned by Caesar as current among the Celts in Briton. In the Irish *Book of Rights* ring-money is stated to have been paid to the King of Aileach by his tributary lords. Gold and silver rings varied in size and weighed from a pennyweight to sixteen ounces.

The Abbot went on with his reconstruction. But while the work was proceeding during those first years of the twelfth century, the air seethed with rebellious criticism of the Church. What had brought the Munster hordes down upon Derry was still vexing her spirit. The clergy were fully aware of what was taking place. It was happening too universally to be ignored. They fought their battle with churches. It was a building age. There was a passion for the erection of sacred edifices. Ireland was only in the fashion. She had seven of them in one valley, Glendalough. They gave that dignity to the landscape that is seen so poetically in the illustrated Froissarts. The duchies and little kingdoms that could produce these edifices must have had a society to match. Froissart makes us aware of fine ladies in ridiculously exaggerated hats with floating veils, riding on magnificently appointed horses in and out of gateways and citadels. Life was a perfect pageant. Everything was new and bright and of a dazzling brilliance. And the brightest and most dazzling of all were the new churches.

In 1118 the clerical authorities sought to solve the Irish difficulty. At an Ecclesiastical Council held in Rath-Breasil the whole of Ireland was partitioned into dioceses by a Papal Mandate. Keating quotes from the *Annals of Clonmenagh* (a work which has been lost) certain entries which show that this Council was presided over by Giolla Espuic, or Gilbert, who was the *first* Papal Legate ever sent to Ireland. Rome was dealing with the matter directly. It was settled at this synod that 'the bishoprics of Raphoe, improperly referred to as Derry, should extend from the Cataract at Ballyshannon to Shroove Point in Innishowen.'

This quotation proves that there was some dispute about the bishoprics which may have been the cause of the Abbot O'Brolchain's ambition.

It is clear that the air was seething with controversies and criticisms. Storms gathered and threatened. When men turn against their priests the sores fester in their souls. There were three forces which kept Derry rational in this crisis — while the forceful Abbot O'Brolchain was travelling up and down the country and devoting his energies to his cathedral. These forces were a woman, a young man and an old man.

Derry may well have been held back from disaster by the old man alone. Events often have this habit of awaiting the death of an old man. The onslaught of innovation is sometimes checked by a power no stronger than the thin thread of a life that is about to go out. It is a tribute to one who is regarded with reverence, and who is about to leave. This man was such a man. His name was Ardgar and he was a king's son. As a young man he had been celebrated for his courage and integrity. When he was old he was respected for his wealth and for his charity. In the little city of those days, confined within the Abbey walls, there can be no doubt that he was a personality. He was able to stem with his fine character what was grievous and of an urge to others. One can imagine the sphere of his influence — his words and reasoning — to those who visited him.

And then there was a curious thing. The lay *erenach* of that time was a woman! She could not have been a beautiful woman for no mention is made of her looks; and the beauty of a woman never escapes tribute when her position among men is unique. She was neither a queen nor an abbess nor a prostitute for if she had been one of these we should have had her record. She must therefore have been that most wonderful of all things — a good woman. She must have been a clever woman. She must have been chosen upon the fairest grounds of all, her ability. She had a gentle name, Bebinn, or Bébeen. We have no reason to doubt that it belonged to a gentle woman. She certainly could not have been a fool for the times would not have exalted her if she had been. She was probably very capable and reliable and full of wisdom. I like to think of her with a sense of humour, a woman with that deep kindly laughter in her eyes which could blaze, when occasion warranted, into the finest anger. We shall never know now what brought her to a public office. All we can be certain about is that her position was unique and because of that those who were for her must have been passionately for her and those who were against her must have been equally passionate.

Her co-mayor or *erenach* was a young abbot. He was elected at the age of thirty-three. I wonder if he was Gratian to her Teresa, or was he the one who dominated her? He was a brilliant young man. His name was Gelasius and he became Bishop of Armagh. But in those first days of his administration in Derry we can imagine how he stemmed the rising tide in his Derry pulpit, scattering it with his eloquence. He was able to deal with the full argument, to break it up with astute syllogisms so that it had to be won all over again, by its parts.

In 1121, on the evening of a feastday, the Feast of Mochuarog, the old man died. He was seventy-seven.

In 1124 the people rose against the tyranny of the clergy under one of their own princes, the King of Aileach's heir. He and his hosts fought the ecclesiastical forces *within* the walls. He was slain. His blood was spilled by the clergy of the Abbey which Saint Columba had founded in the name of peace. This disaster put an awful silence upon the whole problem for ten years. But the grievances did not die down. They endured. In 1134 the crowds came up again from Munster. The date is significant, for Bebinn, it is recorded in the *Book of the Four Masters*, died that year. She died at the beginning of the year, on March the twenty-third. They waited for her to die, as they had waited for the old man to die. In those days the chivalry of men had certain obediences. Although men of her own tribe and relationship could spill their blood upon the precincts she ruled over, outside princes could not and were held back because she was a woman. It is a tribute to her. Her body was hardly cold in the grave before the fighting broke out and Derry was burned and plundered. As a woman she had maintained peace of ten years' duration.

The ecclesiastical authorities refused to give in. They continued their exactions. When wrongs muster among groups of human beings acts of God sometimes occur by way of punctuation. In 1146 a violent tempest broke out which killed people who were congregated in the Church.

And all this while the Abbot O'Brolchain went steadily on. He was consecrated to his cause. He must have regarded it as a fetish which would, as soon as he had fulfilled it, accomplish a miracle. His cathedral was built and blessed. The Episcopal seat was removed to Derry by synodical decree and he was consecrated as its first bishop.

We have no indications to denote the standard of this cathedral. The *Annals of Ulster* refer to it in 1164 as 'the Great Church of Derry'. There is a later mention, in 1180, of 'a rectory gate which was bestowed upon it by a rich lord, O'Cahan of Krieve, and his wife who was a daughter of the O'Nonorge.'

Exactly three years after Bishop O'Brolchain was consecrated, the storm broke. The urban people clamoured for freedom, for the right to breathe as free citizens. This time they proclaimed their demands with such strength and urgency under the leadership of a nobleman, Murtagh, that the ecclesiastics were compelled to yield. A meeting was convened between the laity and the clergy, between the laic householders and the *com-arba,* or *comharb* — the 'holders of the Church lands'. It was decided and ruled at this memorable convention that 'the houses of Derry should be sundered from the Church; that eighty new houses should be built and the Erlar, or Tributary Wall, extended.'

The word *com-arba* is another with an Egyptian derivation. A *com-arba* was literally a partner in church lands. It is compared to the Arabian *sheriff,* or *sharif,* derived from *araf,* which means a priest or priestly augur.

The Kinel-Owens must have been very clearly associated

with the new system because the four bishops who succeeded Bishop O'Brolchain were known as 'Bishops of Kinel-Owen'. Afterwards the bishops were entitled Bishops of Derry, or Derry-Columcille.

For the first time in almost seven centuries of Christianity the clergy and the laity were separated in Derry. Derry was evolving. The freedom did not sit easily upon her. She seemed unhappy at the breaking of her traditions, as though she kept it upon her conscience. It is surprising how little peace there has been among Christians. When they have not warred against foreigners and authority they have warred against each other. Unrest was the age's symptom. The feudal lords were fighting everywhere for control. Ireland was no exception. In France it was the same. The French found a name for these angers that were nursed between men of the same race: *mauvain-sang*. Bad blood because it was angered between brothers. In 1177 Derry was torn by a scandalous event. She was disrupted by fearful riots which broke out between cousins. Donogh Caire Allain of the Kinel-Owens slew his cousin Niall O'Gormley, lord of Moyhla and Kinel-Enda, in the very heart of the town.

The young Donogh Caire Allain was brought to trial before a tribune. He was 'sentenced to make his peace with God, Saint Columba and the Clergy.' He was obliged to make it not alone for himself but for his posterity. He was made to 'promise his own gifts of amendment as well as the gifts of his sons and posterity for ever.' He gave to the sons of the man he had killed the townland of Donoughmore. He gave them (what was then of very great value) a golden goblet. He was obliged to present the family of his victim 'with a new house'.

But, in spite of penitence, the bad blood had been spilled. Three years later his own son, Randall O'Caire Allain, was killed by a young O'Gormley.

Derry was raided by English Danes, Danes who had settled in England, in 1195, 1197 and in 1203. She repulsed them twice, but the third time she was sacked and burned from 'Saint Martin's Sanctuary to Adamanan's Well'.

She recovered once again. There is a reference to the 'completion of the Great Church of Derry in 1217'. It is not clear if this refers to a restoration after the Danish pillage or whether the work on the Cathedral had been going on continuously.

In 1250 she was struck by another act of God. With no

enemies about and for no visible cause and with the abruptness
of a caprice, the entire upper part of the Cathedral collapsed.
This was regarded as an evil omen. It had the same effect as the
mice in Rome before the Empire fell. It struck through the heart.
It was a good thing that Bishop O'Brolchain was not alive to see
it. He must have loved his church. It is a great pity that we have
no description of it. It is not unthinkable that he pored over the
designs of other churches before he chose its pattern. Perhaps he
communicated with Anselm, the Archbishop of Canterbury.
Perhaps he visited Saint Albans, that pile of slender Roman
bricks that had been built by the Celtic King of Mercia in
memory of Alban — who had served as a soldier in Diocletian's
army. There may have been a very definite link between the
Mercian Celts and the Irish. Ely, which also had its cathedral,
and supposedly derived from Aileach. It is more than probable
that the clergy visited each other. The Church was strongly
bound in the making of doctrine, and writings and arguments
were exchanged. One small significant proof is given of this
tendency by the fact that in 1274, when a Dominican Friary was
founded in Derry by a Prince of Tyrconnell, it was dedicated to
the memory of Saint Thomas Aquinas. It was the year he died.
This proves that both Art and Scholasticism had their adherents
in Ireland.

It is the trifles that give us the atmosphere. All the links are
of value. I think it is Breasted who, in the midst of archaeological details, suddenly mentions a letter written by an Egyptian
conscript (BC), which evokes for us the full measure and pen-
alty of his era. Voltaire scoffed at the veracity of Tacitus. But
Tacitus did not always mistake his facts. He knew, for instance,
that Derry was a name derived from *derg*, an oak.

Poets often give us these intimate little truths. When monks
kept the records they kept them strictly as gentlemen. Neither
time nor effort nor precious materials were wasted upon trifles.
Only the large events were inscribed. It is the poets who tell us
about the women. It is through them that we have been made
familiar with Finn's wife, Gráinne; and 'that huge woman the
King of Greece's daughter'. We know that Maeve ran a cattle-
drive when cattle were worth their weight in gold.

We know definitely that Derry was an ecclesiastical city. Her
entire history was fused with the Church. It was this which
brought her the enmity of England, which began with these

English Danes who had no other goal but her plunder. It was Derry's Roman attachments which drew the wrath of Henry the Eighth upon her. Henry was fighting the Catholics. He stood for the rise of Protestantism. He was anti-Catholic in England. Henry's daughter, Elizabeth, was hemmed in between her Catholic relatives — Mary who had married Philip of Spain, and Mary, Queen of Scots. She was compelled to control the Irish Catholics. She would have been a fool in her own interests if she had not done so. It is an odd stretch of destiny that Derry had to be destroyed between two kings who were not her own: William of Orange and James.

It was to Derry that Elizabeth sent Essex when she made him Governor of Ireland in 1599. He was thirty-two, thirty years her junior. She charged him to 'fortify and garrison Derry'. He was particularly commissioned to keep its representatives 'O'Donnell and O'Neill divided' — the *divide et impera* which Machiavelli had turned into a creed for rulers.

An English *Ordnance Survey Memoir of Londonderry*, made in 1837, states:

> Previous to the fifteenth century Derry and its parishes were inhabited chiefly by the tribe of Kinel-Owen or descendants of Owen. Of these the MacLoughlins, the direct descendants of Owen and the eldest branch of the Northern Hy-Nialls were originally of the highest rank in the kingdom, but sank in the thirteenth century under the rival house of O'Neill and still lower under the O'Dohertys in the 15th. After this period Derry received a portion of the race of Kinel-Connell into its population which thus, until the Plantation of Dowcra, consisted of these two great tribes of the same race, Kinel-Owen and Kinel-Connell.

We can think of Essex in Derry, in the little steep streets, perhaps in the Street of the Clapping Hands. The old names are as full of poetry as the old names in France. We know from his portraits what Essex looked like: a very handsome and noble man, accustomed to the courtesy of life at court. He was a man of taste and culture, one of the finest examples of the England of his time. He set out as emissary to Ireland with the best intentions, eager to fulfil his mission. What happened to him to make him change his purpose? The issue is quite clear: either Essex betrayed his Queen's cause for his own ends, or he betrayed it because he could not help it. He was either a scoundrel or a gentleman.

The argument goes against his personal ends. He was no

Simnel. He was a man of noble birth and his personal ends
could best have been served on the Queen's side. He was very
intimate with her. She was very fond of him. She trusted him. A
man such as Essex could not possibly have betrayed that trust
for a mean motive. His principles must have been involved. He
might have been tired of her as a woman, but that would not
have made him any less her servant as his Queen. Nobody has
ever dared to suggest that he sided with Mary, Queen of Scots,
or with Philip of Spain.

There remains the aspect of this affair which has never been
justifiably considered, the influence of the men and women he
met in Ireland. He had been sent specifically among them to
disrupt them. It had already been proved that they were a
national problem. They were still undefeated. All representatives of the Crown who had been sent among them had been
subjected to their persuasion. They had a genius for breaking
down opposition that was so untouchable and indefatigable
that, in the end, the administration of the city had been removed to London. The 1531 *Civil Records of Derry* have a brief
statement that: 'In 1515 a Charter was granted to the Company
of London and a gilt sword sent to them by the Mayor.'

Derry became Londonderry because she was ruled by a company composed of London ironmongers and drapers. But she
was still unconquered and Essex had to be sent to deal with her.

A State Document, in describing Derry in 1586, gives us an
inkling of the sort of men Essex had to deal with. This Document was sent to Elizabeth.

> . . . it containeth O'Cahan's county. Lieth between Lough Foyle and
> the Bann. The Captain is Roy O'Cahan under the rule and govern-
> ment of Turlough O'Neill, who has 140 horse and 400 foot soldiers
> (*kerns*). He hath buildings in his county upon Lough Foyle side, 2
> strong castles, Castle Roe and Castle Coleraine (Cahan), Castle An-
> agh and Castle Limavady. O'Neill kept a constable and ward to
> receive his share of the fishing. Castle Limavady is near the Dog's
> Leap.

Perhaps Elizabeth imagined that Dog's Leap as she held the
document in her hands. It was a salmon leap. Perhaps she
wondered if O'Neill enjoyed his fishing. This 'Bann' was the
River Boyne that was to seal its name upon the defeat of much.
The Irish called it Banna, or the Bann-abha — the white water.
Ptolemy has a reference to it as Argita, the silver river. It had the

kind of water in which salmon love to live. The arms of the O'Neills consist of a ship, the Salmon and the Hand.

Perhaps Essex went fishing in the silver river! Whatever the spell was he came under it. He fell to the Irish friendship. He came out with these people and not against them. And Elizabeth would not listen to him. She would not be persuaded to such a friendship. She condemned him. I like to believe that, if she had listened to him, all the enmity that has been spilt between England and Ireland would never have happened. She condemned him and made him a lesson for any future failing of the same description. The men who followed Essex took good care not to expose themselves to any similar enchantments.

Lord Mountjoy succeeded Essex as Viceroy. He did not go to Derry. He sent Sir Henry Dowcra to fortify it against O'Neill. Dowcra landed with a British force of 4,000 men. We have his terse, military records:

> On 22nd May Army put in order to march to Derry, four miles up the river, a place in manner of an island, comprehending 40 acres, wherein were the ruins of an old Abbey, a Bishop's House, 2 Churches and an old castle. A river on one side and a bog most uncommonlie wet. This piece of ground we possessed ourselves of.

It was Sir Henry Dowcra who warned Elizabeth about the Armada. He was the one to advocate colonisation. He wished, he explained, 'to make the place an asylum for the English as they were needed for the education of the natives.' He does not state that for over a hundred years all Catholic teaching had been forbidden in this place. It is hard to believe that Derry, which had been a centre of Christianity and under a stable administration for a good thousand years, could lose all that its people had learned. The ins and outs of the struggle which lasted for so many bitter generations cannot be gone into here. Historians of good faith admit that the fight was bitter. The 'Ulidians' were hard to subdue.

To return to my people: in 1586, when Sir John Perrot was the Lord Deputy, the Kinel-Owen territory was broken up and Ulster was 'shired'.

> All that Land now included with the counties of Tyrone and Londonderry, with some extra districts, comprises the great territory of tribeland of the Clan of Cinel-Owen one of whom had early taken the name of O'Neill.

Sir John Perrot 'formed the seven counties of Ulster out of the Cinel-Owen territory. The Tyrone territory was broken up. The Northern part was first named Coleraine, from O'Cahan's county, afterwards it was renamed the County of Derry.'

At first, in the time of Henry the Eighth, the Anglicised version of Termonderry was given as Templederry. It was under King James that a Royal Charter bestowed the affix of London. In the Charter the city is described:

> Its latitude 54°59 N, longitude: 70°19W. The city is on the West or Donegal side of the Foyle, about five miles above the junction of the river with Lough Foyle — on a hill insulated by a broad navigable river. This 'Hill' or island of Derry was selected as the natural *acropolis* of the North.

When Derry was 'incorporated for her London Owners' she was described:

> The incorporation of Londonderry consists of 12 aldermen, 24 Capital burgesses, one chamberlain and 2 sheriffs.
> The state annexed to this city, on the Western bank of the Foyle was originally computed 4,000 acres, divided in two: the Upper and Lower Liberties.
> Upper Liberty: Mr. Alexander Lecky and Mr. Scott. The Lower Liberty, extending from the Bishop's Demesne to the West and North.
> The *main* streets of the city are divided into lots, consisting of 36ft each, measured in front.
> To these were annexed perches in the Island, the peninsula on which the city stands.

It was the London Company which rebuilt the walls. Derry had to keep her walls! The new walls were made of

> . . . lime and stone. The Circuit was 284 perches, at 18ft to the perch. Beside the 4 Gates which contain 84ft, every place in the Wall is 24ft high, 6ft thick.
> The Gates are all battlemented.
> 2 drawbridges, two portcullises. The bulwarks are v. good. Nine of them, add 2 half-bulkwarks.
> For 4 of them there are 4 cannons.
> The Rampart within the city is 12ft of earth.
> 92 houses *within* the Walls.
> The form of the city is that of a parallelogram, longest Northeast to Southwest; streets Northeast to Southeast.
> The length from Bishop's Gate to Shipquay Gate 1,273ft.
> The breadth from Ferry-Quay Gate to Butcher's Gate 635ft.

This is the description, furnished by the clerks of the corpora-
tion to the drapers and ironmongers in London who were to
pay for the bill. 'The top of the Wall,' it was added elsewhere,
'was used as a walk or Mall.' Few men of that London Company were ever to walk upon it.

Today, in 1942, American soldiers are walking upon it. I
wonder how much they know of its history?

King James the First of England bestowed the estates of
Derry and Tyrone by Letters Patent upon Sir Arthur Chichester.

An Irish writer, Kernohan, refers to Chichester as 'one of the
great pro-consuls of his age'.

It was Lord Chichester upon whom fell the confiscation of
the estates. He was responsible for the two English Inquisitions
held in 1609, the year in which: 'The Irish Gentry claimed their
land and were told that it was, according to law, no longer
theirs.'

That was a year of deep tribulation and humiliation. It was a
year of evictions and 'transplantings'. Its disasters inspired the
quiet and scholarly McFirbis to gather up what crumbs he could
from the waste and destruction. He was the last true Irish
scholar who attempted to preserve the ancient history. A
nineteenth-century writer, O'Donovan, wrote:

> Why should we question the ancient history of Ireland? It was a
> history preserved with much care. Historians were numerous.
> They were appointed and governed by laws. If they wrote false-
> hoods they lost their pay-rewards, erre-clan.

He pays tribute to McFirbis. Incidentally he mentions the
'Caire-Allains of Derry as one of the tribe of the Kinel-Owen,
directly descended from Eoghan, ancestor of all the tribes of Tir-
Eoghan, tirone.' The 'Caire-Allains' were still there in the nine-
teenth century. McFirbis entitled his record: *Degrees of the Fileas
— Laws of the Historians.* His manuscript was, at the time
O'Donovan refers to it, in the library of Lord Roden, Ireland.

McFirbis began his work with a prefatory notation:

The Place: College of Saint Nicholas at Galway.

Time:–   That of the religious wars between the Catholics of
             Ireland, Scotland and England, especially the year
             1650.

The Author:– Donald, the son of Gelasius More McFirbis, historian and antiquarian of Leacan McFirbis of Tirragh on the Moy.

Intent:– Glory of God and information for All.

McFirbis gives the list of historians or *shanachies* and the families to whom they belonged:

1: The O'Mulconnys were hereditary Shanachies to the Gil-Murray at Croghan, and to the septs of the same family in Thomon, Leinster and Analy.
2: The McFirbises in Lower Connaught and to the Clan Donnel in Oriel.
3: The O'Duigenana in Ly-lug and Conmaicne Moyrein.
4: The O'Cuirnins with the O'Rourkes.
5: The O'Clercens in Tirone.
6: The O'Clerys and O'Cannans in Tir-Connell.
7: The O'Luinins in Fermanagh.
8: The O'Duinans with the MacCarthys and O'Sullivans.
9: Mac an Gowan with the O'Kennedys in Ormond.
10: The O'Reardons in Ely.
11: The MacCurtius with the MacBroodys in Thomand.
12: The MacGilkellys in Iar-Connaught with the O'Flaghertys.

McFirbis lists these as the outstanding *shanachies*. There were many others. His tribute was written with haste in a time of pressure. He sought to put down in writing all that he remembered that could prove that there had been these institutions. He foresaw that a time was coming when 'the old men would have forgotten these things.'

The first decades of the 1600s were bleak and devastating years. They were Job years for the Irish. The property of the Kinel-Owens was divided by Chichester in his plan for the 'escheated lands' into six counties: Tyrone, Coleraine, Donegal, Fermanagh, Armagh, Cavan. The 'Division' was published in 1609. These Barony Maps of 1609 are still issued, I believe.

These were the years of the Inquisitions. The 'native Gentry' were forced to appear in person before the 'Stranger's Council', and suffer being told what to do with themselves, where to go and where not to go and how to spell their names. The parents of my grandmother's mother were among them. That was when the little silver spoons were hidden in a woman's bosom.

There was no appeal. If the Catholics were hunted and disfranchised in England they were hunted and disfranchised in

Ireland with a double fierceness. John de Courcy and his mail-clad knights wasted and ruined Catholic property and endowed Protestant Churches in the devastated regions.

The Ecclesiastical records of Derry show that, at the time of the Dowcra occupation, part of the old Abbey was still standing. It consisted of a 'round tower Belfry with a silver bell'. The ruins are marked on the maps of the period as having been built on the site of the old monastery of Columcille, in the street of the Long Tower, the Duv-Regles. The Walls of Derry also contained at this time the Friary that was founded in 1274. It was not until after the Siege of Derry, in 1688, that the endowment of this Friary was 'granted to the London Company'. The site of this Friary (as late as 1837) occupied Abbey Street, William Street and Roseville Street. Also at the time of Dowcra, and until 1625, there was an Augustinian Church, of the order of the Canons Regular. No Catholics were allowed to worship in any of these ruins. Prayers were only allowed in the Protestant schoolroom.

In 1633 the Colonists sought to impose their authority by the means which they had destroyed. Where the sword had failed to win the 'natives' to their creed they now sought to impose the dignity of a religious domination. In that year they began the erection of their own cathedral upon the peak of Derry Hill. It crowns it to this day. Derry is still held by her destiny, she is still Temple-Derry. The Colonists were impelled to possess her along her own lines. It was upon *them* that the atmosphere was imposed. They were the ones who had to take on the shape of this place which, according to their own testimony and upon the 'oathes' of the jurors in their Inquisition:

> did, long before any busshops were made in the same kingdom, [receive from] Donell McHugh O'Neale, King of Ireland 635 . . . severall portions of land, and a third of all tiethes . . . for the repairs and maintenynge of a church . . . of *certaine Holy Men* whom they call Sancti Patres and their honour and gloire and that afterwards the Holy Men did give unto severall septs proportions of the same lands and placed one or more in everie parish to hold the same tiethes according to tanistrie, free from all exactions. For that cause these were called termon-lands, or free lands and the tenant thereof sometymes called corbe and sometymes called herenach.

These English jurors were struggling with a foreign language. They were confused by the alternate corbe and erenach. It did not seem to occur to them to interpret these titles as one for the clergy and one for the laity. But the admission is there, in black and white, that Derry had her own Sancti Patres as far back as the seventh century. The English *Ordnance Survey Memoir* admits that 'anterior to Elizabeth, the history of Derry is almost wholly ecclesiastical.'

In 1688 the final bitter struggle of 'Catholics and Protestants' was fought out within the Walls of Derry. Her Siege was the final bitter spite between two kings who claimed the throne of England — the Catholic James and the Protestant William of Orange. The world was once more upon her! The issue really had nothing at all to do with her. She was only its instrument. The Gates of Derry were shut against King James by the Derry Apprentices. Lundy, a Catholic, tried to get them open for the Catholic forces. He was caught and hanged as a traitor. It was his effigy which was burned upon the Walker Monument and which Major and I had to witness with terror in unforgettable twilight.

Exactly a hundred years after the Siege of Derry, the Protestant Bishop Barnard died. Lord Townshend was then Lord Lieutenant. He had his own candidate for the 'bishoprick'. But he was overruled by Lord Shelbourne. The *Dublin Evening News* of 23 January 1768 has this item:

> We can assure the public that the Rt Rev Dr Hervey, Bishop of Cloyne, is translated to the See of Derry.

He was enthroned on 31 March 1768.

The appointment brought Dr Hervey an income of twenty thousand pounds sterling a year. It enabled him to live like a petty prince both at home and abroad. His interests were so wide and varied that he was sometimes accused of being a 'freethinker' and sometimes of being a 'papist'. He spent a good deal of his time on the Continent where he visited the Pope, Pope Clement XIV, at Rome and Voltaire at Ferney. It is said that he went to Rome to confer secretly with the Vatican upon the state of the Irish Catholics. He is credited with the appointment of the Catholic Dr McDevitt to the See of Derry. Dr McDevitt was celebrated for his scholasticism. He had been educated in Paris, at the Irish seminary and the Collège des Lombardes.

Dr Harvey had, as Ahn told my mother, 'a passion for the Giant's Causeway', for all basaltic formations. A visit to Vesuvius had awakened this passion for geology. He visited the rocks of Auvergne and Languedoc, Northern Italy and the

Grisons. He corresponded for years with the Count de Salis of the Chateau Bondo, in the Grisons. The Count, who was a Count of the Holy Roman Empire, was of Irish descent through his mother. Dr Hervey employed several Italian naturalists and he travelled on horseback with one of these, the Abbé Fortis, through remote parts of Dalmatia where basaltic traces were to be found. He wrote a letter to Emma Hamilton in which he told her that he 'had crossed from Italy to Dalmatia, through Manfredonia to Spolata,' which he found to be 'a modern city built in the precincts of the palace of Diocletian.'

He returned to his diocese in 1772 with an Italian artist, Bitio, a native of the Dolomites.

This was the Protestant Bishop whose exploits Ahn remembered as a child. He was extremely interested in architecture and knew a great deal upon the subject. He was responsible for the beginning of the restoration of the Long Tower which made the marriage of Ahn's parents possible. It was because of his influence that my great-grandfather was able to build his house — the house with the damson tree in the garden — for the girl he loved. It was built upon part of the site of the old Friary that had been founded in 1274. It was sacred earth to him and his bride. He must have had his own gifts, this young man, judging by the friendships he attracted. He was the son of poets. His name, McNulty, was an Anglicised version of Mac-an-Ollain which means the son of an ollain or poet. He was the first Catholic allowed to 'come down into the city' after the Dowcra occupation. The girl he married was one of those Erenach Kinel-Owens who, for a thousand years, had never lived out of the city. It is no wonder that they felt that they belonged to it. She had been given the little silver spoons directly from those who had stood before the 'Stranger's Council' to change their name to Smith. The silver spoons had been given to Ahn who had given them to my mother. I remember Ahn as an old lady in her nineties. I remember the thin spoons; I saw them with my own eyes; held them in my own hands in the Glendermott attic, kneeling on the floor beside the Saratoga trunk.

My mother was the link with Ahn. Ahn was the one to whom the past was told. She had a marvellous memory. She carried things in her mind. She was educated at the knees of wonderful and learned men. She told my mother that she remembered her father in the long summer evenings, sitting under the tree with a bishop on either side of him — a Catholic and a Protestant bishop. Between those three men all the conflict of the times was reasoned. Ahn remembered the discussion of the Test Act. She remembered the Emancipation Act. Although he died when she was hardly more than an infant she remembered the stories about Dr Hervey, and how he rode to Dublin 'in a Puce Coat wearing white gauntlets with gold fringes'. Her father said he was a 'glorious scamp of a Bishop and a glorious friend to have on your side.'

But it was Jane, the rebellious daughter, the one who heard least of all perhaps as a child, who returned to her native place because 'its stones were in her blood'. It was the worldly and ambitious Jane who was drawn back to her roots and the full meaning of her people. She founded a convent there, the Nazareth House. She endowed the Catholic College. Jane never did anything upon a private scale. She never did anything quietly. She did not die quietly. She was a person of destiny. It is remarkable that she should receive her deathblow in the cathedral to which she had given generous gifts — the cathedral which had taken long over a hundred years to erect. It must have been a symbol to her, for beneath her fierce exterior Jane was the one who dreamed dreams and not only dreamt them but set them going. She was the active principle in what had become quiescent. It was Jane who brought my mother from New York to Derry. It was her act that caused me to be born there, to belong to these women whose secret pride was the strong wind in which I was reared.

I have tried to set down honestly the gradual process by which I came to know them. In the chaos and hazard of human life much is lost, but it is the unforgotten that endures and becomes the symbol. Those little silver spoons that had been carried in a woman's bosom were as much a symbol to my people as that silver bell in Saint Columba's belfry that stood when all about it was in ruins. They were the touch upon the past.

Nothing could have been more disastrous than for them to be taken from my family. I remember the stricken look in my mother's eyes when she was told that *everything* in the house had been sold. The auctioneer who had asked her so commandingly to 'permit him to know what he was doing', nefariously ignored all her reservations on the day of the sale. Everything that Mother had wished to keep had been sold to strangers.

It was indeed a '*Cherry Orchard*' sale, the yielding of a final possession. It left us with our spirits standing naked against the world, struck down with a terrible uncertainty. It was my moment of farewell, although I did not strictly know it for what it was at the time. It has come back to me many times. It returns with the words of an old song:

> Farewell Faughan, Farewell Keenaght
> Farewell all for I must leave you
> Farewell my hills and farewell my mountains
> Farewell my plains and farewell my fountains.

Farewell my Faughan, my road with the roses above the plain of Aileach, roses that caught in my hair as a child.

Biographical Note

Kathleen Coyle
b. Derry, 1886; d. Philadelphia, 1952

The summer at the Giant's Causeway, planned by Kathleen's mother Catherine at the end of *The Magical Realm*, was to prove the last sojourn in Ireland for the Coyles as a family. This biographical note summarises the main events of Kathleen's life from when she first left her home country at the age of twenty. It has been compiled with the aid of Michelle Ripley, Kathleen's daughter, to whom I am extremely grateful.

In 1906, Kathleen, her mother and grandmother left Derry for Liverpool where they lived in straitened circumstances alleviated only by Kathleen's income from a job in the local library. When, on leaving school, Kathleen's younger brother James failed to secure employment in London, Kathleen persuaded her mother to let her try the capital herself. She promptly found work in the office of *The Statesman*, then edited by W.T. Stead. Kathleen resettled the family in London and helped to find employment for her two sisters on recalling them from their Belgian convent. W.T. Stead was instrumental in introducing Kathleen to writers and political activists. Among her acquaintance was Rebecca West who encouraged Kathleen in her first attempts at writing fiction. West would later write in a preface for Kathleen's novel *Liv* (1928) that she was 'impressed, and almost alarmed by her endowment of poetic sensitivity.'

Kathleen resisted the attempts of Stead to involve her as a medium in the spiritualism which interested him, but she did join the Theosophical Society where she found an attitude to literature where symbol was considered literal truth, which is recognisably congenial to her developing sensibility as described in *The Magical Realm*. Exposed in London to the burgeoning socialist movement and the campaign for women's suffrage, Kathleen began attending socialist meetings in Dublin after returning to Ireland circa 1911. She was often in the company of her friend, writer Desmond Ryan (later secretary to Pearse and combatant in the 1916 rising), who had also returned from London. At one such meeting Kathleen met Charles O'Meagher, a committed socialist from a working-class County Westmeath family. They married in 1915 and by 1920 had had two children, a boy and girl named Kestrel and Michelle. The marriage, however, was not a success, and its eventual disintegration, coupled with a growing disillusionment about methods used in the cause of labour, led Kathleen to leave O'Meagher and to return to London with her children sometime that year.

The post-war situation in London made it difficult for Kathleen to obtain work. Employers were now encouraged to favour returned soldiers and women who had taken an active part in the war effort, and Kathleen's ally, W.T. Stead, had drowned in the sinking of the Titanic. Having spent a brief time with her mother and sister, who as increasingly devout Catholics were unsupportive of her situation, Kathleen decided to try to earn her living by writing. She found a foster home for her children for a time and within two years had produced her first two novels. *Piccadilly* and *The Widow's House* were published by Jonathan Cape, London and by E.P. Dutton, New York in 1923 and 1924 respectively.

These works were characterised by Rebecca West as having that 'shadowy quality' which 'appears when a writer has not yet found the subject of which his inner self really wants to write'. If they do bear the mark of being the early work of a writer concerned mainly with writing for the market, they also encompass the theme of the spiritual dimension in individual suffering — a key theme of Coyle's literary work — and they succeeded in earning the funds that enabled her to move to the continent with her children in 1923. She initially chose Antwerp but her sights were set on France where she would live from 1926 to 1936 after a time spent travelling. She later wrote in *Twentieth Century Authors* that she chose France 'because it was a country which gave real food to intellectuals, no matter how poor they were. It gave liberty and depth to the spirit.'

Kathleen's move to Paris in 1926 was helped by introductions into literary society from her Antwerp-based contacts. She soon established a friendship with philosopher Gabriel Marcel, and among their shared interests were the interpretation of Henri Bergson's writings and discussion of the implications of new philosophies for Christian thinking. Kathleen moved on the fringes of celebrity throughout this decade. Her usually precarious cash-flow was alleviated for a number of years by a stipend from American banker Arthur Karns. She counted critic Louis Gillet and Catholic thinker and novelist Charles du Bos among her friends and attended the latter's Sunday gatherings which were frequented by many of the English-speaking intelligentsia living in Paris. It was Louis Gillet's daughter Louisette who translated the edition of *A Flock of Birds* published in French in 1932. Either through Gillet, or perhaps through her Irish friends Padraic and Mary Colum, Kathleen also became acquainted with James and Nora Joyce and was an occasional visitor to their apartment. She recounts later in an article for *Tomorrow* magazine how she discussed his daughter Lucia's condition with Joyce, an incident indicating Coyle's interest in the new psychology when she says, 'I thought her eye-weakness was, perhaps, symptomatic of her sympathy for her father. Cases of such indications occur.' ('My last visit with James Joyce', *Tomorrow*, Vol. 10, No. 2)

This period of relative financial stability meant that Kathleen could entertain at her home and regular visitors included mystery writer Marie Belloc-Lowndes, Blanche Knopf (spouse of publisher, Alfred), American poets Stephen Vincent Benét and Robert Nathan, and American naturalist novelist James Thomas Farrell, as well as her publishers Jonathan Cape and John McCrae of E.P. Dutton, New York. Kathleen constantly had to find ways to create the working time she needed to write. She enrolled her children in a progressive boarding school in Switzerland for a number of years and during the summers would obtain au-pair help, often by offering to a daughter of some of the many White Russian migrants to Paris a working holiday in Brittany where she rented a cottage for the season.

Between 1926 and 1936, Coyle published nine novels, several short stories and a poetically written psychological fantasy entitled *There is a Door*. Of this period, her finest and most lauded works are *Liv* (1928), a Jamesian story of a young Norwegian woman's foray into Paris and her realisation that it is both terrible to be young and terrible to love, and the subsequent book *A Flock of Birds* (1930), which explores the personal crisis of an Irish mother whose son will hang for a Republican murder. By the early 1930s, however, her benefactor Karns had died and Kathleen's habit of spending what she earned left her under tremendous financial pressure. She wrote *The French Husband* — a genre romance — in eleven days, and *Morning Comes Early* — a highly melodramatic tale — in three weeks. Not appreciating that book sales were affected by the post-war depression, Kathleen had a major quarrel with E.P. Dutton over lack of royalties, and her financial position was made even more precarious by travel to her mother's funeral in 1932 and subsequent trips to London to deal with family arguments over her none-too-large legacy.

Having left Paris in the early 1930s, Kathleen spent some time in Antwerp before American friends with an eye on the situation in Europe helped to raise funds enabling her to travel to the United States in 1937. She was accompanied by her daughter Michelle and would be joined two years later by son, Kestrel. In New Hampshire, Kathleen was accepted into the group of artists, musicians and writers collectively known as the McDowell colony. She was helped to assimilate by writer and critic William Rose Benét, brother of Stephen and widowed husband of poet Elinor Wylie. Wylie was notorious in the American literary world chiefly for her abandonment of her son and first marriage for another man, and Coyle later based the character of Victoria Rising in *Immortal Ease* on this poet whom she understood as embroiled in a relentless quest for an authentic way to live.

Having temporarily left E.P. Dutton, Kathleen published with Harper and Brothers the nostalgic reminiscence of *Brittany Summer* (1940) and animal-story *Josephine* (1942), which were easily received on both sides of the Atlantic, although her novels from the 1930s onwards were more favourably received in the United States than elsewhere. During the Second World War, encouraged by agents Otis and Mackintosh, Kathleen placed many of her stories with the widely circulated *Redbook Magazine*, which paid between $800 and $1,000 per publication. This source of income enabled her to maintain a decent apartment in Greenwich Village, New York, where she had moved after her stay in New Hampshire.

The New York city literary circle in which Kathleen moved included both Benét brothers, Mary and Padraic Colum and

Blanche Knopf, as well as some of the English-speaking exiles whom she had known in Paris, including Charles du Bos, who now held a chair at the University of Notre Dame. After 1949, Kathleen's source of income from magazine publication began to fail as writers returning from war increased the available competition. Kathleen, however, did not give much credence to this factor and became bitter in rejection towards the editors of the *Redbook* whom she accused of telling her how to write.

Desiring a change from New York, Kathleen moved in the late 1940s to Princeton, New Jersey. There she enjoyed the academic atmosphere and used her relative financial freedom to further her life-long interests in Joan of Arc and Saint Paul. She also began a study of Rimbaud, one of her favourite poets, and made translations of a number of his poems. In demand to write reviews and articles, especially for *Tomorrow* magazine edited by Irishwoman Eileen Garrett, she worked consistently although her health was failing. When admitted to hospital a day before she died of advanced cancer, she brought with her the notes towards a further volume of autobiography on which to work. She died on 25 March 1952 with a number of projects unfinished, including her study of Rimbaud and a planned play set in Philadelphia. Her body of publications by then included thirteen full-length novels, a novella, some anecdotal tales, several short stories and a volume of autobiography. She had been translated into French and Italian, had appeared on the *New York Times* bestseller lists (with the novel *Immortal Ease*), and an appreciation of her life and work appeared in that paper four days after her death.

Kathleen Coyle's concern with the events in a life which give shape and substance to an individual soul or 'self' permeates all her novels, even those of less ambition. Her commitment to charting the spiritual development of the suffering individual is a linking factor through all her work. *The Magical Realm* (1943), her last published work gives fullest autobiographical expression to this, amounting to a vividly impressionistic portrait of the artist's developing sensibility.

Kathleen Coyle was a spirited and tenacious woman who deceptively appeared frail and timid. Her daughter Michelle recalls how visitors would comment on her physical grace and beauty, sometimes not noticing her lameness until it was pointed out. Kathleen protected her privacy, preferring to ignore requests for information on her life and work. She prided herself that she had managed to provide for her family through her writing and, in the process, had also kept up some of the gentility of her childhood environment. Coyle's few self comments are indicative of these values and a fitting end to this short biographical note. 'Writing . . . was my only outlet and means of expression. I was good for nothing else', she opines in *Twentieth Century Authors*, and in an aphorism she enjoyed expressing to her children: 'I am one of those who made bricks without straw'.

Siobhán Campbell

Further Reading

Wolfhound Press have re-issued Coyle's *A Flock of Birds* as part of their classic Irish fiction programme and *Liv* is planned for Spring 1998. Many of Coyle's novels are available in The National Library of Ireland as are the *Times Literary Supplement* reviews of her work. John Cronin includes a chapter on *A Flock of Birds* in *The Anglo-Irish Novel: Volume Two* (Appletree Press, 1992) and a full bibliography and critical analysis of three key novels is available in the NUI Master of Arts thesis at University College Dublin, *Kathleen Coyle: Reluctant Modernist* by Siobhán Campbell.